The Dynamics of Transitional Justice

The Dynamics of Transitional Justice draws on the case of East Timor in order to reassess how transitional justice mechanisms actually play out at the local level. Transitional justice mechanisms – including trials and truth commissions – have become firmly entrenched as part of the United Nations 'toolkit' for successful post-conflict recovery. It is now commonly assumed that, by establishing individual accountability for human rights violations, and initiating truth-seeking and reconciliation programmes, individuals and societies will be assisted to 'come to terms' with the violent past and states will make the 'transition' to peaceful, stable, liberal democracies. Set against the backdrop of East Timor's referendum and the widespread violence of 1999, this book interrogates the gap between the official claims made for transitional justice and local expectations. Drawing on a wide range of sources, including extensive in-depth interviews with victims/survivors, community leaders and other actors, it produces a nuanced and critical account of the complex interplay between internationally sponsored trials and truth commissions, national justice agendas and local priorities. *The Dynamics of Transitional Justice* fills a significant gap in the existing social science literature on transitional justice, and offers new insights for researchers and practitioners alike.

Lia Kent is a Postdoctoral Fellow in the School of International, Political and Strategic Studies at the Australian National University.

Transitional Justice
Series Editor: Kieran McEvoy
Queen's University Belfast

The study of justice in transition has emerged as one of the most diverse and intellectually exciting developments in the social sciences. From its origins in human rights activism and comparative political science, the field is increasingly characterised by its geographic and disciplinary breadth. This series aims to publish the most innovative scholarship from a range of disciplines working on transitional-justice-related topics, including law, sociology, criminology, psychology, anthropology, political science, development studies and international relations.

Titles in this series:

Transitional Justice, Judicial Accountability and the Rule of Law
Hakeem O. Yusuf (2010)

The Era of Transitional Justice: The Aftermath of the Truth and Reconciliation Commission in South Africa and Beyond
Paul Gready (2010)

Identity, Reconciliation and Transitional Justice
Nevin Aiken (2012)

Corporate Accountability in the Context of Transitional Justice
Sabine Michalowski (2013)

The Judiciary and the Politics of Transition: Saviours, Scoundrels, Scapegoats
Marny Requa (2013)

Truth, Denial and Transition: The Contested Past in Northern Ireland
Cheryl Lawther (2013)

The Dynamics of Transitional Justice

International Models and Local Realities in East Timor

Lia Kent

Routledge
Taylor & Francis Group
a GlassHouse Book

First published 2012
by Routledge
2 Park Square, Milton Park, Abingdon, Oxon, OX14 4RN

Simultaneously published in the USA and Canada
by Routledge
711 Third Avenue, New York, NY 10017

A GlassHouse book

Routledge is an imprint of the Taylor & Francis Group, an informa business

British Library Cataloguing in Publication Data
A catalogue record for this book is available from the British Library

Library of Congress Cataloging in Publication Data
Kent, Lia.
The dynamics of transitional justice : international models and local realities in East Timor / Lia Kent.
p. cm.
Includes bibliographical references.
ISBN 978-0-415-50436-2 (hardback)
1. Transitional justice—Timor-Leste. I. Title.
KNW5046.8.K46 2012
320.959870l'1—dc23

2011052527

ISBN: 978–0–415–50436–2 (hbk)
ISBN: 978–0–203–11743–9 (ebk)

Typeset in Garamond
by RefineCatch Limited, Bungay, Suffolk

If justice doesn't come, we will still dream of justice, we will still scream for justice.

(José, Liquica)

No justice . . . seems possible or thinkable without the principle of some responsibility . . . before the ghosts of those who are not yet born or who are already dead.

(Derrida 1994: xix)

Contents

List of figures

Acknowledgements

Many people have helped to sustain me throughout the writing of this book. Jennifer Balint, Dianne Otto and Julie Evans devoted enormous time and energy to this project in its first incarnation as a PhD thesis at the University of Melbourne. The Arts and Law Faculties at the University of Melbourne provided me with much-needed financial support for fieldwork. Eve Darian-Smith and Kieran McEvoy also provided invaluable advice, and the encouragement I needed to embark upon a book. Much of the book was written while I was a Postdoctoral fellow at the Australian National University. I am grateful to many people at the ANU for making me welcome, in particular colleagues at the State, Society and Governance in Melanesia programme, who provided me with the time, space and collegial atmosphere needed to complete the project. Deserving of special mention are Sinclair Dinnen, Gordon Peake, Nicole Haley, Richard Eves, Sue Ingram, Pyone Myat Thu, Graeme Smith and Sue Rider, for stimulating conversations, encouragement and, at times, much-needed distraction.

I am deeply grateful to the many East Timorese people who took the time to talk to me about the difficult topic of justice. This book would not have been possible without their openness and generous contributions, which profoundly shaped this project. I hope, in some small way, the chapters that follow do justice to their experiences. Special thanks must go to José (Zeka) Moniz's family in Covalima, and to Angelo and family in Lautem, who provided warm hospitality and all manner of helpful advice. Ana Maria and her family greatly assisted me with contacts, motorbike transport and advice in Liquica.

I benefited enormously from the support and advice of friends and colleagues in Dili, who enriched my understanding of East Timor and helped to make the research process far less solitary than it would otherwise have been. Thanks in particular to Keryn Clark for friendship and for always offering a place to stay. Megan, Nela and Naomi at the International Center for Transitional Justice very generously allowed me to use their office facilities from time-to-time and were a source of invaluable information and advice. I am also grateful to Ben and Alison, who very generously sub-let their house in Dili to me in

2007, and to Faviola, Arti, Tuta and family in Taibessi, for being my family away from home. I also benefited greatly from discussions with Sophia Cason, Mark Harris, Jon Cina, Joaquim Fonseca, Anthony Goldstone, Charles Scheiner, Kerry Brogan, Anjet Lanting, Sara Niner, Lisa Palmer, Adérito Soares, Annemarie Devereux, Soren Blau, Michael Leach, Isabel Guterres, Fidelus Magelles, Josh Trindade and Hugo Fernandes. Pat Walsh deserves a particular thank-you for sharing his deep insights and for patiently answering my questions on many occasions. I am also indebted to Bu Wilson, Susana Barnes, Matthew Abud, Damian Grenfell, Megan Hirst, Manuela Long Pereira and Nesam McMillan, who read and provided helpful comments on draft chapters. Tom Davis very generously put in long hours to read the book in its entirety and made helpful suggestions.

I am profoundly grateful to family and friends in Melbourne for supporting me throughout this project with love, encouragement and much needed diversions. Particular thanks to my parents, Desleigh and Randall. Finally, to Tom, I am grateful to you in more ways than I can express. It was your love, patience, humour and unwavering belief in me, that sustained me.

Parts of this book have been previously aired in earlier forms. Parts of Chapter Six appeared in 'The Politics of Remembrance and Victims' Rights in East Timor', in Michael Leach, Nuno Canas Mendes, Antero B. da Silva, Alarico da Costa Ximenes and Bob Boughton eds *Hatene kona ba/Compreender/Understanding/Mengerti* Timor-Leste, Hawthorn: Swinburne Press, 2010, and in 'Local Memory Practices in East Timor: Disrupting Transitional Justice Assumptions', *International Journal of Transitional Justice* 5(3) 2011.

Permission has kindly been granted for the use of the following images, photos and poetry extracts in the book: the aerial photo of Dili after the post-referendum in the Introduction was taken by Ross Bird; the photo of the veterans' medals ceremony in Chapter 4 was taken by Edith Bowles; the photo of the Community Reconciliation Hearing in Chapter 3 was supplied by the CAVR archives; the photo in Chapter 3 of East Timorese President Xanana Gusmao meeting Indonesian presidential candidate former General Wiranto in Bali was supplied by Picture Media/Reuters and was taken by Dadang Tri; the photo in Chapter 6 of the CTF demonstration was supplied by La'o Hamutuk. The map of East Timor was provided by Cartographic Services, ANU College of Asia and the Pacific, the Australian National University. Jill Jolliffe granted permission to reproduce the poem 'Foho Ramelau' by Fransisco Borja da Costa, in Chapter 4.

Lia Kent
December 2011

Glossary of terms

Acronyms

ABRI	*Angkatan Bersenjata Republik Indonesia* (Indonesian Armed Forces)
AMP	Alliance of the Parliamentary Majority
CAVR	*Comissão de Acolhimento, Verdade e Reconciliação* (Commission for Reception, Truth and Reconciliation)
CNRM	*Conselho Nacional de Resistência Maubere* (National Council of Maubere Resistance) (1988–1998)
CNRT	*Conselho Nacional de Resistencia Timorense* (National Council for Timorese Resistance) (1998–2001)
CNRT	*Conselho Nacional de Reconstrucao Timorense* (National Council for the Reconstruction of Timor-Leste) (2007–current)
CRP	Community Reconciliation Process
CRRN	*Concelho Revolutionário de Resistência Nacional* (National Council for Revolutionary Resistance) (1981–87)
CTF	Truth and Friendship Commission
FALINTIL	*Forças Armadas de Libertação Nacional de Timor-Leste* (Armed Forces for the National Liberation of East Timor)
FOKUPERS	Women's Communication Forum
FRETILIN	*Frente Revolucionária de Timor-Leste Independente* (Revolutionary Front for an Independent East Timor)
ICC	International Criminal Court
ICTJ	International Center for Transitional Justice
ICTR	International Criminal Tribunal for Rwanda
ICTY	International Tribunal for the Former Yugoslavia
SCIT	Serious Crimes Investigations Team
SCIU	Serious Crimes Investigations Unit
TNI	*Tentara Nasional Indonesia* (Indonesian National Army)
UDT	*União Democrática Timorense* (Timorese Democratic Union)
UN	United Nations
UNAMET	United Nations Assistance Mission in East Timor

UNMISET	United Nations Mission of Support in East Timor
UNMIT	United Nations Integrated Mission in Timor Leste
UNOTIL	United Nations Office in Timor Leste
UNTAET	United Nations Transitional Administration in East Timor
Yayasan Hak	Rights Foundation

Non-English terms and phrases

Adat	Custom
Ai farina	Cassava
Aldeia	Hamlet
Cadeira	Chair/position
Chefe de Aldeia	Hamlet chief
Chefe de Suco	Village chief
Ema Bo'ot	Big people (ie, the political leadership)
Funu	Conflict
Laran Moras	Sick inside/worried
Lian Nian	Lit. the 'owner of the words' (customary leader)
Lulik	Sacred
Malae	Foreigner
Matebian	Ancestors/ghosts of the dead
Mate Restu	Remains of the dead
Moe	Shy/ashamed
Nahe Biti	Lit. 'stretching the mat' (customary dispute resolution process)
Povu Ki'ik	Small people (ie, ordinary people)
Rate La'ek	Empty graves
Suco	Village
Tau matan ba	To watch over/look after
Terus	Suffering
Uma Lulik	Sacred house

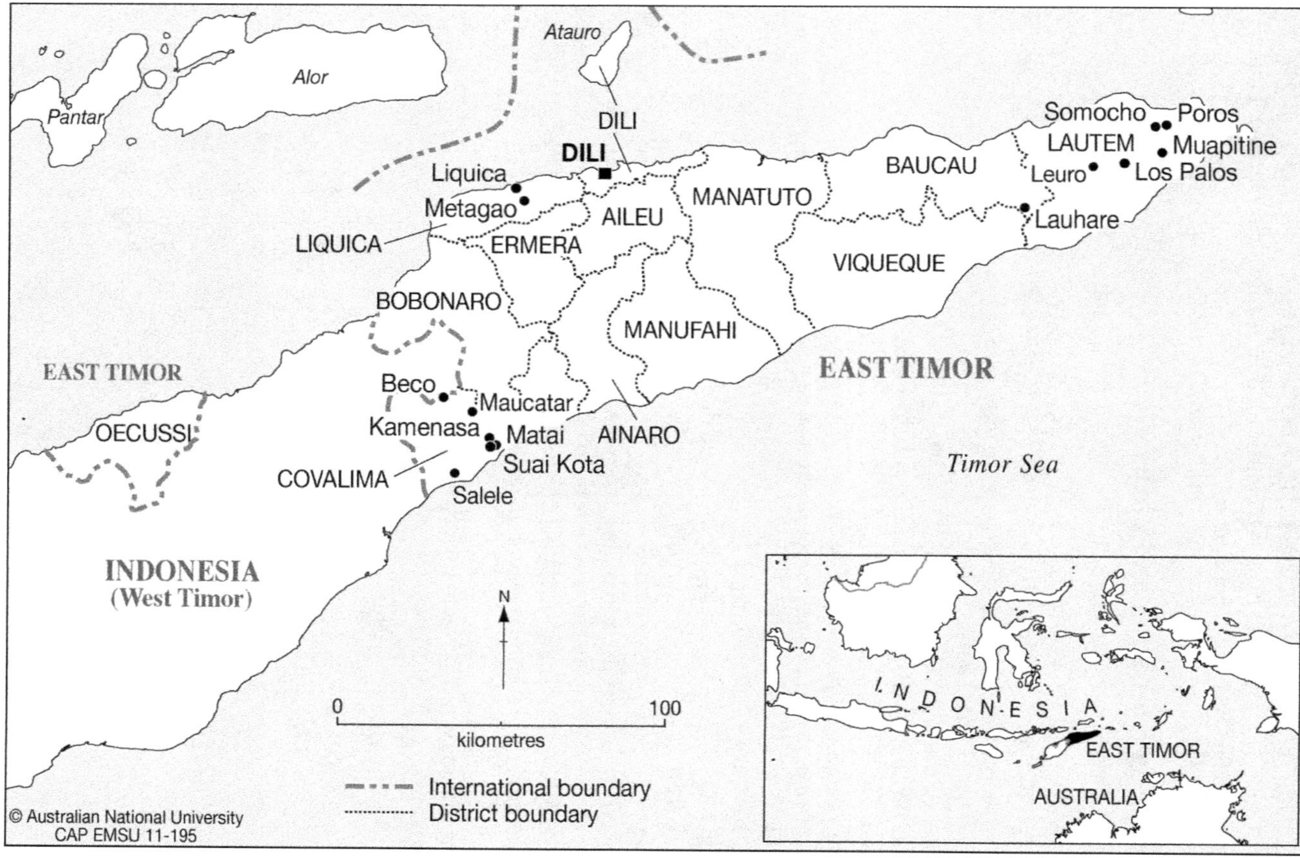

Map of East Timor (Cartographic Services, ANU College of Asia and the Pacific, the Australian National University)

Introduction

The global celebration of transitional justice and the East Timor reality

On a hot, muggy afternoon in the sleepy town of Liquica, East Timor, I sit down to speak with José on the veranda of his modest home, a few blocks from the church where the massacre of April 1999 occurred, in which more than sixty people were killed by the *Besi Merah Putih* (Red and White Iron) militia group. As we drink sweet, black coffee, José begins by explaining to me the origins of the long machete scar that begins behind his ear and runs diagonally down his neck. He tells me how he managed to survive the militia's assault and protect his young son by covering him with his body. After recounting his survival story, José turns quickly to his preoccupation with the present. José is well educated, and was employed by the Commission for Reception, Truth and Reconciliation (CAVR) as a victim support worker. He also told his own story as part of the CAVR's truth-seeking process, and has been interviewed on numerous occasions by serious crimes investigators. José expresses deep frustration at the lack of practical outcomes from transitional justice and says that he feels the government has 'lied' to him. 'We keep creating commissions but we don't have a solution,' he says. José speaks forcefully about his desire for the Indonesian military who orchestrated the massacre to be brought to justice. Another of his main preoccupations is his machete wounds, which still cause him pain and headaches, and worry about how he will pay for his child's schooling. 'I can't work hard because of my injuries. But my child needs to go to school so what can I do?'

In the district of Covalima a few weeks later – the site of another horrific church massacre, in September 1999 – I am introduced to two members of a local widows' group called *Mate Restu* (leftovers from the dead). Both women had been interviewed by serious crimes investigators a number of times and had participated in the CAVR's truth-seeking and reconciliation process. The women now have stalls at the local market selling basic items such as instant noodles, sugar, cigarettes and condensed milk. When I request an interview with them, they make clear their desire not to speak to me. As we sit perched on wooden boxes inside their small market stall, the women ask, 'What are we to talk about? Whether we talk or not it is just the same. It just wastes our time.' 'Many people have come and taken our information', they say. 'What we want is justice. And we need the government to provide assistance for our children to go to school.'

There is a profound sense of frustration and disappointment with the lack of 'results' from the transitional justice process in East Timor. This disjuncture between the rhetorical claims made for transitional justice and the local expressions of disenchantment with its achievements is something I have been constantly struck by throughout my experiences in East Timor – first as a human rights officer during the United Nations Transitional Administration in East Timor (UNTAET) period, and later as a researcher. I wondered how it was that a process that claimed for itself the capacity to deliver 'justice', to establish the 'truth' and foster reconciliation and nation-building, could engender such disillusionment amongst those whose interests it purported to serve. While some of the reasons, I knew, related to the political constraints under which East Timor's transitional justice process was established – which resulted in an inability to hold high-level members of the Indonesian military to account – I also thought that this disparity might reflect deeper issues. My intuition was that the ways in which transitional justice mechanisms conceptualise conflict, justice and transition did not encapsulate the complexities and lived realities of these issues. It was this that drove me to explore the divergence between the official claims made for transitional justice and community discontent in greater depth.

Transitional justice mechanisms – including trials and truth commissions – have become firmly entrenched as part of the United Nations (UN) 'toolkit' for successful post-conflict recovery. It is now commonly assumed that by establishing individual accountability for human rights violations, and initiating truth-seeking and reconciliation programmes, individuals and societies will be assisted to 'come to terms' with violent pasts, and states will make the transition to peaceful, stable, liberal democracies. Set against the backdrop of East Timor's referendum and the widespread violence of 1999, this book unsettles these assumptions by exploring the social and political realities of transitional justice in East Timor. It seeks to unravel the complex interplay between internationally sponsored trials and truth commissions, the nation-building and justice agendas promoted by East Timor's political elite, and local priorities, practices and expectations of justice. In doing so, it aims to contribute to a more nuanced and grounded understanding of the complexities of both 'justice' and 'transition' in East Timor.

While the findings of this book are specific to East Timor, they also have broader applicability. Despite burgeoning scholarship in the transitional justice field, relatively little attention has been paid to the ways in which local communities engage with, and seek to make sense of, these concepts and practices within particular social, political and cultural contexts. Examining these dynamics can help to unsettle the 'seductive' assumptions (as per McEvoy 2008) that pervade the discourse and practice of transitional justice, and may also open up new and unexpected possibilities (see Shaw and Waldorf 2010). Most importantly, it can contribute to a more nuanced appreciation of the intricate and long-term justice issues facing individuals, communities and societies emerging from debilitating periods of conflict.

The aims of this book are both practical and scholarly. I hope that this book will be of interest to practitioners involved in the design, establishment and implementation of transitional justice mechanisms, as well as scholars, justice activists and non-governmental organisations (NGOs). Specifically, I hope that the findings of this book may assist these actors to reflect more deeply on the possibilities and limitations, contradictions and silences of transitional justice, and stimulate an interest in the development of more locally informed responses to complex legacies of violence.

The remainder of this chapter sets the scene for the in-depth exploration of the encounter between transitional justice norms and practices and local realities in East Timor that occupies the rest of the book. It first charts the global expansion and celebration of transitional justice discourse and practice, and situates East Timor's transitional justice process within these developments. It then provides a brief background to the establishment of the UN-sponsored transitional justice process in East Timor, which included a serious crimes investigations and prosecutions process (Serious Crimes Process) and a Commission for Reception, Truth and Reconciliation (CAVR). I finish by outlining a number of the institutional shortcomings of this process that have contributed to widespread dissatisfaction amongst the community.

The global celebration of transitional justice discourse and practice

It has become almost a truism to assert that societies emerging from protracted periods of conflict need to find ways of 'coming to terms' with past human rights abuses. In recent decades, a set of mechanisms and tools known as 'transitional justice' has been developed to assist states to confront the wrongdoings of repressive predecessor regimes and thereby make the shift from violent pasts to peaceful futures. Although transitional justice may encompass a broad range of measures such as reparations policies, institutional reform, lustration (the vetting of public officials), memorialisation, and reforms to police, prisons and judiciary, the most popular mechanisms are criminal trials and truth commissions. Transitional justice is more than just a collection of tools or mechanisms, however; it is also a 'discourse' that assumes a relationship between the promotion of the liberal values of individual rights and liberties, the rule of law and democracy, and the achievement of peace and stability in post-conflict societies. These assumptions are often taken for granted by transitional justice policymakers.

There is now a celebration of transitional justice practice – reflected in the proliferation of international courts and tribunals around the globe, including the recently created International Criminal Court (ICC), and the growing number of truth commissions. Indeed, as Stanley (2009: 56) observes, forty international courts and tribunals and over thirty-five truth commissions have been established over the last three decades. The emergence of non-governmental institutions, such as the International Center for Transitional Justice, in New York, and the birth of a new academic journal, the *International Journal for Transitional Justice*, are further testament to the growing popularity of transitional justice practice and discourse (see Moon 2008: 3).

The proliferation of transitional justice mechanisms has gone hand in hand with an expansion of the discourse regarding what these mechanisms can accomplish. Once viewed simply as a means of contributing to the redress of past violations and the development of an official historical record, transitional justice is now also claimed to facilitate broader processes of societal transformation and to contribute to ambitious goals such as reconciliation, nation-building and peace. Through the official investigation and public exposure of past human rights abuses, transitional justice is claimed to provide a rite of political passage towards the creation of a liberal political order that embeds values such as the rule of law and the rights of individuals.

Recent years have also seen a shift away from the dichotomous debate about the relative merits of truth commissions versus trials. Previously, proponents of truth commissions argued that the broad and flexible mandates of these mechanisms made them more 'victim-centred' than the adversarial and confrontational nature of judicial proceedings, and that they promote accountability, deterrence, reconciliation, truth and the rule of law more successfully than criminal tribunals (see Waldorf 2006: 16). By contrast, those who favour trials suggested that criminal accountability for human rights abuses provide more 'just' outcomes for victims than truth commissions, thereby creating a firmer basis for societal reconciliation. There is now a growing recognition that trials and truth commissions can positively complement each other and, recent transitional justice processes, including those established in East Timor, Argentina, Peru and Sierra Leone, have adopted a combination of mechanisms (see Lambourne 2009: 33; Leebaw 2008: 102; UNSG 2004: 9).

The current era is also marked by an apparent shift away from 'one-size-fits-all' approaches to transitional justice, towards a greater emphasis on 'local context'. Evidence of this can be seen in the 2004 report of the UN Secretary General, *The Rule of Law and Transitional Justice in Conflict and Post-Conflict Societies*, which calls for greater attention to indigenous and informal processes for administering justice or settling disputes on the basis that this will help to make transitional justice processes more meaningful to informal populations (UNSG 2004: para 36). The enthusiasm for incorporating local justice practices into formal transitional justice processes is apparent in the UN-sponsored truth commissions of both East Timor and Sierra Leone (Shaw and Waldorf 2010: 15; Waldorf 2006: 3).

In a different way, the renewed attention to local context is reflected in the UN's growing embrace of 'hybrid' or internationalised tribunals. Located within the country where the crimes were committed, and comprising both national and international staff and judges, hybrid tribunals are sometimes claimed to promise greater local legitimacy than international tribunals: they are said to be more economically sustainable, to contribute to the capacity-building of domestic legal systems and to make justice more meaningful to victims due to their proximity to the community (see, for example, UNSG 2004; OHCHR 2006). Hybrid tribunals, which have now been established in Kosovo, Sierra Leone, Cambodia and East Timor, can arguably also be understood as a response to what has been termed 'tribunal fatigue' within the UN and donor community, as a result of the expense and duration of international criminal trials (see, for example, UNGA 1999).

Somewhat paradoxically, alongside the UN's apparent eschewing of a 'one-size-fits-all approach' to transitional justice is the growing link between transitional justice and UN-sponsored state-building projects in states incapacitated due to conflict (see, for example, Fritz 2005). Transitional justice has become firmly entrenched as an essential component of the UN 'toolkit' for successful post-conflict recovery, underscored by the UN Department of Peacekeeping Operation's (UNDPKO) establishment of a Security Sector Reform and Transitional Justice Unit, the production of a number of UN documents and 'tools',[1] and the UN's sponsorship of recent transitional justice mechanisms, including those in East Timor and Sierra Leone.[2] This has meant that post-conflict states are now 'expected, encouraged or even coerced' to adopt transitional justice mechanisms (Subiotic 2009: 21). These developments can be seen as part of the surge in UN efforts to promote the 'rule of law' around the globe: a concept that the former UN Secretary General Kofi Annan has described as being at the very heart of the organisation's mission (UNSG 2004: 4).[3] Indeed, since the early 1990s, the UN and other international organisations have promoted transitional justice, human rights,

1 Recent UN documents include the 2004 report of the UN Secretary General, *The Rule of Law and Transitional Justice in Post-Conflict Societies* (UNSG 2004) and the 2006 publication of a series of *Rule of Law Tools for Post Conflict States* by the Office of the High Commissioner for Human Rights designed to help UN field missions and administrations emerging from conflict to establish transitional justice mechanisms (OHCHR 2006).

2 While East Timor's truth commission was established by the UN itself, in the case of Sierra Leone it received explicit endorsement from the UN. Various UN agencies have also provided transitional justice assistance and advice in countries such as Liberia, Afghanistan, Bosnia, Burundi and Herzegovina (Study by the Office of the United Nations High Commissioner for Human Rights on human rights and transitional justice activities undertaken by the human rights components of the United Nations system, UN Doc E/CN.4/2006/93, 7 February 2006 available at http://www.ictj.org/en/where/region3/507.html (accessed 2 February 2012)).

3 The UN Secretary General defines the rule of law as 'a principle of governance in which all persons, institutions and entities, public and private, including the State itself, are accountable to laws that are publicly promulgated, equally enforced and independently adjudicated, and which are consistent with international human rights norms and standards. It requires, as well, measures to ensure adherence to the principles of supremacy of law, equality before the law, accountability to the law, fairness in the application of the law, separation of powers, participation in decision-making, legal certainty, avoidance of arbitrariness and procedural and legal transparency' (UNSG 2004: 4).

the rule of law, good governance and democratisation as a key strategy of intervention, peacemaking and reconstruction in conflict and post-conflict societies (Humphrey 2005: 204; see also Carothers 2003; Sriram 2007). The assumption is that by granting an extensive role to the 'international community' in restructuring political, legal and economic systems, and introducing internationally recognised legal standards, post-conflict states will be assisted to become stable, liberal democracies that respect human rights and are integrated into the global economy (Paris 2004: 5; Rajagopal, 2008: 1346). These assumptions were certainly evident during the UN's post-conflict reconstruction of East Timor, which took place under the auspices of the UN following the 1999 referendum, and which, on the eve of the new nation's independence, was claimed as a 'success story'.

East Timor: from colonialism to 'transition'

The year 1999 was one of both extraordinary hope and terrible violence for the East Timorese people. While a UN-sponsored referendum on 30 August ushered in East Timor's transition to independence, and brought to an end the twenty-four-year oppressive Indonesian occupation of the territory, the year was also marred by killings, the burning and destruction of thousands of houses, and mass displacement. The primary perpetrators of this violence were East Timorese militia, mostly young men who had been armed and trained by the Indonesian military. Yet it is important to locate the events of 1999 within a much longer history of violence, disadvantage, poverty and exploitation that encompasses the Indonesian occupation and the period of Portuguese colonisation that preceded it. Considered in this light, the idea of 'transition' begins to lose its temporal certainties, and the concept of 'justice' comes to mean more than the prosecution of perpetrators of the 1999 violence (Figure I.1).

From the seventeenth century, East Timor was valued for its resources of sandalwood and coffee. Nonetheless, as one of the most remote of Portugal's colonies, it was relatively neglected, and received limited economic and political investment until the late nineteenth century (Taylor 1999: 1–3). At this point, Portuguese rule became more intrusive as the colonial power sought to consolidate its control over the territory in order to more systematically exploit its resources. One strand of its strategy involved the expropriation of large areas of agricultural land from local rulers to cultivate coffee and copra as cash crops for export, a system that was maintained by various methods of coercion, including a head tax and forced labour (Molnar 2010: 35). Another component pivoted around the introduction of policies to undermine the indigenous system of political alliances based on kinship and to replace it with a new administrative system (Taylor 1999: 10–11). The combined impact of these policies on East Timorese society was profound: the forced production of cash crops undermined the production of less profitable food crops that were vital to

Figure I.1 Aerial view of Dili after the post-referendum violence of 1999 (Ross Bird)

the food security of the East Timorese (Ramos-Horta 1987), while the creation of a system of government that deliberately pitted 'loyal' *liurai* (chiefs) against rebellious ones deepened pre-existing divisions amongst the population and fostered new ones (Taylor 1999: 11–12; Robinson 2010: 6).

The Second World War exacerbated the debilitating conditions in which much of the East Timorese population lived. Following Japan's attack on

Pearl Harbor in December 1941, Australian, British and Dutch troops took 'pre-emptive' action by landing in Portuguese Timor, concerned that Japan might use it as a base to launch attacks against Australia (CAVR 2005a: Part 3, 10). After Japan's invasion of Timor on 19 February 1942, many East Timorese fought alongside Australian soldiers, paying a heavy price for doing so. By the time the Japanese surrendered, some 60,000 East Timorese, or 13 per cent of the population, had died as a result of the war, most of East Timor's main towns and villages had been destroyed, livestock levels were greatly reduced and large numbers of people were starving (Taylor 1999: 14). As in other parts of Asia, there had also been widespread sexual slavery of East Timorese women by Japanese soldiers (ETAN 2008). As Gunn (1999: 235–7) highlights, despite the fact that many ordinary East Timorese suffered immensely during the war, there has never been an international investigation into war crimes committed by Allied or Japanese soldiers, nor have war reparations been paid to the East Timorese people.

After the war, Portuguese administrators re-established their control over the territory, even while many other southern nations were undergoing decolonisation (Molnar 2010: 37). East Timor remained a highly unequal society with a very limited infrastructure. For example, it was not until the 1960s that the capital city Dili was provided with electricity. By 1974, only a few main streets of Dili had been paved, while piped fresh water and medical facilities were not provided to towns beyond Dili until the early 1970s (Ramos-Horta 1987: 22). Education was also restricted: only one public high school existed in the territory in the early 1970s and 90 per cent of the population remained illiterate (Hughes 2009: 34; see also Gunn 1999: 247). Only a small number of privileged Portuguese-speaking *assimilados* (assimilated natives) were able to access seminary education. Educated in Portuguese history and literature, members of this elite group were also among the first nationalists in East Timor, and some went on to play key roles in the independence movement (Molnar 2010: 43–4).

The overthrow of the Caetano regime in Portugal in 1974 stimulated the growth of political parties in East Timor. Among the most prominent were the radical pro-independence FRETILIN (*Frente Revolucionária de Timor-Leste Independente* / Revolutionary Front for an Independent East Timor) and the more conservative UDT (*União Democrática Timorense* / Timorese Democratic Union), which favoured eventual independence, but only after a lengthy period of transition under Portuguese tutelage. In August 1975, in the context of covert Indonesian operations aimed at bringing about East Timor's integration with Indonesia, these parties were engaged in a brief, but brutal, conflict, which is often described as a civil war. After winning a military victory, FRETILIN declared East Timor's independence on 28 November 1975. The new nation was then invaded and occupied by Indonesian forces nine days later, and was subsequently incorporated into Indonesia as its 27th province. A tenacious armed and clandestine resistance struggle – which is discussed in Chapter 4 – was waged over the next twenty-four years.

Although the Indonesian invasion of East Timor in 1975 was widely condemned by the UN, the international community largely turned a blind eye to the repressive nature of the occupation. Many Western states acquiesced to the invasion, and played an ongoing role in sustaining the Indonesian occupation because it served their economic and strategic interests. Perhaps the most vigorous supporter of the Indonesian regime was Australia, which doubled its military assistance to Indonesia between 1975 and 1981, and granted *de jure* recognition to Indonesia's annexation of East Timor, necessary for its negotiations with the Indonesian government over the rights to the oil and gas deposits in the Timor Sea (Nevins 2002a: 629). Meanwhile, the United States continued to supply arms to Indonesia for use in maintaining 'internal security' (Nevins 2002a: 630).

According to credible estimates, the Indonesian occupation resulted in the deaths of an estimated 100,000–200,000 people out of a population of less than 800,000 (see Robinson 2003: 16; CAVR 2005a: Part 6; Kiernan 2003). While some deaths were the direct result of military assaults, more people perished of illness and starvation after being displaced, herded into camps or forcibly moved into Indonesian military-controlled resettlement villages, which, strategically, were located in zones far from areas of resistance (Taylor 1999: 84–92; Robinson 2010: 51). Poor conditions in resettlement villages, minimal supplies of food and medicine, and inadequate water sources were compounded by strictly curtailed freedom of movement and agricultural activities. These factors led directly to a devastating famine in the late 1970s, which claimed thousands of lives (Taylor 1999: 93; Robinson 2010: 51; CAVR 2005a: Part 7.3, 67). Throughout the occupation, the East Timorese population also endured arbitrary imprisonment, torture, assault and rape, repeated displacement, lack of access to basic needs including health care, and ongoing restrictions on freedom of movement (CAVR 2005: Part 7). Another pervasive feature of the occupation was the extensive militarisation of East Timorese society. A key aspect of the Indonesian regime's counter-insurgency approach involved the systematic recruitment of East Timorese into combat battalions, paramilitary groups and civil defence forces, and their employment as spies and informants, tactics that worked to undermine social bonds and to sow fear and distrust within local communities (see Robinson 2010; Larke 2009: 654; CAVR 2005a: Part 4).

The 1991 Santa Cruz massacre, in which up to 273 East Timorese lost their lives, many of them young people, marked a turning point in international awareness of Indonesian atrocities. Although similar atrocities had taken place before, what was different about Santa Cruz was that the actions of the Indonesian military were filmed by a British photojournalist who then managed to smuggle the film out of the country. The events were then shown worldwide (Taylor 1999: xiii). Nonetheless, real change was possible only following Indonesia's President Soeharto's fall from power in 1998 in the wake of the Asian Economic Crisis. The new President, B.J. Habibie, then unexpectedly announced his government's intention to conduct a referendum in which the people of East Timor would choose between autonomy within Indonesia and independence. Following negotiations between the UN and the Indonesian government, the United Nations Mission in East Timor (UNAMET) was established to organise a referendum. Despite evidence that the Indonesian military and police forces were collaborating with local militia groups to intimidate voters against voting for independence, the Indonesian police were put in charge of ensuring security for the referendum (Robinson 2010: 106). As the referendum date approached, the violence escalated and, on 6 April, members of the *Besih Merah Putih* militia group attacked a group of people who had taken refuge in the Catholic church compound in the town of Liquica. As many as sixty people were killed by militia as Indonesian military, police and Paramilitary Brigade (Brimob) troops stood by. Not long afterwards, on 17 April, militia members rampaged through East Timor's capital, Dili, killing more than a dozen people.

Despite the climate of intimidation, 99 per cent of registered East Timorese voted in the referendum. Within days of the announcement of the results, however, which demonstrated that an overwhelming majority of East Timorese people were in favour of independence, the territory was subjected to an intensified campaign of violence and abuse. Over 1,000 people were killed, houses and villages were burned and destroyed, around 400,000 people were displaced (including more than 200,000 into West Timor), and all significant government and commercial basic infrastructure was destroyed (OHCHR 2000; CAVR 2005a: Part 7.5, 48). A particularly brutal massacre took place in the town of Suai, Covalima, the day after the announcement of the referendum results, on 6 September 1999, when up to 200 unarmed civilians were killed at the *Nossa Senhora do Rosário* (Our Mother of Rosario) church, including refugees who had been sheltering in the church, together with three priests (Figure I.2). On 8 September, UNAMET was forced to withdraw most of its personnel from the territory due to grave concerns about their security, and it was not until 20 September that a multinational military force known as the International Force for East Timor (INTERFET) was deployed, under the operational command of Australia, to restore order (see UNSC 1999b). The UN then assumed the administration of East Timor, through the UN Transitional Administration for East Timor (UNTAET), until formal independence was declared on 20 May 2002.

The UNTAET mission represented one of the most ambitious state-building projects undertaken by the UN. Going beyond traditional peacekeeping and peace-building mandates, UN state-building is directed at 'constructing or reconstructing institutions of governance capable of providing citizens with physical or economic security' (Chesterman 2004: 5). In the case of transitional administration, these ends are accomplished by 'assuming some or all of the powers of the state on a temporary basis' (Chesterman 2004: 5). The

Figure I.2 Suai church, where up to 200 people were killed on 6 September 1999 (Lia Kent)

UNTAET mission was more expansive than previous UN transitional administrations because it represented the first time that the UN had exercised full sovereignty over territory independently of any parallel local authority (Chopra 2002: 28; Chesterman 2002: 46). As the UN Secretary General noted in early 2000, 'never before has the United Nations attempted to build and manage a state' (UNSG 2000a: para 64). Security Council Resolution 1272 establishing UNTAET gave the mission 'overall responsibility for the administration of East Timor' and the power 'to exercise all legislative and executive authority, including the administration of justice' (UNSC 1999a). With funding provided from the assessed contributions of UN member states and the voluntary contributions of foreign donor states and multilateral institutions, UNTAET was responsible for a daunting array of tasks. These included providing security and maintaining order, rehabilitating infrastructure, establishing an effective administration, assisting in the development of civil and social services, supporting capacity-building for self-government and reconstructing the justice sector (UNSC 1999a). The World Bank, in co-operation with the Asian Development Bank, had responsibility for facilitating economic reconstruction and development, and focused on the sectors of health, education, agriculture, transport, power and water supply, and private sector development (see Rohland and Cliffe 2002). East Timor's transition to independence was expected to take two to three years.

Dealing with the past

In response to widespread condemnation around the world of the post-referendum violence, UN statements, resolutions and reports were imbued with strong language about the need for criminal prosecutions of those responsible for the 1999 violence (see UNSC 1999a; UNSC 1999b; UNCHR 1999). This would be essential, it was argued, to provide 'justice' to the East Timorese and to facilitate a successful transition to democracy by acting as a deterrent against future abuses and helping to entrench a strong 'rule of law' culture. Thus the Security Council Resolution establishing INTERFET in September 1999 condemned all acts of violence and demanded that those responsible by brought to justice (UNSC 1999b).

Less explicitly, the prosecution of serious crimes perpetrators was also viewed as important to the international community as a whole, to restore basic 'universal values' that had been undermined by the Indonesian government's flagrant breach of the Security Council Resolution that had entrusted security for the referendum to the Indonesian police. Thus a report by the UN's High Commissioner for Human Rights, also in September 1999, concluded that:

> To end the century and the millennium tolerating impunity for those guilty of these shocking violations would be a betrayal of everything

> the United Nations stands for regarding the universal promotion and protection of human rights.
>
> (UNCHR 1999: para 48)

Despite these robust statements, there had been little pre-planning about how prosecutions would take place and who should take responsibility. To provide further guidance on these questions, a UN Commission of Inquiry (COI) visited the country in September 1999. It produced a report that, like that of the UN High Commissioner for Human Rights, was emphatic that the UN had a 'special responsibility' to ensure that the crimes committed in 1999 would not go unpunished, especially as Indonesia had breached a binding Security Council Resolution (OHCHR 2000: para 147). The COI report recommended the establishment of an international criminal tribunal along the lines of those created for the former Yugoslavia and Rwanda. In his letter of 31 January accompanying the COI report, UN Secretary General Kofi Annan endorsed the COI's findings, underscoring that 'the United Nations ha[d] an important role to play in this process [of bringing perpetrators to account] in order to protect the integrity of Security Council actions' (UNSG 2000b).

Yet, rather than following the COI's recommendation and establishing an international criminal tribunal, the Secretary General – responding to assurances from the Indonesian government – recommended that the Indonesian courts must first be given an opportunity to investigate and prosecute perpetrators in Indonesia. He justified this by explaining:

> The main thing is to put people on trial and make them accountable . . . If the Government has the capacity and the willingness to do it and is doing it, you don't want to create another tribunal.
>
> (UN Secretary General Kofi Annan, in Linton 2001: 213)

At the same time, the Secretary General declared that he intended to strengthen UNTAET's capacity to conduct investigations and to collaborate with the Indonesian processes, and, in April 2000, a Serious Crimes Investigations Unit (SCIU) was established in East Timor comprising international civilian and police investigators. The SCIU was mandated to investigate certain 'serious crimes', defined as genocide, crimes against humanity and war crimes, as well as certain domestic crimes including murder, torture and sexual offences. Two months later, in June 2000, a specialised 'hybrid' or internationalised tribunal was established, known as the Special Panels for Serious Crimes ('the Special Panels'), which was attached to the Dili District Court. Together, these investigative and prosecutorial functions are referred to as the Serious Crimes Process.[4] A Memorandum of Understanding (MoU)

4 See UNTAET Regulations 2000/11 and 2000/15.

between Indonesia and UNTAET was then signed with the purpose of ensuring co-operation in the exchange of evidence, requests for witnesses and making arrests, and ensuring the transfer of suspects when needed in the investigation and prosecution of serious crimes (RI/UNTAET 2000: Preamble). The MoU reaffirmed the commitment to 'hold accountable the perpetrators of serious violations of international humanitarian and human rights law in East Timor'. In response to international pressure, the Indonesian government eventually created another mechanism – the Ad Hoc Human Rights Court in Jakarta – to try within its own jurisdiction Indonesian perpetrators who had played a leading role in the violence.

UNTAET was also faced with the question of what to do with the thousands of other 'less serious' crimes, including looting, arson, theft and the destruction of property, committed immediately prior to and following the referendum of 1999. It was clear that the nascent domestic legal system, with its limited infrastructure and inexperienced legal actors, would not be capable of dealing with all of these issues. A related preoccupation at this time of both UNTAET and members of the East Timorese political elite – namely, leaders of the *Conselho Nacional de Resistência Timorense* (National Council for Timorese Resistance/CNRT)[5] – was how to ensure the safe return of the 120,000 Timorese who remained displaced in West Timor, who had the capacity to cause continuing instability. To respond to these concerns, in June 2000, UNTAET's Human Rights Unit, together with Uppsala University from Sweden, organised a workshop on transitional justice mechanisms to consider truth commission options, at which representatives of the International Center for Transitional Justice (ICTJ) provided expert advice (Larke 2009). The East Timorese leadership was also considering options for a truth commission and, in August 2000, a Congress of the CNRT recommended the need for a 'Commission for Resettlement and National Reconciliation', which should 'undertake fact finding to collect detailed data' (CNRT 2000a). The UNTAET Human Rights Unit then took the lead in convening a Steering Committee, which led to the establishment of the *Comissão de Acolhimento, Verdade e Reconciliação* (Commission for Reception, Truth and Reconciliation/CAVR), in July 2001, as an independent statutory body, by a legal act of the UN (UNTAET 2001). The body was then formally recognised within the East Timorese Constitution.

The CAVR had three main stated aims. The first was to establish the 'truth' about the twenty-four-year Indonesian occupation, by collecting statements

5 CNRT was formed in 1998 and was the major coalition of East Timorese political groups that resisted the Indonesian occupation of East Timor. The two most powerful among its constituent parties were FRETILIN and UDT. The president of CNRT was Xanana Gusmão. José Ramos-Horta – CNRT's international spokesman – was another powerful figure. CNRT was disbanded prior to the August 2001 elections.

from individuals throughout the nation and conducting public hearings. The second was to encourage the 'reception' and reintegration of former militia members who had committed so-called 'less-serious' crimes during 1999 back into their communities through an innovative community reconciliation process (CRP), which incorporated local dispute resolution practices. The third aim was to prepare a final report containing findings and recommendations to be presented to East Timor's President and Parliament following independence. Although it was developed quite separately from the Serious Crimes Process, the CAVR was nonetheless expected to play a complementary role and, in particular, the CRP was expected to relieve the pressure on an overburdened and underdeveloped East Timorese legal system.

While the Serious Crimes Process invoked 'universal' human rights values and the rule of law as means of addressing the past and deterring future human rights abuses, the CAVR promoted the values of community reconciliation and healing through truth-telling and restorative justice. It was also assumed that the CAVR's work would have other benefits: that enabling victims to tell their stories would help to restore their dignity, and that establishing the truth about East Timor's repressive past would contribute to national reconciliation, democracy and state-building, and act as a deterrent against future abuses. These multilayered expectations were articulated by the UNTAET Transitional Administrator, Sergio Viera De Mello, in January 2002:

> [The CAVR is a] vitally important initiative for the country. It will provide the East Timorese people with an official ear to listen to their grievances and acknowledge their past suffering. It will provide them with a historical record that is based on the experiences and stories of the people themselves. It will bring together those who have been in conflict in the past and give them a way forward, an opportunity for grievances and long-lasting reconciliation. It will further the cause of justice by offering a mechanism for dealing with many of the violations that were committed in this country during past conflicts, without burdening the court system that is already addressing the most serious cases.
>
> (Sergio Viera De Mello, in Huang and Gunn, 2004: 30)

In many ways, then, the transitional justice approach adopted in East Timor resonates with recent trends in transitional justice discourse and practice. Transitional justice was a central component of the UN's post-conflict reconstruction 'toolkit' applied to East Timor and, in addition, represented one of the first examples of an attempt to combine criminal prosecutions with a truth commission. Representing a shift away from international tribunals (in spite of lobbying by East Timorese leaders and human rights groups for this model), East Timor's 'hybrid' Special Panels for Serious Crimes were established as an adjunct to the domestic legal system; they comprised both East Timorese and international judges, and governed by a mixture of Indonesian and international law. This model was purported to combine the strengths of an international tribunal with the benefits of local prosecutions (Katzenstein 2003: 245–6). The CAVR, and in particular, the innovative CRP, represented a deeper attempt at engaging with East Timor's local context by building on pre-existing, village-based, dispute resolution practices. Endowed with an ambitious mandate, the transitional justice process as a whole was expected to accomplish a daunting range of goals, which included providing 'justice' to victims and their families, fostering healing, reconciliation and nation-building, acting as a deterrent to future human rights violations, and protecting the integrity of the UN itself.

Recent studies have shown that this approach had a number of fundamental flaws. A key issue was Indonesia's lack of co-operation with the UN's hybrid Serious Crimes Process; this meant that suspects based in Indonesia, among them senior members of the Indonesian military, could not be prosecuted. Relying on the Indonesian judicial system to prosecute war criminals also proved to be poor judgement on the part of the UN. Widely condemned as a failure by the international community, the Ad Hoc Human Rights Court indicted eighteen people, all of whom were eventually acquitted (Cohen 2003). By contrast, the CAVR has been judged to be more successful. Its nationwide community reconciliation process (CRP) adjudicated almost 1,400 cases of minor crimes, while, as part of its truth-seeking function, the CAVR held a series of hearings that were highly participatory and were broadcast widely on the radio and television. Yet many have questioned the extent to which the CAVR has responded to East Timorese expectations of justice, given that none of the principal Indonesian perpetrators of serious crimes have been arrested or prosecuted (Larke 2009; Kent 2004; Pigou 2004; Stanley 2009; Nevins 2005; Robinson 2010).

Following the conclusion of trials by East Timor's Special Panels in May 2005, and the completion of the CAVR's final report in late 2005, the slogan 'No reconciliation without justice' continues to be a rallying cry for national human rights NGOs and local victims' groups, who are waging persistent and vocal campaigns demanding prosecutions of the Indonesian military and reparations for victims. The enduring nature of these campaigns – which call attention to unfinished business and 'unreconciled' experiences – gives a preliminary sense of the widespread community disillusionment with the transitional justice process, and with the limited form of 'justice' it has provided. In the chapters that follow, I interrogate the dissonance between community expectations and institutional rhetoric in greater depth by unravelling the intersections, and at times collisions, between diverse narratives of justice circulating within the international, national and local spheres.

Producing a 'thick' study of transitional justice: methodology and conceptual approach

This book sets out to contribute what McEvoy refers to as a 'thick' exploration of transitional justice (McEvoy 2008: 17). In contrast to 'thin' or positivist studies, which emphasise the formal, instrumental or normative aspects of transitional justice, 'thick' explorations focus on its complex, multilayered and actor-oriented dimensions (ibid). They seek to engage with the messiness of transitional justice, including how globalised concepts and processes are given meaning in specific places and times, and how they may be reshaped in unexpected directions (see Shaw and Waldorf 2010: 3–4).

The book intentionally focuses on the *local* dynamics of transitional justice in East Timor. This emphasis means that the empirical material upon which the book relies is oriented primarily towards capturing the views of East Timorese survivors (as opposed to those of international state-builders, East Timorese leaders and transitional justice advocates). In other words, the book does not set out to provide a detailed examination of the political dynamics and conflicting narratives that played out *within* the UN and the transitional justice institutions themselves (although this would be a very interesting story in itself). Thus, while Chapters 1, 2, 3 and 4, which examine international and national justice narratives, draw on some interview material, they rely primarily on a critical analysis of key texts and documents including newspaper articles, speeches, press releases and UN reports. In reading these texts, I engage with a range of critical approaches to international law that seek to shed light on the deeper relations of power and particular worldviews that underpin the so-called 'universal', liberal assumptions of transitional justice *discourse*. I argue that these assumptions lead to particular retributive justice and restorative justice responses to conflict that may foreclose other, more nuanced ways of thinking about, and responding to, conflict. These power relations and exclusions may not always be visible to those who are formally involved in the practice of transitional justice, no matter how laudable their intentions.

The methodology for Chapters 5 and 6, which examine local justice narratives, draws on the results of extensive fieldwork. I seek to provide rich information about survivors' perceptions of the transitional justice process and to show how these perceptions are informed by the multiple, locally embedded meanings of justice. These chapters draw, in particular, on the findings of interviews conducted in the districts of Covalima, Lautem and Liquica over two fieldwork visits in 2007 and 2008. I conducted in-depth semi-structured interviews with approximately 100 individuals, primarily 'victims' or 'survivors' who had participated in the Serious Crimes Process or the CAVR, as well as community leaders, including *Chefes de Suco* (village chiefs) and *Chefes de Aldeia* (hamlet chiefs). These interviews were supplemented with informal conversations and observation. An analysis of fieldwork findings helps to further unsettle the liberal, universal assumptions of transitional justice discourse by showing how these processes are given meaning within specific political and social contexts (see also Dembour and Kelly 2007b). As Darian-Smith makes clear, empirical methodologies – and specifically ethnographic methodologies – are well placed to explore these intricacies because they illustrate that the 'law is not monolithic and universalistic in practice, that it does not correlate to any one culturally discreet unit, and that it is not devoid of sites of resistance, challenge and modification' (Darian-Smith 2004: 556).

Conducting cross-cultural research, particularly with individuals who have experienced violence and regarding painful subject matter, presents many ethical challenges and is fraught with issues of power and representation. The challenge, as post-colonial scholars have identified, is for researchers to seek to 'decolonise' their research practices (Tierney 2003: 306; Smith 2003: 7; Moreton-Robinson 2000). As Tierney acknowledges, while a commitment to 'naming' silenced lives or 'writing back' those who have been marginalised by dominant discourses is part of a decolonising approach, this, in itself, is insufficient (Tierney 2003: 306). What is needed is for researchers to engage in a process of 'reflexivity' in order to interrogate their own views and values and challenge Western research orthodoxies, which are often considered to be authoritative, neutral and universal (Rigney 2001: 3; see also Moreton-Robinson 2000; Tierney 2003).

A key aspect of a reflexive approach is an acknowledgement of the constructed nature of the research process, including the fact that researchers are not objective, impartial, recorders of facts, but have their own conceptual frames and worldviews, and interpret and mediate the data in a number of ways (Elliot 2005: 20; see also Tierney 2003). It also seeks to render visible, and challenge, the relations of privilege and power inherent in the research process (Tierney 2003; see also Stanley 2009: 16). Far from disavowing possibilities for change, this process can enable researchers to think more deeply about *what* they write and *why* they write (Tierney 2003: 318). The need for reflexivity is particularly important in the context of research on traumatic events, where trauma victims frequently become the objects of 'voyeuristic or triumphalist fascination' (Radstone 2007: 23), and where there can be a tendency to assume that providing an opportunity for interviewees to 'speak' may help be healing or therapeutic (Stanley, 2009: 13; see also Radstone 2007: 22). As Stanley observes, researchers can exacerbate experiences of marginalisation and inequality by turning stories into a 'commodity' for external consumption (Stanley 2009: 14–16; Tierney 2003: 318). Storytellers, she writes, 'can regularly lose ownership over their stories, a point intensified by unequal resources and access to global information flows' (Stanley 2009: 16).

Informed by these insights, where possible I attempt to consider the way in which my status as a white, female researcher from Australia – who speaks

Tetum – may have been perceived by interviewees, in order to unsettle assumptions about my 'neutral' and 'objective' status. This included being attentive, during fieldwork, to the reasons why some survivors may have expressed annoyance, or weariness, about the prospect of being interviewed, and why some of those I approached did not wish to speak to me. I also sought to understand why other individuals approached the interview task with a particular urgency, and recounted their stories in the style of a *testimonio* (testimony) in order to make a particular claim on my attention (see also Tierney 2003: 298–9). Like Stanley (2009: 15), who conducted research with East Timorese torture survivors, I found that, for many of my respondents, the interview process was not considered as an end in itself, but a form of political agency that was connected to a desire for concrete changes in their everyday lives. Reflecting on these issues led me to be particularly aware of the responsibilities inherent in the privileged role of 'researcher'. This entailed accepting that my role was not that of an 'objective' and 'neutral' recorder of facts, and that my position of privilege gave me a responsibility to be more than a 'spectator' to people's experiences (see Scheper-Hughes 1995). It meant that, where possible, I tried to assist individuals by clarifying basic facts about the transitional justice mechanisms and passing information back to these bodies regarding requests for information, public hearing books and feedback on certain cases.

Conceptually, the book works from a critical analysis of 'discourses' and 'narratives'. I understand discourse as a regulated way of thinking about and representing an issue through written and verbal forms, as well as socio-cultural practices (see, for example, Fairclough 1995). As Fairclough (1995: 82) has observed, discourses do not just represent the world, but are also ideologically invested because they contribute to the reproduction of relations of power. Some discourses can also be described as narratives. These are 'discourses with a clear sequential order that connect events in a meaningful way for a definite audience and thus offer insights about the world and/or people's experiences of it' (Hinchman and Hinchman, cited in Elliot 2005: 3). As Clare Moon (2008) has noted, transitional justice discourses can be understood as discursive narratives, in that they tell a story about 'transition' that has a clear beginning (conflict) and a clear end (peace or reconciliation). This story – which is a narrative of progress – evolves '*as if* in a linear and developmental trajectory' (Moon 2008: 7). Transitional justice narratives also render certain 'subjects' (namely, 'victims' and 'perpetrators') visible, and certain 'truths' (namely, a truth of individual human rights violations) central (Moon 2008: 6).

The public discourses of justice and nation-building promoted by members of the East Timorese political leadership can also be described as narratives. As will become clear in later chapters, these narratives tell their own story of progress, albeit of a very different kind. Theirs is a story of collective struggle and endurance against colonial occupiers and, ultimately, of liberation, in which certain subjects (namely, 'heroes' and 'traitors') are rendered visible. In a similar vein, the views and opinions of East Timorese survivors should be understood as 'narratives'. These tell very different kinds of stories from official narratives. They may be fragmented, non-linear and highly personalised stories, which, unlike official narratives, stress the continuing influence of the past in the present and emphasise a range of intertwined needs. Nonetheless, as will become evident in Chapters 5 and 6, local actors also embrace, transform and resist national and international narratives in a range of ways.

In analysing the views of East Timorese survivors in this way, I am informed by the work of feminist, Marxist, post-structuralist and post-colonial theorists interested in issues of subjectivity and identification. According to these theorists, our sense of self, or subjectivity, is not static, but fluid, and is 'constantly being reconstituted in discourses every time we think or speak' (Weedon 1987: 33). Rather than viewing individuals as autonomous agents who are capable of independently inventing themselves, these scholars understand individual lives as 'constant constructs embedded in societal and cultural forces that seek to constrain some and enable others' (Tierney 2003: 299). They do not assume that interview data provides objective, factual, information, but are interested in what this data reveals about the broader culture, framework and relations of power in which people make sense of their lives, and the everyday practices by which individuals construct and reconstruct their sense of identity (Elliot 2005: 28, 124). Informed by these insights, while I acknowledge interviewees' painful and very real personal experiences of past harm, I recognise that their lives 'cannot be considered independently of their social world and the discourses available to them to understand their experiences' (Powell 2007: 92). I am mindful, too, that local communities may replicate broader social inequities (McEvoy and McGregor 2008b: 9). In addition, I am interested not only in what interviewees say, but in *how* they frame, present and interpret their own stories, and the deeper meanings of these stories. Thus I consider such important questions as what is emphasised and what is left out of these stories? What is the purpose of telling stories? What do those who tell their stories expect from the listener? Who gets to tell their stories and who does not?

Finally, there are several terms I seek to problematise throughout the book. These include the terms 'international', 'national' and 'local'. Although I am interested in analysing the narratives of justice circulating within the international, national and local spheres, I am mindful that these spheres are not bounded and impermeable, but overlapping and interrelated. To suggest that East Timorese victims/survivors operate only in the 'local' sphere, while the staff of the CAVR and the Serious Crimes Process are 'international' and the East Timorese leadership is 'national', may overlook the extent to which international and national narratives circulate locally; international human rights discourses, for example, may be invoked by survivors in making justice claims, while East Timorese civil society organisations often have close links to international human rights organisations such as Amnesty International and Human Rights Watch. These terms may also obscure the extent to which 'local' problems often have global dimensions and causes (Merry 2006a: 212; see also Darian-Smith 2004: 552). East Timor's widespread and entrenched poverty, for example, is closely connected to a history of Portuguese colonialism and Western support for the oppressive Indonesian occupation. Thus, even as I use the terms international, national and local as broad terms of categorisation, I seek to unsettle them by exploring their internal tensions and their areas of intersection.

The terms 'victim' and 'perpetrator' may be similarly problematic. They may be analytically inadequate for attending to the multiple and changing identities that people assumed in the coercive context of the Indonesian occupation, when Indonesian military surveillance seeped into everyday life, permeating relationships, and fostered fear and suspicion amongst neighbours and families. As Shaw and Waldorf (2010: 8) note, the labels 'victim' and 'perpetrator' may also be profoundly depoliticising. The term 'victim', for example, often requires individuals to conform to a particular script of 'innocence' that defines them as 'passive objects of pity' and renders them 'dependent and subject to external interventions' (Gready 2011: 165). In the East Timor context, as I discuss further in Chapter 5, the extent to which an individual chooses to identify as a victim may also be shaped by a range of factors, including socio-economic status, gender and the extent to which they were involved in political resistance activities. Thus, during interviews, many activists and NGO workers did not wish to identify themselves as victims, associating this term with passivity and a lack of agency. To add another layer of complexity, even those who define themselves as victims in East Timor are far from a homogenous group: differences in gender, socio-economic status, political background, and experiences influence perceptions and views about justice. Conscious of these complexities, while I use the term 'victim' (or 'survivor') throughout this book to refer to individuals who had participated in the transitional justice process as a victim, I also seek to unsettle this category by considering who it includes and excludes, and reflecting on the forms of agency it enables and disallows. I also seek to engage with individuals not as passive victims, but as political actors: as 'living and breathing people attempting to make sense of their lives' (Hughes 2009: 21).

The chapters

Chapter 1 sets the conceptual scene for the rest of the book. It begins to unsettle the concepts of 'transition' and 'justice' that are often taken for granted by transitional justice decision-makers. Drawing on the work of critical theorists, ethnographers and social scientists, it questions the idea of 'rupture' between the past and the future, and highlights that 'dealing with the past' is a long-term, contested and inevitably political process. It identifies the limited, legalistic, conceptions of 'justice' that are contained within transitional justice discourse and seeks to broaden them. It argues that more diverse understandings of justice are needed that are socially, historically and culturally situated, and take into account the structural dimensions of violence.

Chapters 2, 3 and 4 explore transitional justice narratives promoted by actors in the international and national spheres. They seek to unravel the interactions, and at times collisions, between these spheres as each competes to provide the 'official' justice response to East Timor's violent past, and, in doing so, to facilitate East Timor's transition from a violent past to a peaceful future. Chapter 2 examines the competing political imperatives that shaped the establishment and operation of the official transitional justice process. Situating East Timor within other relevant international experiences, it considers the complex debates on questions such as reconciliation versus retribution, amnesty and repatriation of refugees that emerged soon after the referendum and traces them into the post-independence period. In contrast to the UN's toolkit approach, which assumed that transitional justice mechanisms could be introduced by international actors operating 'above' the political sphere, this chapter shows that the Serious Crimes Process and the CAVR were significantly marked by political debates over the best way in which to deal with the past, in which pragmatic 'stability' imperatives – informed by Indonesia's strategic influence in the region – came to overshadow retributive justice goals. By unravelling these debates, this chapter unsettles the view that transitional justice in East Timor has been a normative and apolitical process, and challenges the linear notion of 'transition' that assumed that these mechanisms would help to bring about a rupture with the past and foster a new, democratic, order.

Following on from this discussion, Chapter 3 explores the day-to-day operation of the Serious Crimes Process and the CAVR. It argues that multiple factors constrained the ability of the transitional justice mechanisms to meet their own retributive justice and restorative justice goals. Some of these constraints reflected the unique context in which these mechanisms were established – in particular, the stability imperatives discussed in Chapter 2 – while others illustrate some of the more general difficulties faced by trials and truth commissions in attempting to accomplish a range of diverse, and, at times, conflicting goals. This chapter also sheds light on the inherent inability of the transitional justice mechanisms to attend fully to the demands of justice that are *beyond* the law. Among other issues, I demonstrate that the Serious Crimes Process and, to a lesser extent, the CAVR, were incapable of fully responding to the structural dimensions of East Timor's violence. By bringing these multiple constraints to the fore, this chapter sheds further light on the reasons for local disillusionment with the transitional justice process in East Timor.

Chapter 4 turns to an analysis of narratives of justice promoted in the national sphere, through the East Timorese political leadership. These narratives

– which invoke a forward-looking vision of reconciliation-as-forgiveness and social justice rather than retributive justice – are grounded in collective experiences of struggle against the Indonesian occupation. I show that these narratives, and their internal tensions, continue to be reflected in the leadership's statements and approaches to questions of prosecutions, reconciliation and commemoration. By tracing how the transitional justice process has become embedded within a national context in which there are pre-existing debates about the significance of the past, this chapter raises additional questions about the capacity of legal and quasi-legal mechanisms to provide a meaningful form of justice to the East Timorese population, and further unsettles the linear assumptions of 'transition'.

Chapters 5 and 6 explore narratives of justice and injustice promoted in the local sphere, by East Timorese survivors. Chapter 5 draws on in-depth interviews in East Timor to explore the diverse and highly personalised forms of justice that East Timorese survivors sought through participating in the formal transitional justice process, some of which resonated with the underlying objectives of these mechanisms, and others which diverged from them. I show that survivors' conceptions of justice reflect a range of influences including customary belief systems, personal experiences of violence, socio-economic conditions, national resistance narratives and international transitional justice narratives. By carefully attending to the views of survivors, this chapter highlights that recourse to legal and quasi-legal mechanisms alone may never meet historically and culturally situated, and ongoing, demands for justice.

Building on this analysis, Chapter 6 explores how the local practices of East Timorese survivors are unsettling official international and national justice narratives. I show how local actors are pursuing their own, locally grounded, forms of justice by constructing memorials, commemorating massacres and establishing victims' support groups. These practices bring to the fore personal and familial commitments to keeping the memory of past violence alive and invoke customary responsibilities to the ancestors. I argue that some local memory practices can be seen, too, as political struggles for recognition from the state by those who perceive themselves to be left out of the nation-building process. These struggles, which are evident in civil society campaigns for victims' rights and reparations, and in the political tenor of local memorialisation practices, suggest that East Timorese survivors are in various ways reproducing, resisting and transforming 'official' discourses of justice and nation-building. These developments suggest that, in the drive towards 'closure', a new form of politics is beginning to transpire in which 'victims' are emerging as key actors.

Drawing together the key strands of the book, Chapter 7 argues that the pursuit of justice in post-referendum East Timor is a dynamic and ongoing process that is not confined to a specific 'transitional' period. It argues that transitional justice has become part of a nationally and locally engaged conversation about how best to 'deal with the past' that is being shaped and contested by a myriad of different actors, among them the national government and opposition parties, national and international human rights organisations, the UN, victims' groups and other interest groups. Reflecting on this dynamism, I offer some thoughts on what 'rethinking' transitional justice may entail for practitioners, justice activists and scholars, both in East Timor and beyond. My conclusions point to the need for a less 'celebratory' approach to transitional justice scholarship and practice. This approach would acknowledge that justice can never be fully provided by legal and quasi-legal mechanisms, and would conceptualise transitional justice not as a short-term 'project', but rather as part of a fluid, dynamic and locally embedded conversation.

Chapter 1

Interrogating 'transition' and 'justice'

The terms 'transition' and 'justice' are often taken for granted by transitional justice scholars and practitioners, neglecting the assumptions that are embedded within this terms. Now that the core themes of the book have been introduced, this chapter canvasses the conceptual material that will help to explain and structure those themes and the assumptions that underpin them. In particular, I take a closer look at the growing body of critical scholarship on transitional justice. Drawing on a wide range of disciplines, including law, anthropology, criminology, history and sociology, critical analysts have begun to unsettle the claims that trials and truth commissions will assist individuals, communities and nations to 'come to terms with' past conflicts. Engaging with this scholarship, we can begin to posit some explanations for the disjuncture between the official goals of transitional justice and local expressions of disappointment with its achievements in East Timor.

This chapter engages, in particular, with two strands of the critical transitional justice scholarship. The first, which encompasses the work of critical theorists, seeks to unpack the purportedly universal liberal values that underpin transitional justice discourse. These theorists argue that, rather than embodying a series of universal rules and mechanisms that can reveal the truth and deliver an impartial form of justice, the discourse of transitional justice rests upon liberal assumptions that may prevent more complex ways of understanding and responding to past conflicts. By questioning the idea of 'rupture' between the past and the future and highlighting the long-term, contested and inevitably *political* process of 'dealing with the past', their work helps to identify simplistic assumptions about the nature of transition. It also assists in identifying – and broadening – the limited conceptions of 'justice' that are evident in transitional justice discourse by attending to its redistributive dimensions. The second, related, strand of criticism encompasses the work of empirical and ethnographic scholars. By providing a 'bottom-up' approach to the study of transitional justice and exploring how individuals and local communities actually engage with these processes, this scholarship assists in developing more nuanced conceptions of 'justice' that are historically and culturally situated. Before turning to both strands of this scholarship, however, it is important briefly to situate them within key established critiques of the dominant legal, liberal tradition and UN state-building projects in post-conflict societies.

Unpacking the universalist assumptions of international law and state-building

Liberalism claims that the law embodies 'universal' values that 'transcend context, morality and politics' (Otto 1999: 11). Because of the law's concern with the formal equality of all individuals, it lays particular claim to the qualities of 'objectivity, abstractness and neutrality' (Charlesworth and Chinkin 2000: 32). For example, the powerful idea of the 'rule of law', which embodies beliefs that no one is above the law, that all are equal before the law, and that laws should be fairly and consistently applied, stands in 'opposition to tyranny and the arbitrary use of force' (Evans 2005: 58). However, critical legal theorists have demonstrated that the law's supposedly universal values have supported particular elite interests – namely, the interests of Western, affluent males – to the exclusion of others, including women, people of colour and those without property (Otto 1999: 12; Stanley 2009: 63; Mehta 1990). Similar critiques have been mounted of international law, the practice of which has tended to benefit affluent Western countries rather than poorer states (see, for example, Anghie 2005). Even in the area of international criminal law, and despite the emergence of the principle of 'universal jurisdiction', which denotes that crimes against humanity, war crimes and genocide should be punished wherever they occur, it is evident that powerful states have a disproportionate influence over whether, and how, war crimes trials are conducted (Nagy 2008). Moreover, when war crimes trials threaten to become inconvenient to powerful states, they simply do not take place – a recent illustration of this being the failure to investigate potential NATO breaches of the law of war in Serbia (Simpson 2007: 47).

Critiques of liberal accounts of law take a range of forms. Some scholarship questions the extent to which the individualist language of rights and the preoccupation with questions of formal equality and individual liberty are able to address underlying structural inequalities, including the unequal distribution of economic, social and political power, which inhibit the accomplishment of formal rights (see, for example, Gledhill 2003: 212). Feminist scholars similarly argue that the liberal focus on achieving formal equality between men and women in the public sphere, such as in political participation and representation, market services, employment and education, leaves untouched the structural barriers to women's participation. They have noted, too, that the exclusive focus of law on the public rather than the private sphere marginalises the concerns and experiences of many women (Charlesworth and Chinkin 2000: 39). These issues are reflected in international human rights law, which, like national law, has tended to target 'public' state-sanctioned violence, rather than violence that occurs within the home (Charlesworth and Chinkin 2000: 31).

Powerful critiques of international law have also been mounted by post-colonial scholars, who point to the Western origins and cultural bias inherent in the development of the international legal regime (see, for example, Anghie 2005; Fitzpatrick 1992). These scholars reveal how, historically, the universalist assumptions in Western law enabled European states to impose their legal systems in different parts of the empire in order to buttress their power (Darian-Smith 2004: 554; Fitzpatrick 1992). For example, key theorist Anthony Anghie traces the links between colonialism and the development of international law, arguing persuasively that international law contributes to the maintenance of structures of inequality between the European and non-European world (Anghie 2005). He emphasises how notions of cultural difference and 'backwardness' have provided the rationale for the denial of sovereignty to non-European states and paved the way for colonial practices of racial discrimination, economic exploitation and territorial dispossession. These practices were justified by a 'civilising mission', which claimed to educate and develop the underdeveloped and oppressed people of the non-European world in order to incorporate them into the 'universal' civilisation of Europe (Anghie 2005: 3). Despite the granting of sovereignty to non-European states in the era of decolonisation and the dramatic changes to the membership of the UN since 1945, international law continues to be shaped by its colonial origins. This is evident in the way in which international law continues to 'manage' Third World states by requiring them to participate in a global political economy in which they are vastly disadvantaged – in part because of the historical forces that shaped them (Darian-Smith 2000: 820; Anghie 2005: 11). Thus, while they may be nominally 'sovereign', post-colonial states are often dependent on loans, grants, investment and intervention for their survival (Kelsall 2009: 157).

Many of these conceptual threads are taken up in recent critiques of UN state-building projects in post-conflict societies, which seek to promote both political and economic liberalisation as a remedy for civil violence (Paris 2004: 5). Critical scholars have explored the connections between the contemporary liberal state-building project in post-conflict societies and the colonial era, and argue that the former reproduces many of the assumptions of the civilising mission, with international institutions involved in state-building claiming to be 'bearers of progressive human rights and democratic values' (Orford 2003: 158; Anghie 2005: 313). Meanwhile, post-conflict states are commonly characterised as underdeveloped, violent, corrupt, incompetent and primitive (Fritz 2005; Anghie 2005: 317). Like the civilising mission, the project of liberal state-building may also further the interests of powerful states and institutions. For example, while the rhetoric of state-building claims to build liberal democracies by promoting free and fair elections, the rule of law and human rights, the state-building process is nevertheless occurring in contexts where the authority of those states is vastly diminished. These issues are particularly acute in UN transitional administrations, where the UN is temporarily responsible for some, or all, state functions. During the UNTAET period in East Timor, the UN was effectively the government of the country, which, as Chopra has noted, essentially endowed the institution with mandates and powers comparable to a colonial regime (Chopra 2000). Moreover, the promotion of economic liberalisation generally requires post-conflict states to create opportunities for private investment by adopting policies of privatisation, reducing government intervention in the economy, and restricting public spending (Anghie 2005; Paris 2004: 5). The powerful influence of international economic organisations, including the World Bank and International Monetary Fund, on post-conflict states can also impede their capacity to debate national priorities and to respond to the needs of their domestic constituencies (Turner 2008: 139).

UN state-building projects may also rest on a problematic 'transition paradigm' (Carothers 2002), which suggests that post-conflict societies move in a linear fashion from dictatorial rule or conflict towards democracy. Within this paradigm, the organisation of free and fair elections, and the establishment of formal democratic institutions, is assumed to be equivalent to democracy rather than just one of its components, and state-building is promoted as an ostensibly 'technical' exercise (Carothers 2002: 7; Bhuta 2009: 49). As Carothers puts it:

> A whole generation of democracy aid is based on the transition paradigm, above all the typical emphasis on an institutional 'checklist' as a basis for creating programs, and the creation of nearly standard portfolios of aid projects . . . some judicial reform, parliamentary strengthening, civil society assistance, media work, political party development, civic education and electoral programs.
>
> (Carothers 2002: 6)

Technocratic approaches fostered under the transition paradigm pay little heed to the complexities facing post-conflict societies, including their underlying economic, social and institutional conditions and legacies (including their colonial legacies), which affect their ability to become stable democracies (Bhuta 2009). They also elide the fact that the apparently 'universal' idea of the 'state' and its associated institutions is, as Bhuta observes, 'a highly particularised historical product' that has been the result of long-term processes and material endowments, rather than of design (Bhuta 2009: 60–1). The 'transition paradigm' also ignores the potentially destabilising effects of democratic and economic liberalisation processes brought about in a rapid fashion. As Paris's work has shown, post-conflict states often struggle to manage the inequalities and social dislocation that results from opening their markets to the global economy; rapid political and economic liberalisation also has the potential to exacerbate social and political tensions and to increase the likelihood of renewed violence (Paris 2004: 5; see also Orford 1997).

These critiques could be applied to East Timor, where the UNTAET state-building project promoted both democratic and economic liberalisation, and held its exit strategy to be the holding of free and fair elections within a defined period (Beauvaris 2001: 1166). On the eve of East Timor's independence, which occurred after two-and-a-half years of UN transitional administration, and following parliamentary and presidential elections, this mission was pronounced a 'success'. Yet, as Stanley (2009: 140–1) has identified, UNTAET's state-building rhetoric – which accentuated the notions of empowerment, development and human rights, and depicted international donors and international economic organisations as essentially 'charitable' – also embedded a free market model of development that promoted private expansion, foreign investment and export production. Given the extent of East Timor's reliance on subsistence agriculture, this model made living conditions more difficult for many East Timorese by raising the costs of basic goods and increasing food insecurity in the rural areas. Similarly, as Grenfell (2004) observes, although ensuring a fair distribution of resources from the lucrative Timor Gap oil and natural gas deposits could end East Timor's dependence on the aid of the international community, the terms of the division of the Timor Sea – which lies between East Timor and Australia – have largely been set by, and will benefit, Western states such as Australia.[1] Although, as I discuss in Chapter 4, East Timor's economic fortunes (and consequently its policy independence) have changed somewhat since 2007, when the government began to receive oil and gas revenues from the Timor Sea, in the early years of independence the new nation had little option but to remain reliant on external aid. The extent of this reliance is reflected in a World Bank report of 2003, which notes that, at that time, around half of the East Timorese government budget was financed by external assistance and aid amounted to about 60 per cent of the country's GDP (World Bank 2003).

There is some evidence to suggest that, following East Timor's independence, liberal state-building assumptions hindered international policymakers in having a nuanced appreciation of problematic political developments within the new East Timorese government, many of which were connected to deep-seated social cleavages and colonial legacies. The 2006 'crisis', which led to street clashes, looting and other violence, and was precipitated by the government's sacking of around one-third of East Timor's military, was not predicted by most state-builders. In the wake of the crisis, the fact that most

1 The Timor Sea dispute is driven by conflicting claims around where a maritime boundary should be placed between Australia and East Timor. Australia has refused to engage in negotiations regarding a permanent maritime boundary (which, under international law, might mean that certain lucrative oil fields are deemed to lie within East Timor's exclusive economic zone) and will negotiate only about revenue-sharing (see La'o Hamutuk 2007).

international media and political commentary identified the East Timorese as responsible for the violence also indicates that the UN has given little consideration to the way in which its approach to state-building may have exacerbated tensions within post-conflict East Timor (Stanley 2009; Curtain 2006). At the very least, the transition paradigm, which assumes that 'democracy' can be transplanted in societies with diverse histories, cultures and institutional legacies, and can be introduced as part of a technical 'checklist', may be part of the problem.

Unpacking 'transition'

Transitional justice discourse shares many of the assumptions of the liberal state-building project. Key amongst these is the belief that, by fostering democratic institutions and free markets, introducing the 'universal' values of the rule of law and assisting societies to 'come to terms' with their past, states will make the 'transition' to peaceful, stable, liberal democracies (Sriram 2007; Moon 2008). Thus, as Claire Moon (2008: 19) has identified, transitional justice discourse is informed by an underlying narrative of 'transition' or 'progress' that symbolises the shift from an illiberal to a liberal regime, or from violence and peace. Invoking Enlightenment values of 'reason, progress, improvement and redemption' (Colvin 2008: 416), transitional justice discourse is built upon the notion of 'breaking with the past', and establishes a definitive sense of 'now' and 'then' (Nagy 2008).

As Moon has observed, this narrative of transition underpins the assumptions of both criminal trials and truth commissions, in that each mechanism purports to offer a particular form of resolution to violence (Moon 2008: 19). Thus criminal trials are informed by a prominent retribution narrative, which is based on the idea of 'settling accounts' through acknowledgement of individual criminal responsibility and punishment (Schaap 2005: 18; Moon 2008: 19). By promoting the values of human rights and respect for the rule of law, generating trust in legal institutions and acting as a deterrent to future criminality, criminal prosecutions are expected to contribute to a shift away from a culture of impunity, and mark a break between the past and the present. By contrast, truth commissions are imbued with a restoration/reconciliation narrative that promotes the resolution of conflicts through restorative justice and truth-telling (Moon 2008: 19). Truth commissions are based on assumptions that public witnessing of the truth about human rights abuses and the creation of an 'agreed-to' historical record of the past will contribute to individual and social healing, build shared values, foster reconciliation, and mark a definitive rupture between the past and present orders (Colvin 2003). Like retribution narratives, then, the language of reconciliation purports to provide its own form of resolution to conflict, whereby populations can be 'healed' through therapeutic storytelling.

Both retribution and restoration/reconciliation narratives can be 'seductive' (McEvoy 2008: 19–20) in that they purport to provide a simple solution to complex historical and political problems. They lead policymakers to view transitional justice mechanisms as 'technical' projects that are short term in nature, embody 'universal' values and are transferrable to a variety of locations. This tendency, which is exemplified by the inclusion of transitional justice as part of the UN's recommended 'toolkit' for successful post-conflict recovery, can be problematic in that it fosters the perception that trials and truth commissions can be orchestrated from 'above' the political sphere, and obscures the extent to which these mechanisms are often the product of compromise, limited domestic choice and conflicting policy agendas (Rajagopal 2008; Fritz 2005; Simpson 2007: 24–5; Bhuta 2005: 245–71; McEvoy 2008: 11).

Contesting these assumptions, a number of critical theorists have called attention to the fact that transitional justice processes are themselves embedded within the political sphere rather than being 'neutral' (see, for example, Simpson 2007: 24–5; Bhuta 2005; Dembour and Kelly 2007b: 12–15; Leebaw 2008). This is not a new debate. In 1964, political theorist Judith Shklar argued persuasively that criminal trials should be viewed as one technique for social control and reform, and should be judged in comparison to other methods of 'doing politics' (Shklar 1964: ix). Similarly, the critical legal studies movement that emerged in the 1970s challenged the view that the law is rational and objective, and argued that law cannot be separated from politics (Charlesworth and Chinkin 2000: 34). The question to ask of criminal trials, then, is not whether they are 'legal' or 'political' tools, but *whose* interests are being advanced and what *kind* of politics are being pursued (Shklar 1964: 145; see also Bhuta 2005). Yet the seductively simple claims of transitional justice may make it difficult to ask these questions, by obscuring tensions between disparate policy agendas and conflicting transitional justice goals, and depicting transitional justice mechanisms as universal, technocratic and neutral.

Fritz has argued that the promotion of transitional justice mechanisms as apolitical is particularly problematic in the context of UN-sponsored initiatives (Fritz 2005). UN-sponsored initiatives are seen as part of the 'standard operating procedure when addressing post-conflict situations in the developing world', and so are much less likely than nationally sponsored processes to acknowledge the politics and compromises that are entailed (Fritz 2005: 330). Promoted as standardised procedures rather than as the product of limited domestic choice, UN-sponsored transitional justice initiatives are presented as the 'optimal' blueprint (Fritz 2005: 330). Similar critiques have been mounted of internationally sponsored 'rule of law' initiatives, which, as Chandler (2004a: 581) has argued, are also particularly likely to ignore the difficult, long-term political discussions and negotiations that are required to build an inclusive political community. Consequently, the imposition of solutions 'from above', irrespective of the specificities of the political context, and often without an agreement with the people of an afflicted state, frequently produces mechanisms that are 'internationalised but isolated from their societies' (Chandler 2006: 166).

These dynamics can be readily observed in East Timor, where transitional justice mechanisms, sponsored by the UN, attempted to provide a framework for understanding the conflict and to offer a means of resolving it. During the UNTAET period, UN statements and pronouncements reflected a prominent retributive justice narrative, stressing individual criminal responsibility as a means of addressing East Timor's legacy of conflict. This narrative was embodied in the Serious Crimes Process. A less prominent restoration/ reconciliation narrative was also evident. Reflected in the establishment of the CAVR, it emphasised that community-level reconciliation hearings and therapeutic truth-telling could assist East Timor to make the transition from a violent past to a peaceful future. Both of these narratives were informed by a 'meta-narrative' of progress or transition that permeated the post-conflict reconstruction process as a whole, and which portrayed East Timor as transforming into a modern, liberal state. On the eve of the new nation's independence, it also presented East Timor as a UN 'success story'. As will be discussed further in Chapter 2, these narratives disguised, at least partially, underlying tensions and political conflicts between different sections of the UN, and between the UN and the East Timorese leadership, over the best way in which to 'deal with' the past. While such tensions were exposed in debates over the relative priority to be accorded stability issues (such as building diplomatic and economic relations with Indonesia) over criminal justice issues (such as individual accountability for human rights violations), they were then obscured by seemingly neutral assertions about the importance of transitional justice, the rule of law and therapeutic reconciliation. Moreover, the establishment of these mechanisms 'from above' the political sphere did little to encourage the process of discussion and consensus-building that was necessary to give the East Timorese people a sense of involvement in the nation-building process. Thus, as I discuss in Chapter 2, despite the claims of local ownership embedded within the transitional justice model, there were limited opportunities for local East Timorese, including elite politicians, to debate the establishment of the Serious Crimes Process in particular and, to a lesser extent, the CAVR. Moreover, as shown in Chapter 3, both transitional justice mechanisms were envisaged as short-term 'projects' with specific designated 'deliverables'; this has meant that little attention has gone into thinking about how to foster an *ongoing* space for inclusive public debate about justice questions following the conclusion of the two mechanisms.

By unsettling the concept of 'transition', then, the work of critical transitional justice theorists has shown that this concept is unable to encapsulate – and may even work to obscure – the complex issues involved in building a shared political community in the wake of mass violence. Their insights suggest the need to rethink the assumptions of transitional justice as providing a solution to past violence, which assumes clear starting and end points and a pre-existing 'toolkit' of responses.

Unpacking 'justice'

A key way in which transitional justice mechanisms are assumed to assist conflict-ridden societies to make the transition to a liberal, peaceful, democratic order is by providing 'justice' to victims of violence. Yet what do we mean by justice? As scholars have long observed, justice is an amorphous and elusive concept that can be interpreted and experienced in a myriad of ways (Mani 2002; Dembour and Kelly 2007b; Henry 2005: 238; Franke 2006).

Within transitional justice discourse, justice is generally understood as retributive justice or restorative justice. Retributive justice stresses the importance of establishing individual responsibility for human rights violations and bringing those responsible to legal account. Advocates of retributive justice contend that criminal prosecutions are a moral obligation owed to victims, and that this process contributes to their healing process by publicly acknowledging and punishing the perpetrator who committed the wrong against them. Prosecutions are also claimed to benefit the broader society by deterring criminality, preventing a repetition of violations in the future and instilling public confidence in the 'rule of law'.

By contrast, proponents of truth commissions draw on restorative justice theory, which emphasises face-to-face mediation between offenders, where 'offenders offer atonement and victims reciprocate with forgiveness' (Waldorf 2006: 14). Rather than focusing on individual guilt or punishment, restorative justice views the problem as one of the whole community, and is interested in rebuilding broken relationships and restoring 'community' (Huyse 2003: 111). As Huyse explains:

> Restorative justice is thought to handle wrongdoing differently: it works with the full participation of the victim and of the relevant communities in discussing the facts, identifying the causes of misconduct and the defining sanctions. The ultimate aim is to restore relations as far as possible, both between victim and offender and within the broader community to which they belong.
>
> (Huyse 2003: 111)

As Kiss (2000: 71) observes, restorative justice proponents also claim that this approach is more effective at providing a 'victim-centred' form of justice that restores the dignity of victims than criminal prosecutions. Their argument is that truth commissions provide a more supportive space for victims to share their painful memories of violence than is possible in criminal trials (see Kiss 2000: 69; see also Minow 1998: 58). One of the reasons for this is that the focus of trials on individual perpetrators, their strict requirements to establish the requisite level of 'proof' of the elements of each crime, and their rules of evidence mean that victims are merely witnesses and are unable to tell their own personal narrative. These factors also mean that criminal trials are inevitably less participatory and accessible than truth commissions (Minow 1999: 58; Kiss 2000: 69; Allen 1999).

Despite their differences, advocates of both retributive and restorative justice share a belief in the need to 'recognise' and respond to human rights violations committed against individual victims (Franke 2006). This emphasis is grounded in the liberal legal tradition, which, as previously noted, stresses the importance of acknowledging individuals as rights-bearing subjects and is attentive to questions of formal equality (Douzinas 2002; see also Stanley 2009: 40). Thus criminal prosecutions are said to provide a form of recognition – a public recognition that wrongs were committed against victims. The rule of law and principle of equality before the law are claimed to help to achieve a kind of public recognition of individual victims as equal right-bearers, with the ability to make claims (Halderman 2007). Similarly, enabling victims to tell their stories – for example, through a truth commission process – can be seen as a commitment to recognising past harms committed against them, acknowledging their dignity as individuals and recognising them as citizens with rights. The production of an historical record of the past via a truth commission report, or trial judgments, may be similarly understood as providing a credible, publicly sanctioned form of recognition of survivors' experiences. Reparations programmes, which may be included as part of retributive or restorative justice approaches, can also be understood, at least in part, as a form of recognition. A reparations programme can be a means of recognising victims' suffering and its ongoing effects, and restoring victims' dignity and self-worth (De Greiff, 2006; see also Verdeja 2006). Indeed, de Greiff (2006: 461) goes so far as to suggest that reparations are the 'material form of the recognition owed to fellow citizens whose fundamental rights have been violated'.

The emphasis on recognition within the transitional justice literature draws on a broader body of work, including that of theorists Charles Taylor (1994) and Axel Honneth (1995; 2001). Both Honneth and Taylor have drawn attention to the centrality of recognition as an aspect of justice at both the individual and societal levels. Honneth (2001: 43) emphasises that the precondition of a just society is the recognition of the personal dignity of all individuals. Individuals, according to Honneth, have a deeply rooted human need to be recognised as bearers of a distinctive identity. Similarly, Taylor (1994) has described recognition as a 'vital human need', and has argued that the *denial* of recognition can be experienced as an acute form of *in*justice, which can become an important source of motivation for political mobilisation, resistance and conflict (see also Markell 2007).

By the same token, critical scholars and activists have drawn attention to the circumscribed nature of recognition that trials and truth commissions are able to provide. They have commented, for example, on the inescapable tension that exists between the requirements of the criminal law to recognise survivors as 'subjects of the law' and the desires of survivors to be recognised as individuals with their own unique life histories. Franke, for example, observes that the strict rules of evidence of criminal trials and the requirements to establish the requisite level of 'proof' of the elements of each crime circumscribe the avenues for survivors' participation and storytelling, and undermine possibilities for the recognition of their unique experiences and grievances (Franke 2006: 813–18). Similarly, Mertus highlights that, through the criminal justice process, survivors come to 'wear the stamp of potential witness; they become conduits through which investigators make their case' (2000: 144). In the process of 'piecing together facts to prove the crime', investigators and prosecutors cannot 'return the survivors' rightful claim to subjecthood' (Mertus 2000: 144). In other words, in criminal trials, the story belongs to the court rather than the survivor, and in the shaping of witnesses narratives to suit the needs of a particular audience, survivors may be disempowered, their voices silenced rather than validated (Henry 2009: 125).

While truth commissions are not constrained by the narrow boundaries of the criminal law, they have their own institutional purposes, which shape the way in which individual stories are received and reported. Individuals' experiences, for example, may be recognised insofar as their stories conform to broader nation-building narratives of 'reconciliation'. This prioritises stories of catharsis, reconciliation and healing over stories of revenge, and retribution and unfinished business (Rawski 2002: 3). In addition, truth commissions may also produce reports that are overly legalistic, which reduces individuals' complex experiences of conflict to a series of isolated human rights violations (Ross 2003b: 176). In this sense, both trials and truth commissions demonstrate the limits of institutional forms of recognition and that shaping individual's experiences to conform to broader institutional imperatives may subsume them under the 'larger principles which their testimony helps establish' (Franke 2006: 821).

Further to the issue of constrained forms of recognition, scholars have also criticised the way in which transitional justice processes recognise individuals either as 'victims' or 'perpetrators' (Ross 2003b). At one level, becoming identified as a victim can open up new avenues and opportunities of political expression, and can empower individuals to make claims upon the state. The recognition of victims as citizens with rights can be an important means of enabling them to resume lives that are not determined by their prior victimhood (Verdeja 2006: 122–3; Wilke 2007: 482). Yet, as previously discussed, the term 'victim' may be constraining, in that it fails to acknowledge individuals as political actors (Shaw and Waldorf 2010: 8). Thus, as Taylor notes, in reconfiguring individuals into 'innocent or transgressing individuals with individual rights and obligations', trials and truth commissions may flatten the terrain of human agency, including individuals' collective struggles, ideals and political motivations (Taylor, in Ross 2003b: 176). Similarly, in her detailed study of women's experiences of the South African Truth and Reconciliation Commission (TRC), Ross observes that the Commission created two possible speaking positions: one could either 'speak', thereby making known one's experiences of violation and actively claiming the subject position of victim, or remain silent, thereby remaining 'unrecognised' (Ross 2003b: 172). South African political activists did not always wish to embrace the subject position of 'victim', yet were given little option.

Another strand of criticism focuses on the way in which recognition-based justice sidelines questions of 'social justice' or 'redistributive justice', an example being issues of political and economic exclusion that often underlie conflicts and continue into the post-conflict period (Mani 2002: 127–8; Stover 2005: 199; Stanley 2009: 7). It builds on a broader body of work, including that of political theorist Nancy Fraser. Fraser (2000; 2003) has been influential in calling attention to redistribution as an important dimension of justice, arguing that a sole focus on 'recognition' can divert attention away from struggles for structural equality and socio-economic transformation by focusing on individuals' identities, rather than what they need to live a 'good life' (2000: 100). Rather than viewing recognition and redistribution as mutually exclusive alternatives, Fraser develops a two-dimensional justice framework that accommodates both claims for social equity and claims for recognition of difference. This framework revolves around the concept of 'status parity', which seeks to ensure that all members of society are able to interact as peers (Fraser 2003: 9).

In the context of transitional justice initiatives, it is apparent that more emphasis is accorded to recognition than redistribution (see Franke 2006). Transitional justice mechanisms are generally unable to grapple with the issue of redistribution of resources, except insofar as they can consider the question of 'reparations' (see, for example, Miller 2008: 278; Lambourne 2009: 42). A singular focus on reparations may be problematic in itself, by simplifying what is required for the resolution of complex economic issues (Miller 2008: 278), and focusing on the past harm rather than the present and future needs of survivors (Lambourne 2009: 42). The broader state-building context in which transitional justice processes often take place, in which economic growth and liberalisation may be foregrounded at the expense of issues of equity and social justice, can make these omissions more obvious.

The salience of these critiques is supported by the East Timor experience, where questions of redistribution were excluded from the transitional justice process, except insofar as the CAVR established a very small-scale 'urgent reparations fund' to provide small one-off payments of assistance to the 'most vulnerable victims' and made recommendations in its final report for a more comprehensive reparations scheme. In addition, as previously noted, the transitional justice mechanisms were implemented within the context of a broader state-building programme that promoted a narrow economic growth model, which exacerbated economic hardship in the rural areas.

The exclusion of redistributive justice from the mandates of trials and truth commissions is reflective of the general invisibility of *structural* violence within transitional justice discourse and the dominant liberal legal tradition in general. According to Johan Galtung (1994), structural violence refers to the structural or systemic violence that is caused by social structures or social institutions when individuals are prevented from meeting basic needs such as food, housing, health care and water. This violence is 'built into the very social, political and economic systems that govern societies, states and the world' (Galtung, Jacobsen and Brand-Jacobsen 2002: 17), and is connected to class, race and gender inequalities (Farmer 2003: 42–3). Structural violence is manifested and made real in the 'everyday' experiences of 'infant mortality, slow starvation, disease, despair and humiliation', which frequently remain 'invisible or misrecognised' due to our tendency to view it as part of the status quo (Scheper-Hughes and Bourgois 2004: 2; see also Nevins 2005: 189–90). As Scheper-Hughes expands:

> Structural violence . . . refers to the invisible *social machinery* and oppression that reproduces pathogenic social relations of exclusion and marginalisation via ideologies and stigmas attendant on race, class, caste, sex and other invidious distinctions. Structural violence erases the history and consciousness of the social origins of poverty, sickness, hunger and premature death, so that they are simply taken for granted and naturalized, and no one is held accountable, except, perhaps, the poor themselves.
>
> (Scheper-Hughes 2006: 287–8)

In East Timor, the effects of structural violence during the Indonesian occupation (and the earlier period of Portuguese colonisation) are strikingly evident in the widespread poverty, malnutrition, maternal mortality, illiteracy and domestic violence that are prominent features of the post-conflict state.

While transitional justice mechanisms focus on recognising and addressing certain kinds of 'direct' violence – namely, widespread human rights violations, such as crimes against humanity, genocide and war crimes, including cases of murder, torture, rape and physical assault – they give little attention to the more 'everyday' experiences of poverty, disadvantage, exclusion and inequality (Stanley 2009: 63; see also Humphrey 2003; Nevins 2002b; Nagy 2008). The emphasis on direct as opposed to structural violence is also reflected in the narrow temporal and geographic boundaries of trials and truth commissions, and their concentration on individual perpetrators (Nevins 2002b; Nagy 2008). The focus on direct violence fosters assumptions that extraordinary violence occurs within a specific time and place, and is caused solely by individuals. For example, war crimes trials tell a story of 'bad men doing evil deeds'; questions of structural violence are peripheral (Simpson

2007: 157). While truth commissions have broader scope to explore a wider range of experiences, they also tend to focus on direct rather than structural violence. Ross (2003b), for example, has exposed the way in which the South African TRC reduced the understanding of violence to that which is inflicted on the body; in relation to women, this led to a focus on experiences of sexual violence. One effect of this was to deflect attention away from the 'everyday' violence of apartheid, including poverty, and the broader context of racial discrimination in which this violence occurred:

> Rather than commencing from the historical grounds of the constitution of the subject under Apartheid, the Commission considered its subject in terms of the violation of particular rights. The effect is an 'even-handedness' that presumed to offer a neutral and objective stance towards violence and its documentation by stripping away context and condensing suffering to its traces on the body.
>
> (Ross 2003b: 176)

Similarly, Rombouts argues that the TRC's restriction of the definition of 'victim' to victims of killings, abductions, torture or severe ill-treatment created a 'hierarchy of harms', and left many victims of the apartheid system (for example, victims of the pass laws and deportation) beyond the scope of the TRC (Rombouts 2002: 224–7). Nagy makes the additional point that ignoring structural violence also has a gender dimension, in that the violence that women often experience in societies that are militarised and unequal, including violence in the home, may be unrecognised (Nagy 2008: 286).

Another effect of the focus of on direct violence committed by individual perpetrators is that the role and responsibilities of indirect perpetrators, bystanders and institutions, including international actors, can be obscured (Border 2003; Meister 2002; Leebaw 2004; Orford 2006; Moon 2008; Ross 2003a; Nevins 2002b; Mamdani 2001b). For example, in the context of South Africa, Mamdani (2001b) has suggested that the TRC's focus on direct violence committed by individual perpetrators against victims obscured the *systemic* nature of the apartheid regime, in which certain individuals and groups benefited economically at the expense of others. Similarly, in the case of Iraq, Nagy argues that the restriction of the transitional justice time frame to the period of Saddam Hussein's regime in Iraq glosses over broader justice issues, such as the illegality of the US-led invasion and the human rights abuses committed by US soldiers at Abu Ghraib (Nagy 2008: 281). In the context of East Timor, Nevins (2002b) has argued that the temporal and geographic boundaries of the Serious Crimes Process constructed an impression that the twenty-four-year conflict between Indonesia and East Timor was a 'local' conflict, and obscured the role of nations such as Australia in regularly covering up evidence of abuses committed by the Indonesian military and actively aiding and abetting the Soeharto regime in its occupation.

The focus on direct forms of violence committed within narrow temporal and geographic frames can also have the effect of representing the 'international community' as the 'saviour' or solver of conflict-related problems (Hughes and Pupavac 2005; Orford 1999; 2003; Colvin 2008). By constructing an impression that violence is a 'local' problem, populations may be pathologised – portrayed as 'sick' and 'traumatised', or as 'backward' and trapped in cycles of violence perpetuated from generation to generation (Hughes and Pupavac 2005; Pupavac 2004). This can obscure a more complex analysis of the causes of conflict. As Hughes and Pupavac write:

> The portrayal of conflict as emerging from the darkest realms of the psyche of the Other, who must be protected and healed by Western instrumental rationality and care, obliterates a political and economic analysis of the causes of conflict and their effects in favour of either military suppression or sympathetic smothering.
>
> (Hughes and Pupavac 2005: 887)

These observations can be readily applied to East Timor, where the focus of the transitional justice process on East Timorese and Indonesian actors has arguably depicted the violence of the Indonesian occupation as a 'local' conflict, which bolstered the UN's image as a humanitarian and benevolent problem-solver and contributed to the construction of the post-conflict reconstruction 'success story'.

The work of critical justice scholars is important, then, because it tests the dominant legalistic definitions of justice and draws attention to its redistributive dimensions. It also expands the 'frame' of justice questions beyond individual perpetrators and the nation state by considering the global context of violence, including the role of international actors and economic institutions. By highlighting the limits of legal forms of recognition, this scholarship can help to shed light on why East Timorese survivors may be dissatisfied with the transitional justice process. I want now to turn to the work of ethnographic scholars and social scientists who have reflected on the disjunction between legal possibilities and the demands of justice by illuminating the diverse, socially and historically situated meanings of justice. This scholarship highlights the importance of going beyond the law, and theories of the 'just' society in general (Sarat and Kearns 1996: 12), to consider how justice gains its meaning in specific local contexts.

Justice from below

A good starting point for thinking about the diverse meanings of justice, and the elliptical and paradoxical relationship between law and justice, is the work of influential philosopher Jacques Derrida. For Derrida, justice can never fully be provided by law and is always something we strive towards – it is always 'yet to come':

> Law is not justice. Law is the element of calculation, and it is just that there be law, but justice is incalculable, it demands that one calculate with the incalculable.
>
> (Derrida 2002: 244)

Derrida and other scholars have argued that one of the reasons for the distinction between law and justice is that law itself is intimately connected with violence in a number of ways. The state and its laws, for instance, are founded in violence – most modern states emerged as a result of war, revolution, rebellion or occupation. Moreover, the law relies on violence to 'enforce' its decisions, for example through police, armies and prisons (Derrida 2002: 252; see also Douzinas 2000: 330; Sarat and Kearns 1996: 13). Given these factors, legal justice can never be 'pure' or complete, and is always corrupted to some extent. A related reason for the gap between law and justice is that there is an inherent tension between the demands of the law to follow a set of general rules or principles – to 'categorise and calculate' – and the demands of justice, which require a response to a unique and specific situation or individual, and which cannot be captured in any generality (Derrida 2002: 245; see also Callinicos 2008: 82). As Derrida explains:

> How to reconcile the act of justice that must always concern singularity, individuals, groups irreplaceable existences, the other or myself as other, in a unique situation, with rule, norm, value, or the imperative of justice that necessarily have a general form, even if this generality prescribes a singular application in each case?
>
> (Derrida 2002: 245)

Another, related, reason for the gap between law and justice in the context of post-conflict initiatives is that transitional justice mechanisms are required to mediate a myriad of conflicting interests, including the interests of individual victims, the international community and the national government (Haslam 2007: 59). The goal of providing recognition to individual victims, for example, may be in tension with the requirements of criminal tribunals to contribute to international jurisprudence on war crimes or crimes against humanity. Truth commissions may face similar conflicts between their goals of contributing to 'national' reconciliation and restoring victims' dignity (Leebaw 2008: 115). As I discuss in Chapter 3, these competing demands can be discerned in East Timor. And, as I show in Chapter 5, the dislocation between law and justice was further compounded by the fact that the 'justice' demanded by East Timorese survivors did not always correspond to the 'justice' envisaged by the transitional justice mechanisms.

Despite the gap that exists between law and justice, Derrida suggests that the two concepts are intricately intertwined (Derrida 1999: 72–3). This means that it is always necessary to negotiate between the law, which is always 'conditional', and justice, which is always 'unconditional' (Derrida 1999: 72–3). Douzinas extends this point further by drawing a distinction between two kinds of justice – 'legal justice' and 'transcendent justice':

> When law violates its established procedures; when it does not recognise or uphold principles of equality and dignity – the law acts unjustly according to its own internal criteria. We can call this the first type of injustice, legal injustice; it is negative, internal to the law and operates when the law does not match its own standards and principles. But throughout history, another type of transcendent justice has appeared, to which the law as a whole is accountable. The law of the polis has been judged from the position of the cosmos, with its universal but absent principles and found wanting.
>
> (Douzinas 2007: 291)

For Douzinas, although the law has the capacity to provide 'legal' justice, by adhering to the principles of equality and dignity, it can never fully provide 'transcendent' justice. This is partly because demands for justice stem from the victim's sense of *in*justice, which is the 'name given to the symptoms of social exclusion, domination or oppression' that the law can never fully address (Douzinas 2000: 332). Douzinas makes the point that, to begin thinking about 'justice', we need to start by listening to individual's subjective experiences of *in*justice, rather than by developing abstract theories of 'justice' in general. As will become clear in later chapters of this book, the subjective experience of injustice is a critical element in understanding the various meanings of 'justice' in East Timor.

The insights of these theorists, then, illuminate the inherent tension between justice and the law: while it is necessary to negotiate the demands of justice through the law, and to call the law to account in relation to its established procedures and principles, we must remain aware, as Sarat and Kearns (1996: 12) argue, that the requirements of justice necessarily involve more than compliance with legal procedures, the application of abstract legal principles and theories of the 'just' society in general. This means considering, but also going beyond, questions of recognition and redistribution. Importantly, these scholars do not call for justice to be 'jettisoned from legal discourse' (Sarat and Kearns 1996: 11). Rather, they remind us that justice is a vast subject that is both within and beyond the law, and illuminate the difficulty of constructing a universal theory that is capable of grasping its myriad dimensions (Sarat and Kearns 1996: 11).

A number of recent empirical and ethnographic studies on transitional justice have highlighted the disjunction between law and justice in very grounded ways by focusing on the divergence between the official goals of transitional justice mechanisms and community expectations. By exploring the operation of trials and truth commissions in specific locations, and attending to the experiences, priorities and perceptions of local people, this scholarship acts as a much needed corrective to the 'celebratory impulse' (Scheper-Hughes 2004: 27) that fuels the tendency to portray transitional justice as having the capacity to 'resolve' complex legacies of conflict. Some studies have shown, for example, that local communities may understand 'justice' very differently from the way it is defined by official institutions. Thus, in his detailed ethnographic study of the interaction between the Special Court for Sierra Leone and the local community, Tim Kelsall shows that because Sierra Leoneans have different ideas of 'social space and time, causation, agency, responsibility, evidence and truth telling' from those employed by the court, the application of international justice has been a 'fraught affair' (Kelsall 2009: 17). Similarly, in his study of witnesses who testified before the ICTY, for instance, Stover found that they were often pursuing an idea of 'justice' that diverged markedly from the ICTY's official version. Although the vast majority of witnesses supported war crimes trials, justice was also considered to include:

> the return of stolen property, locating and identifying the bodies of the missing, capturing and trying *all* war criminals . . . securing reparations and apologies; leading lives devoid of fear; securing meaningful jobs; providing their children with good schools; and helping those traumatized by atrocities to recover.
>
> (Stover 2005: 115)

Other studies examine the everyday localised acts of survival through which individuals and communities seek to reconstruct their lives and rebuild relationships in the wake of protracted conflict (Das and Kleinman 2001; see also Das 2003; Das 2007). Rather than looking for a 'grand narrative of forgiveness and redemption', Das and Kleinman are attentive to what they term the 'small local stories' which illuminate how communities are 'experimenting with ways of inhabiting the world together' (Das and Kleinman 2001: 16). This ongoing process of 'remaking a world' occurs at the levels of the family, friends, neighbourhood and community and does not presume closure:

> There is no pretence here at some grand project of recovery but simply the questions of how everyday tasks of surviving – having a roof over your head, being able to send your children to school, being able to do the work of the everyday without constant fear of being attacked – can be accomplished.
>
> (Das 2003: 300)

In the context of this rich scholarship, relatively little attention focuses on the complex ways in which local communities engage with, and seek to make sense of, official transitional justice concepts and practices within particular social, political and cultural contexts.[2] Yet, as Shaw and Waldorf identify, it is necessary to examine these dynamics, because they can not only show us how the foundational assumptions of transitional justice break down, but may also open up new, and unexpected, possibilities (Shaw and Waldorf 2010). Thus, as the work of Sally Engle Merry highlights, when global mechanisms and concepts interact with localised understandings, a process of 'vernacularisation' needs to occur to translate those ideas and practices so as to be compatible with local value systems (Merry 2006). Given the complexities involved in this translation process and the 'friction' (Tsing 2005) that is generated when transnational, regional, national and local processes intersect, it is important to consider how individuals and local communities negotiate with, appropriate, contest and seek to transform transitional justice discourse and practice (Hinton 2010; Dembour and Kelly 2007b). Ethnographic and empirical studies can help to show, then, that rather than being 'juggernauts that prevail over all before them' (Shaw 2007: 186), 'official' transitional justice processes are reshaped and given meaning in specific contexts, where they engage with pre-existing local understandings of justice.

As this analysis of ethnographic and empirical scholarship suggests, in the context of mass harm, justice is an elusive concept that may have multiple socially embedded meanings; justice is also contested concept that is constantly being negotiated within particular social and political constraints (Dembour and Kelly 2007b: 21). The salience of these observations is apparent in the East Timor context, where a number of competing narratives of justice are circulating, and where national and international discourses of justice both inform, and are challenged by, local actors.

These perspectives and concepts provide the starting point for the investigation of local experiences of the transitional justice process presented in the latter part of the book. As I discuss in Chapters 5 and 6, East Timorese survivors have responded to the transitional justice process in a range of complex ways that are beyond simply accepting or rejecting official processes. Transitional justice concepts – including ideas of retributive and restorative justice, victims' rights and reparations – have been introduced in a context in which there are multiple, localised meanings of justice, some of which are influenced by the ongoing significance of customary beliefs. Transitional justice concepts have been reinterpreted and 'vernacularised' within the context of pre-existing value systems. Outside the formal, internationally mandated

2 Important exceptions include the work of Wilson (2001a); Shaw (2007); Shaw and Waldorf (2010).

transitional justice process, the reconstruction of ordinary life and the imagining of a collective future is also occurring through the re-establishment of relationships and social bonds that were fractured during the Indonesian occupation, as well as the reburial of loved ones who died during the conflict, the conducting of ceremonies to put the spirits of the deceased to rest and the construction of monuments to keep the memories of the past alive. The prevalence of these practices highlights the highly personalised, locally grounded and *ongoing* process of resuming everyday life, and of pursuing 'justice' in the aftermath of conflict, fundamentally challenging attempts to mark a clear break between the past and the future.

Chapter 2

Stability versus retributive justice

Unpacking the UN's East Timor 'success story'

> In the rather chaotic history of UN peacekeeping operations, where results have not always matched the efforts of the international community, East Timor stands as an undeniable success. In two and a half years, from November 1999 to May 2002, this totally devastated country was entirely reconstructed – rather I should say: constructed – and brought to independence.
>
> (Jean Christian Cady, deputy Special Representative of the Secretary General of the United Nations in East Timor, quoted in Goldstone, 2004: 83)

On the eve of the East Timor's independence in May 2002, the UN and international donors were claiming the post-conflict reconstruction of the new nation as a 'success', a story of progress in which a 'totally devastated' country had made the transition to independence, with the UN's assistance, in a remarkable two-and-a-half-year period. As a key component of the UNTAET state-building project, the transitional justice process – namely, the Serious Crimes Process and the Commission for Reception, Truth and Reconciliation (CAVR) – was seen as helping to create this success story.

In this chapter, I dig beneath the UN's East Timor 'success story' to unearth some of the debates that emerged in the post-referendum period and following independence about how best to respond to the violence of the past. While the narratives promoted by the UN's toolkit approach implied that the transitional justice mechanisms could be introduced above the national political sphere, this chapter uncovers a far more complex story. I demonstrate that the establishment and operation of East Timor's transitional justice process involved a fraught process of negotiation between and amongst an array of international and national actors, which brought to the fore specific interests and multiple views about the best way in which to deal with the past. In this process, stability concerns, which revealed Indonesia's economic and strategic influence in the region, came to overshadow retributive justice goals. In bringing these tensions to the surface, I argue that the 'success story' did not accurately represent, and to some extent worked to obscure, the fundamentally *political* nature of transitional justice negotiations.

The externally devised transitional justice process and the East Timor 'success story'

As already observed, current international approaches to post-conflict reconstruction and peace-building appear to be infused with the belief that transitional justice processes can be implemented independently from the national political sphere by external actors such as the UN. Transitional justice mechanisms – underpinned by narratives of retribution and reconciliation – purport to offer universal, apolitical and/or therapeutic responses to legacies of conflict. These mechanisms are often devised in the context of UN state-building programmes, which are assumed to be ostensibly 'technical' exercises that promote open market liberalism and electoral democracy, and are underpinned by a 'transition' paradigm. In line with this, the UN and international donors assumed a pivotal role in the establishment and operation of East Timor's transitional justice process, promoting it as a key means of dealing with the legacy of violence from the Indonesian period and fostering the new nation's transition to peaceful, democratic nationhood. Following the 1999 referendum, UN statements and reports were imbued with a retributive justice narrative, portraying the Serious Crimes Process as a means of combating impunity and restoring 'universal' human rights values and the rule of law. As the CAVR began to take shape, a secondary narrative of reconciliation or 'restorative justice' also became evident in these statements, promoting the CAVR as a means of fostering individual healing and national reconciliation through truth-telling.

The conceptualisation of East Timor's transitional justice process as short-term, apolitical and externally driven was evident in UNTAET's limited attempts to engage with the political leadership of the CNRT, and the community more generally, about the form that this process would take. As previously discussed, in the aftermath of the post-referendum violence, human rights activists and some East Timorese leaders had expressed strong views that the UN Security Council should establish an international criminal tribunal, similar to the ICTY and ICTR, to pursue prosecutions of high-level Indonesian perpetrators of serious crimes. Instead, UNTAET, as the governing authority of East Timor, created the 'hybrid' Special Panels for Serious Crimes (Special Panels), which were linked to a specialised Serious Crimes Investigations Unit (SCIU) located within UNTAET.

On the face of it, it would appear that UNTAET's decision to establish a hybrid tribunal reflected a commitment to the principles of national and local 'ownership'. Given the absence of an independent national East Timorese government, however, the creation of the Special Panels was entirely the initiative of the UN administration, and was accomplished by the means of a Regulation issued by UNTAET rather than via a treaty (Reiger and Wierda 2006: 12). This may well have contributed to the East Timorese government's lukewarm support for, and later disowning of, the Serious Crimes Process (Reiger and Wierda 2006: 13). The potential benefits of including East Timorese judges on the Special Panels were also undermined by the lack of provision by UNTAET of essential capacity-building and training to East Timorese jurists, most of whom had little, if any, practical experience. Further exacerbating these problems was the fact that UNTAET did not undertake meaningful consultation with East Timorese jurists regarding significant issues such as the adoption of Regulation 2000/15, which determined what law would apply in the adjudication of serious crimes (Linton 2001: 150). As a consequence, many East Timorese judges felt disenfranchised by the international staff (Chiam 2008: 215).

In contrast to the Serious Crimes Process, those involved in the establishment of the CAVR were committed to the principles of local and national ownership. This was reflected in the composition of the Steering Committee co-ordinated by the UNTAET Human Rights Unit to develop the CAVR's terms of reference and structure, which included representatives from the CNRT, East Timorese human rights NGOs, women's groups, youth organisations, the Catholic Church, the Association of ex-Political Prisoners, FALINTIL,[1] UNTAET and the UNHCR. The Committee also made specific efforts to design an institution that was not a simple replication of previous truth commission models, but would resonate with East Timorese cultural values and practices; this was most evident in the design of the innovative Community Reconciliation Process (CRP), which is discussed in Chapter 3. The Committee also sought to ensure a transparent process for the selection of national and regional commissioners, by canvassing recommendations in all thirteen districts of East Timor and amongst the refugee community in Indonesian West Timor (CAVR 2001). Despite these efforts, it is fair to say that there had not been extensive community involvement in the initial decision to establish the CAVR. Although community consultations were undertaken by the Steering Committee in each of East Timor's districts in late 2000 and early 2001, the decision to establish a truth commission was already a fait accompli by this point, which meant that these meetings were based on a predetermined agenda. Consultations were not undertaken with the East Timorese refugee community in West Timor, primarily because of concerns about the safety of Steering Committee members.[2]

1 FALINTIL (*Forças Armadas de Liberatação Nacional de Timor-Leste* Armed Forces for the National Liberation of East Timor) was the armed wing of FRETILIN until 1987, when it became a non-partisan 'national' army.

2 These concerns were very real, given that, in September 2000, three UNHCR staff were killed by East Timorese militia in an attack on their office in Atambua (interview with Pat Walsh, former CAVR adviser, Melbourne, 13 December 2011).

Although East Timorese political leadership of the National Council for Timorese Resistance (CNRT) was supportive of the idea of a truth commission (reflected in the recommendation of the CNRT Congress, in August 2000, for the establishment of a 'Commission for Resettlement and National Reconciliation' – CNRT 2000a), it was the UNTAET Human Rights Unit that took the initiative to develop the concept further. Indeed, Stahn (2001: 956) makes the observation that although the UN had actively supported the creation of truth and commissions in other countries, East Timor was the first case in which it had acted formally as the founding authority of such an institution. This approach, she suggests, went against the previously held view that truth commissions should be established by democratically elected governments if they are to be perceived as nationally legitimate (Stahn 2001: 956).

Once it was established, the CAVR operated as an independent statutory body, and hence became more nationally 'owned' over time. East Timor's first President, Xanana Gusmão, demonstrated his support for the CAVR through his willingness to meet regularly with the national commissioners and to take part in public hearings.[3] Nonetheless, as discussed further below, Gusmão increasingly made it clear that his view own view of reconciliation (which favoured amnesty for serious crimes) differed from that promoted by the CAVR (which stressed the complementarity of reconciliation and retributive justice efforts). Within the CAVR itself, despite the recruitment of an overwhelmingly East Timorese staff, it was apparent that international advisers and consultants exerted a considerable influence on the direction of the organisation, regardless of their best intentions and commitment to participation.

Some groups in society also remained wary of the CAVR. As acknowledged by former adviser to the CAVR, Pat Walsh, East Timorese leaders in Indonesian West Timor who had voted against independence did not take up the CAVR's invitation to participate, due to a belief that the process would be used as a 'witch-hunt against the 20 percent who voted for continued integration with Indonesia' (Walsh 2011: 181). Some church and human rights leaders were also initially lukewarm in their support for the CAVR. Although, over time, their mistrust abated, some expressed initial concerns that the CAVR was an internationally driven initiative that would divert resources away from prosecutions.[4] Indeed, one of the stark differences between the CAVR and the South African Truth and Reconciliation Commission (TRC) was that the East Timorese bishops declined to play an active role in the CAVR, although this may also have been a reflection of the enormous demands

3 Ibid.

4 Interviews with Frank Brennan SJ, former director of the Jesuit Refugee Service East Timor, Melbourne, 10 July 2009, and Aderito de Jesus Soares, East Timorese academic and human rights advocate, Canberra, 8 June 2008.

being made upon their time in the post-referendum period.[5] The fact that the political leadership and church hierarchy were grappling with a multitude of issues amid the raw and chaotic aftermath of the referendum was itself a reason why some civil society leaders were of the view that this was not the right time to be considering a truth commission.[6]

These issues relating to ownership of the transitional justice process were exacerbated by UNTAET's problematic approach to state-building as a whole. Following a power struggle between the UN's Departments of Political Affairs (DPA) and Peacekeeping Operations (DPKO), responsibility for the planning and operation of UNTAET had been given to the DPKO. This decision exacerbated the tendency of UNTAET to rely on standardised, externally devised solutions, as the DPKO was accustomed to short-term military operations and had little experience of long-term state-building missions (Suhrke 2001: 7). One of the consequences that flowed from this was that little thought went into creating mechanisms for Timorese participation in UNTAET; these were only gradually added as East Timorese leaders, NGOs and donor governments pressed for greater 'Timorisation' (Suhrke 2001: 1–2, 4). Adding to the tendency to overlook East Timorese participation was the fact that UNTAET's budget was financed by assessed (or non-voluntary) contributions from UN members, which meant there was pressure to complete the mission as soon as possible and, by early 2001, the date for independence was set for 20 May 2002 (Suhrke 2001: 10). The period during which the transitional justice mechanisms were established was thus marked by a considerable degree of antagonism between UNTAET and East Timorese political and civil society leaders, many of whom perceived, quite rightly, that they were being excluded from key decision-making processes.

Despite these problems with East Timorese participation, the transitional justice process was central to the UN's rhetoric that its short-term, externally devised state-building programme could effectively respond to East Timor's complex legacy of conflict. Alongside the project of political and economic liberalisation, transitional justice was a key component in a narrative that saw East Timor as undertaking a linear 'transition' from conflict and oppression towards a liberal, democratic state. As already observed, on the eve of East Timor's independence, the reconstruction process was being spoken of in celebratory terms. This was evident in the comments made by the then UN Secretary General, Kofi Annan, that UNTAET had had a 'truly historic mandate' and that 'few would have imagined that a de novo public administration could have been established within just 30 months' (UNSG 2002: 15). Donor states were also quick to claim their own role in East Timor's

5 Interview with Pat Walsh, former CAVR adviser, Melbourne, 13 December 2011.

6 Interview with Aderito de Jesus Soares, Canberra, 8 June 2008.

success story, such as when then Australian Foreign Minister Alexander Downer enthused that:

> Australia was involved from the outset. We participated in the first UN monitoring mission, UNAMET . . . We led the INTERFET mission which restored security in East Timor in the dark days of 1999. And we have contributed a great deal to the UN Transitional Administration in East Timor (UNTAET).
>
> (Downer, 15 May 2002, in Nevins 2005: 147)

For the UN (and more specifically the DPKO and Security Council), there was much at stake in the construction of this success story. As one of the UN's most expansive state-building missions, UNTAET represented the first time that the UN had assumed a governance role independently of any local authority (Chopra 2002: 28). In this context, East Timor's transition to nationhood within a two-and-a-half-year period reflected the UN's own success as an international institution. The importance of this was augmented by the fact that the UN's reputation was particularly fragile at that point in time. UNTAET was established in the wake of UNAMET, which had failed to protect the East Timorese people following the referendum, as a result of being forced to leave the territory due to Indonesia's flagrant breach of the Security Council-mandated 5 May Agreement. In this context, the success story narrative enabled the UN to re-establish its reputation and credibility, and reinforced what Orford (2003: 171–5) refers to as the UN's 'heroic' mission.

Beneath the UN's self-proclaimed story of accomplishment, with its celebration of the capacity of transitional justice to address past wrongs and facilitate East Timor's transition to independence, a more complex debate over the interplay between prosecutions, reconciliation, stability and nation-building was unfolding. To begin to unpack this, I explore some of the tensions between retributive justice goals and stability imperatives that emerged early in the period of UNTAET administration.

The UNTAET period and the emergence of the stability narrative

Despite the prominence of the UN's retributive justice rhetoric, soon after the referendum it was apparent that the idea of formal prosecutions was being shadowed by a powerful 'stability' discourse that was emanating from sections of the UN and some East Timorese leaders. This was reflected in the emerging tensions – both explicit and implicit – at UN headquarters level, within UNTAET, and between UNTAET and the East Timorese leadership. While some voices promoted the need to strengthen diplomatic ties with Indonesia, to support the democratisation efforts of then President Abduraman Wahid and to ensure the security of East Timor's borders, others argued that individual accountability for human rights violations was fundamental to deterrence and to entrenching a strong 'rule of law' culture.

The emergence of these debates and contradictory messages can be understood as reflecting the extent to which, as Harris-Rimmer (2010) observes, decision-making on transitional justice is often marked by friction between conflicting 'legalist' and 'realist' narratives. Generally speaking, a legalist position characterises certain international crimes, such as war crimes, torture, genocide and crimes against humanity, as violating *jus cogens* norms: 'peremptory and non-derogable norms which are fundamental to the interests of the international community' (Harris-Rimmer 2010: 17). Given this, it is argued that there is a non-negotiable obligation to prosecute those responsible. By contrast, a realist position posits that an insistence on prosecutions is both anti-democratic and potentially destabilising, and that compromises may need to be made to establish a lasting peace (Harris-Rimmer 2010: 17–18).

The dichotomous nature of this debate, however, to some extent obscures the complex and often conflicting policy dilemmas facing states emerging from protracted periods of conflict, and the extent to which those who promote legalist and realist positions may be driven by a blend of motivations, including domestic, regional and international political considerations. For example, as Sriram and Ross (2007: 62) observe, the US government's legalist decision to promote a particular 'hybrid' Special Court model for Sierra Leone is inextricably linked to its hostility towards the International Criminal Court (ICC). Moreover, even where states are willing to make a clear condemnation of human rights abuses, they may be reluctant to offer any practical help, or even to honour pledges of support that they make (Mallinder 2008: 340). This reluctance was seen in the lack of concerted international activity following the declarations by the US Congress that the crimes committed in Darfur amounted to genocide. Realist arguments may also be informed by a diverse range of motivations, as is made clear in Mallinder's work on amnesty laws. As she observes, states may make arguments against prosecutions and for the need for amnesties for varied and often multiple reasons, including as a reaction to internal unrest, to shield state agents from prosecution, or on the basis of 'national unity' or 'peace and reconciliation' justifications, which may merge with arguments for the need to 'close the books' on the past and focus on the future development of the country (Mallinder 2008: 43, 50, 404). These motivations, however, are rarely fully transparent (Mallinder 2008: 404).

Many of these complex motivations were discernable in the early transitional justice debates in East Timor. To some extent, the rise of the realist stability narrative can be understood, in part, as a product of the new nation's unique context. This was a context in which the former oppressive Indonesian regime, although no longer officially present *within* the country, maintained a strong influence as a powerful neighbour (Bhuta 2001: 173). An antagonistic Indonesia was perceived as a threat to the future security and viability of East Timor, particularly given the vulnerability of East Timor's land and sea borders and its fragile economic position. Stability concerns were also motivated by fears that too much pressure on Indonesia could threaten the repatriation of hundreds of thousands of East Timorese refugees from Indonesian West Timor. As an UNTAET official in East Timor explained in late 2000, 'Everyone here recognises that it's in no one's interests to rock the fragile political position of President Wahid' (Agliomby 2000). Compounding these difficulties were the vast social, economic and infrastructural tasks facing those involved in the reconstruction of East Timor, and the widespread and chronic poverty affecting much of the population. In this context, both UNTAET and the East Timorese leadership viewed the restoration and maintenance of regional peace and stability as critical to the viability and development of the new nation state (Larke 2009: 655).

At the level of the UN Security Council, the stability discourse was also fuelled by other preoccupations, namely, the importance of maintaining Indonesia's position as a key ally of powerful Western states. The value accorded to Indonesia's economic and strategic influence in the region assumed even more prominence following the terrorist acts of 11 September 2001, when Western states began to seek Indonesia's assistance in the so-called 'war on terror' (Huang and Gunn 2004: 24). These events provided impetus for the US to resume military ties with Indonesia and to support the *Tentara Nasional Indonesia* (TNI/National Indonesian Army), which was seen as a stabilising force within the country (Bhuta 2001: 176; Huang and Gunn 2004: 24). Soon after 9/11, then US President George Bush and Indonesian President Megawati Sukarnoputri agreed to resume regular meetings between the militaries of the two countries. Thereafter, the US government lifted its embargo on sales of non-lethal military items to Indonesia and provided millions of dollars for counter-terrorism measures to Jakarta (Huang and Gunn 2004: 24). Other US allies were similarly focused on rebuilding strategic alliances with Indonesia, including the Australian government, which was intent on restoring the relationship following the prominent role it had taken in encouraging and supporting the East Timor referendum (Bhuta 2001: 176).

Tensions between stability and retributive justice goals came to the surface in the attempts that were made soon after the referendum to encourage refugees in West Timor to return to East Timor. In early 2000, hundreds of thousands of refugees remained living in militia-controlled camps across the border, and UNTAET, UNHCR and the East Timorese leadership considered it necessary to repatriate them in order to reduce the security risk on the border. The situation was complex, in that refugees were believed to have fled for a range of different reasons. Some left simply to avoid the 1999 violence, while others were thought to have been forced to leave by militia members for later use as a 'bargaining chip' (Dolan and Large 2004: 12). It was also believed that a number of refugees were former militia members. In this context, the potential for returnees to suffer retribution at the hands of their local communities was viewed as a real concern, particularly as the longer people remained in West Timor, the greater the likelihood that their community members in East Timor would be convinced of their involvement in violent acts during 1999 (Dolan and Large 2004: 21).

The perceived urgency of repatriation led the United Nations High Commission for Refugees (UNHCR) and UNTAET to sponsor a series of so-called 'reconciliation' activities that were designed to build trust amongst refugees and their communities in East Timor, reducing the likelihood of retribution and facilitating repatriation. These activities included organised reconciliation meetings at the border, the facilitation of letter exchanges between family members on both sides of the border, and visits to refugee camps in West Timor by cultural and sports groups from East Timor. They also involved more contentious 'Go and See' visits for notable militia leaders, initiated by the UNTAET Chief of Staff in close co-operation with Xanana Gusmão, with the full endorsement of the Special Representative of the Secretary General (SRSG). These visits – which were defended as a means of facilitating the return of large numbers of refugees – involved meetings between the UNTAET Chief of Staff and senior militia leaders, and, in some cases, the wining and dining in expensive Dili restaurants of leaders who were perceived to be politically useful in encouraging other refugees to return (Dolan and Large 2004: 88; Katzenstein 2003: 275). One of these meetings, which involved Nemesio de Carvalho, the former deputy commander of the Mahidi militia in Ainaro, where many atrocities had been committed in 1999, was credited with leading to the return, in September 2001, of some 800 persons to the village of Cassa, Ainaro (Dolan and Large 2004: 18; ICG 2011a: 3).[7] Some officials from the SCIU were also involved in these negotiations and, on one occasion, two senior SCIU staff members went to West Timor to negotiate the conditions for the return of the Carvalho brothers, both of whom were militia leaders who held considerable power amongst the refugee community (Katzenstein 2003: 275). Former public defender, Sylvia de Bertodano, describes the less-than-successful negotiations that occurred in this case, following the return of one of the brothers to East Timor in October 2001:

> He was brought before the court as a suspect, released on bail, and was having dinner with the Chief of Staff and senior prosecutors at a restaurant in Dili the same evening. His brother, Cancio, persuaded the UN to

7 According to the International Crisis Group, Nemesio de Carvalho now states he came back 'ready to face justice', but has not faced trial and has not reported to the courts since 2006 (ICG 2011a: 3).

> appoint and pay for a private defence counsel for him as a condition of his return. Having secured this unique privilege, he nonetheless failed to return in January as promised, citing unspecified 'technical reasons' for his decision to stay in West Timor.
>
> (Bertodano, quoted in Katzenstein 2003: 275)

Some SCIU prosecutors expressed fierce opposition to these meetings and negotiations, arguing that the agenda of wooing militia leaders – some of whom were suspected of committing serious crimes – undercut their efforts to pursue investigations (King's College 2003: para 273). Their primary concerns revolved around the fact that informal arrangements had allegedly been made between the UNTAET Chief of Staff and the Prosecutor General to delay or prevent the issuance of arrest warrants and indictments against key militia leaders (ibid; Harper 2007: 192). As these deals became public, they fuelled mounting criticism that UNTAET was giving mixed messages about whether or not those charged with serious crimes would be prosecuted (King's College 2003: para 273). These policy contradictions were not resolved until March 2002, when the UNHCR published its 'Policy of Justice and Return Procedures', which clarified the relationship between prosecutions of serious crimes on the one hand, and reconciliation and the return of refugees on the other (Dolan and Large 2004: 88; Harper 2007: 192–3). Even after this clarification, a memorandum from the SRSG explained that individuals suspected of serious crimes were not to be arrested at the border or transit centres, but at a time determined by the SCIU Prosecutor, and that these arrests should only be made with 'due regard to local sensitivities and bearing in mind the overall goal of promoting further returns' (Dolan and Large 2004: 88–9). In other words, UNTAET's approach towards returnees continued to involve a balancing act between stability concerns and retributive justice goals.

Amongst the East Timorese leadership, the preoccupation with stability concerns was reflected in an emerging discourse of 'reconciliation'. Despite having made emphatic demands soon after the referendum for the establishment of an international criminal tribunal to bring Indonesian military generals to trial (see CNRT 2000a; CNRT 2000b), the East Timorese leadership began progressively to signal a growing reluctance to pursue prosecutions for both Indonesian and East Timorese perpetrators, and, increasingly, to consider various forms of amnesty that could be granted after independence. Amongst the foremost proponents of a reconciliatory stance was the charismatic former resistance figure and then leader of the CNRT, Xanana Gusmão. Stressing the values of 'forgiveness and forgetting', Gusmão's reconciliation narrative differed from that promoted by the CAVR, which emphasised the complementarity of truth-seeking, reconciliation and retributive justice. Thus, soon after the referendum, Gusmão began to promote a 'South African-style' reconciliation process in which the leaders of pro-autonomy political parties and organisers of the violence would return to the scene of their crimes and receive amnesty in exchange for confession. For example, as he explained in an interview in the *Sydney Morning Herald*, in December 2000:

> I don't deny the need for justice . . . People sometimes say if you don't punish these people you will allow a political party to do the same, because everyone now knows there is no justice. I myself don't believe in this process . . . My problem is that if you try the militia, one or two immediately, the others will not come . . . I'm thinking of a process of reconciliation here that can avoid instability in the future and one that people can accept . . . I will not say no to justice, but in a process maybe like South Africa.
>
> (Gusmão, quoted in Dodd 2000)

Gusmão began to express frustrations that such an approach was not viewed by the international community to be acceptable in East Timor:

> Nobody in the world said to [Nelson] Mandela 'your commission of truth and reconciliation is unacceptable', everybody applauded it . . . To us [East Timorese], it seems there are demands.
>
> (Gusmão, quoted in Dodd 2000)

Gusmão's reconciliatory narrative was closely tied to the promotion of a forward-looking development agenda through which he argued the need for social justice rather than retributive justice. Improving people's living standards, Gusmão began to argue, would enable people to move on with their lives and forgive, which a narrow focus on 'formal justice' through the judiciary, trials, punishment and prison, would not. Gusmão also began to question the resources that were being spent on imprisoning East Timorese militia, suggesting that these funds would be more effectively used to improve the living standards of all citizens:

> These men, they will go to trial, they will go to prison. Who will pay for their daily life in prison? The money that you pay in taxation, instead of going to teachers and nurses, will go to prisoners. Do you accept this?
>
> (Gusmão, quoted in *Time Asia* 2001)

Pragmatic stability considerations were a clear driving factor behind Gusmão's reconciliatory narrative, in that he and a number of other East Timorese leaders did not see the prosecution of leading Indonesian military figures – many of whom were still in active service with the TNI – as being in the nation's best interests (Bhuta 2001: 173). The prosecution of lower-level East Timorese militia was also viewed as problematic, in that it would dissuade other militia from returning to East Timor, thereby causing continued instability on the West Timor border. Gusmão's increasing emphasis on reconciliation over retributive justice was also undoubtedly informed by the East Timorese leadership's growing awareness that the UN Security Council was turning a deaf ear to their requests for the establishment of an international criminal tribunal, and a consciousness of their inability to tackle the issue of Indonesian impunity on their own. It was soon apparent, for example, that the UN's initial decision to rely on Indonesian co-operation with the Serious Crimes Process had been fundamentally misguided. In spite of its signing a memorandum of understanding in which it had agreed to 'the widest possible measure of mutual assistance in investigations or court proceedings' (RI/UNTAET: 2000), by early 2001, the government of Indonesia was openly ignoring repeated requests from the SCIU for assistance and extradition of persons within its jurisdiction (Cohen 2002: 7). This meant that the Serious Crimes Process would, in effect, only be able to prosecute low-level militia leaders present in the territory of East Timor (Katzenstein 2003: 274). However, according to a former SCIU staff member, UNTAET was unwilling to bring political pressure to bear on the Indonesian government through the UN Security Council or foreign embassies.[8]

The UN Department of Peacekeeping Operations (DPKO) and UN Security Council were similarly reluctant to publicly pressure the Indonesian government to halt, or drastically reform, its own flawed prosecutorial process. Although the Indonesian government eventually established an Ad Hoc Human Rights Court to prosecute Indonesians responsible for serious crimes in East Timor during 1999, the mandate of the Court was limited to the events that occurred between April and September, and restricted to crimes committed in Dili, Liquica and Suai. The Indonesian Attorney General then limited the scope of the tribunal even further by announcing that attention would be given to only five specific cases (Burchill 2009: 282). The promised trials were also repeatedly delayed.[9]

The absence of serious UN commitment to a retributive justice agenda was also reflected in the under-resourcing of the Serious Crimes Process (which was funded by a combination of assessed and voluntary contributions of states). The level of under-resourcing is made clear when one compares the annual budget of the Serious Crimes Process, which stood at US$6.1 million in 2002 and US$7–8 million in 2004–05 (Cohen 2006: 5), with those of the Extraordinary Courts in Cambodia, which were budgeted at just under US$19 million per year, the Special Court in Sierra Leone, which was costed at US$16 million per year, and the ICTY and ICTR, which each has an annual budget of about US$100 million (Stanley 2008: 173).

8 Interview with former SCIU investigator, Melbourne, September 2009.

9 Although Indonesian officials had announced in August 2001 that court hearings would begin in October, it was then announced in October that the judges would not be named until December (La'o Hamutuk 2001).

No one involved should have been surprised about these emerging issues. A myriad of UN reports had been drawing attention to the problems of the Serious Crimes Process for some time, among them a November 2000 report of a Security Council Mission to East Timor and report of the High Commissioner for Human Rights in 2001 (see UNSC 2000; UNCHR 2001). When UNTAET's mandate was extended in January 2001, the UN Security Council emphasised the need for measures to address the shortcomings of the Serious Crimes Process 'with a view to bringing to justice those responsible for serious crimes in 1999' (UNSC 2001: para 8). Yet, in the context of competing political imperatives, member states of the UN Security Council, and the donor community more generally, appeared to be more interested in avoiding a challenge to Indonesia and maintaining the image of UNTAET as a 'success' than acknowledging and tackling the resource problems and fundamental political constraints of the Serious Crimes Process. Instead, as Stanley observes, the Serious Crimes Process became a convenient 'smokescreen' by means of which donor governments could demonstrate their support for prosecutions while still maintaining diplomatic relations with Indonesia (Stanley 2009: 97; Stanley 2008: 170; see also Aarons 2008: 87). In other words, while the Serious Crimes Process was useful to donor governments, UNTAET and the UN Department of Peacekeeping Office (DPKO), insofar as it furthered their interests by contributing to the construction of the UNTAET success story, it remained largely a token gesture that never had their full support (Katzenstein 2003: 272).

In this climate of competing imperatives, the CAVR fared better than the Serious Crimes Process. Indeed, the institution received significant financial support from countries including Japan, which contributed close to US$1 million, followed by the United Kingdom, which contributed approximately US$931,300 (CAVR 2005a: Annex 3).While this funding success was due in large part to the efforts of CAVR advisers, it was perhaps also the case that the CAVR's emphasis on local reconciliation was attractive to donors because it did not present a threat to diplomatic relations with Indonesia. In this sense, like the Serious Crimes Process, the CAVR was useful to donor states, the UN DPKO and UNTAET insofar is it also contributed to the post-conflict reconstruction success story. By supporting the CAVR, the UN could demonstrate its commitment to justice and reconciliation, and to the principles of participation and local ownership, while disguising its reluctance to challenge Indonesia or adequately support the Serious Crimes Process. Over time, members of the East Timorese political leadership – many of whom had initially been very 'hands-off' – also began to engage with the CAVR, perhaps because they came to view it as more complementary to their own priorities than the Serious Crimes Process.[10]

10 Interview with former CAVR staff member, Dili, 6 July 2008.

Throughout the UNTAET period, then, the propensity of the UN and donor states to portray East Timor as a success story of post-conflict reconstruction (and the promotion of the transitional justice process as a key component of this), masked – at least partially – the multiple competing priorities and interests that were at stake. In particular, it disguised the fact that the transitional justice process was being increasingly hamstrung by the drive by UN Security Council members to prioritise diplomatic relations with Indonesia over retributive justice goals. The emerging ascendancy of the stability discourse resulted in a weakened Serious Crimes Process, but found some complementarity with the goals of the CAVR. In the context of waning international support for prosecutions of the Indonesian military, it was not surprising that the East Timorese leadership began increasingly to promote a 'forward-looking' reconciliatory narrative.

Post-independence tensions

Following East Timor's formal independence, in 2002, the political imperatives that were discernable during the UNTAET period became more obvious, with both the UN and the new East Timorese government increasingly distancing themselves from responsibility for pursuing prosecutions of the Indonesian military. For its part, the new East Timorese government solidified its 'forward-looking approach' towards building diplomatic relations with Indonesia during the independence celebrations of 19 May 2002, when newly elected President Xanana Gusmão and Indonesian President Megawati Sukarnoputri appeared together on stage together with their hands joined in a victory salute. In his speech, Gusmão spoke of 'twenty-four years of difficult relations', which he suggested were the 'result of a historical mistake which now belongs to history and to the past' (Gusmão, quoted in Nevins 2005: 154).

Nonetheless, the East Timorese leadership was not always united on this issue. In general, there was broad agreement between the governing party FRETILIN,[11] led by Mari Alkatiri,[12] and key CNRT political figures Xanana Gusmão, East Timor's first President,[13] and José Ramos-Horta, East Timor's first Foreign Minister,[14] about the need to maintain cordial ties with Indonesia,

11 FRETILIN won 57 per cent of the vote at East Timor's first general election, held under UN auspices in August 2001, prior to formal independence

12 Following independence, on 20 May 2002, Mari Alkatiri became East Timor's first prime minister, governing from 2002 to 2006. He was forced to step down following the crisis of 2006.

13 Presidential elections were held on 14 April 2002. Xanana Gusmão won 83 per cent of the vote.

14 José Ramos-Horta was East Timor's foreign minister from 2002 to 2006. In 2006, he served as prime minister for a short period following the resignation of Mari Alkatiri. He became East Timor's second president after the 2007 presidential elections.

and to develop trade and co-operation. Yet, compared with the President and Foreign Minister, Prime Minister Alkatiri was less publicly outspoken about making calls to forgive and forget, and more willing to continue stressing the responsibilities of the international community to hold Indonesian perpetrators to account. Thus, in May 2003, prior to his first official visit to Indonesia, Alkatiri expressed frustrations with the Indonesian Ad Hoc Human Rights Court. Labelling the process a 'theatre', he stated that an international tribunal should be established in a neutral country, stressing that this was primarily the obligation of the UN, which he accused of 'washing its hands' of prosecutions (*Joyo Indonesian News* 2003; Jolliffe 2003). He also criticised the UN for abdicating its responsibilities in relation to the indictment of Indonesian General Wiranto (discussed in further detail below). However, it seems likely that Alkatiri was chastised by other Timorese leaders (or international donors) for these comments, because, on the eve of his departure for Jakarta in June and in response to requests from Indonesian diplomats to clarify these statements, he reversed his position by suggesting that the reports were inaccurate and that the government was ready to correct this mistake (Unidjaja 2003). The issue was further complicated by separate visits to Jakarta soon after by Gusmão and Ramos-Horta, both of whom emphasised that the East Timorese government did not intend to pressure Indonesia in regards to prosecutions (Jolliffe 2003).

The government's increasingly 'forward-looking' approach to building relations with Indonesia was taking shape in the context of the UN mission's downsizing. Following independence, UNTAET was replaced with a 'patchwork' of smaller successor missions (Federer 2005: 106), the first of which was the United Nations Mission of Support in East Timor (UNMISET).[15] Although some notable attempts were made to improve the functioning of the Special Panels and the management of the SCIU (see Cohen 2006), there was little additional commitment of resources, extension of time, or strengthening of the mandate of the Serious Crimes Process following independence. According to the initial UNMISET 'implementation plan', based on a set of purportedly 'achievable milestones', investigations were to be completed by 31 December 2002 and trials completed by the end of 2003, when the mission itself was initially due to conclude (UNSG 2002). Compounding the problematic nature of this plan was the fact that the flaws in the Indonesian Ad

15 UNMISET was initially given a one-year mandate, which was later extended until 20 May 2004, and followed by a further extension until 19 May 2005. The mission was then replaced by the United Nations Office in East Timor (UNOTIL), a much smaller mission, from May 2005 to August 2006. Unlike UNTAET, UNOTIL was not a peacekeeping mission, but a political mission. Following the violence of April/June 2006, the UN Security Council established a new, expanded mission, called the United Nations Integrated Mission in Timor-Leste (UNMIT), which was given a far-reaching mandate to assist the country in overcoming the consequences and underlying causes of the violence.

Hoc Human Rights Court established in Jakarta had become glaringly apparent. Although twelve trials eventually took place between March 2002 and August 2003, and six defendants were found guilty in the first instance, all six were acquitted on appeal (ICTJ and Kontras 2011).

The overshadowing of retributive justice goals by stability imperatives is no better illustrated than in the controversy that surrounded the indictment of General Wiranto. On 24 February 2003, the SCIU issued an indictment against General Wiranto, the Minister of Defence and Security and Commander of the Indonesian Armed Forces at the time of East Timor's referendum, charging that he was responsible under international law for the crimes against humanity of murder and deportation, under the doctrine of command responsibility. In response, Indonesian Foreign Minister, Dr Hassan Wirajuda, announced that his government would 'simply ignore' the indictment (Detik Com, quoted in Harris-Rimmer 2008: 191). Shortly after this, UNMISET attempted to absolve itself of responsibility for the indictment, declaring that it had been issued through the prosecution service of East Timor and not the UN (UN News Centre 2003). The head of the SCIU, Siri Frigaard, was also reportedly directed by UN headquarters to take the UN logo off the indictment papers after they had already been issued, which she refused to do. As Stanley notes, although the UN's position was technically correct, it was disingenuous, as the UN had set up the judicial process and the SCIU was staffed by UN employees (Stanley 2008: 177; see also Hirst and Varney 2005: 25). The East Timorese government responded by declaring that the indictment was the work of the UN and not of East Timor, and followed this by declining offers of overseas aid for the funding and staffing of the Serious Crimes Process (Hirst and Varney 2005: 25; Katzenstein 2003: 268–9; Harris-Rimmer 2010: 138).

Tensions mounted after the Special Panels for Serious Crimes issued its warrant on 10 May 2004 for the arrest of General Wiranto, who, by this point, was a front-runner in the election campaign for the next President of Indonesia. Not long after this, President Xanana Gusmão and Indonesian President Megawati Sukarnoputri met and agreed that outstanding human rights issues between the countries should be resolved through a 'reconciliatory approach' (Hirst and Varney 2005: 25). These actions influenced the East Timorese General Prosecutor, who had been originally supportive of the indictment. Reversing his position, he presented a motion to the Court seeking to have the indictment against Wiranto 'revised' (Hirst and Varney 2005: 26). Although this motion was refused by the Special Panels, at the time of writing, the General Prosecutor has still not forwarded the warrant to Interpol.

Despite these developments, reports of the UN Secretary General to the Security Council continued to demand that those responsible for serious crimes should be brought to justice (see, for example, UNSC 2004a). In May 2004, a UN Security Council Resolution reaffirmed the 'fight against impunity', yet in the very same paragraph it gave the SCIU until November 2004 to complete all investigations and the Special Panels until 20 May 2005 to conclude trials (UNSC 2004b: para 8). After this time, all remaining cases would be relinquished to East Timor's Ministry of Justice, which, under the growing case load of ordinary crimes and civil disputes, was already extremely overburdened (Katzenstein 2003: 272). Moreover, the UN had no official plan of action for dealing with the hundreds of outstanding indictments. Indeed, as Cohen (2006) notes, the UN defined 'success' for itself as completing its pending cases and handing over its files to the Timorese government, and no further cases ready to go to trial were progressed after mid-2004. In other words, the decision to end the Serious Crimes Process was not because the Special Panels had dealt with all of the available cases, but was due to a decision by the UN Security Council to 'successfully complete' the East Timor mission (Cohen 2006: 4).

Not long after shelving the Wiranto indictment, the East Timorese and Indonesian governments agreed to establish their own bilateral Commission of Truth and Friendship (CTF). Following the meeting between Presidents Gusmão and Sukarnoputri in May 2004, Gusmão met with General Wiranto (Figure 2.1), hugged him as an 'act of reconciliation' and reportedly referred to him as a 'dear friend' (Hirst and Varney 2005: 25). Foreign Minister Ramos-Horta then put forward a proposal for an 'International Truth and Reconciliation Panel', which was to be composed of eminent persons from Asia (Hirst 2008: 11). The concept evolved into a proposal for a bilateral CTF, which was publicly announced by the Presidents in March 2005.

The CTF was a clear indication of the East Timorese leadership's outright rejection of a retributive justice approach, and the promotion of a nation-building agenda that stressed moving on from the past and building diplomatic relations with Indonesia. Unlike the CAVR, the CTF was designed specifically as an alternative to prosecutions, rather than as a complementary approach. Confined to addressing the violence of 1999, the CTF was empowered to seek the 'conclusive truth' in order to contribute to a 'definitive closure of the issues of the past [that] would further promote bilateral relations' (CTF 2005: para 8). The CTF's mandate also emphasised the need to establish 'institutional responsibilities' rather than to identify and assign individual blame, and while it had the power to recommend amnesties and rehabilitation of those 'wrongly accused', it was precluded from recommending prosecutions. Writing very frankly of the pragmatic intent of the CTF, the Timorese co-chair of the Commission, Dionisio Babo-Soares, stated:

> Issues of interest seem coincidentally to match well (Timor Leste is interested in joining ASEAN and needs Indonesian help, whereas Indonesia needs Timor Leste to improve its image abroad and also to approach the USA to lift its ban on selling technical stocks of armaments to Indonesia, etc).
>
> (Babo-Soares, in Hirst 2008: 12)

Figure 2.1 East Timor President Xanana Gusmão and Indonesian presidential candidate, former General Wiranto, in Bali on 29 May 2004 (Dadang Tri/Reuters/Picture Media)

Not surprisingly, the CTF was heavily criticised by Indonesian, East Timorese and international human rights organisations, who viewed it as another device to sidestep the issue of prosecutions. The UN also declined to participate in the CTF, citing concerns about its amnesty provisions, in particular the lack of clear criteria for when amnesty would be recommended, including in relation to the international crimes of crimes against humanity and war crimes (Hirst 2008: 16). More specifically, critics saw the CTF as an attempt by the East Timorese government to divert attention away from the proposal of the UN Secretary General to appoint a UN Commission of Experts (COE) to review transitional justice developments, which, it was anticipated, would recommend reconsideration of the establishment of an international criminal tribunal. These suspicions were reinforced by the Foreign Ministers of Indonesia and East Timor, who issued a joint press release stating that 'In the light of the initiative of the Heads of States of

Indonesia and Timor-Leste [to establish the CTF], the said initiative of the UN Secretary-General [to appoint a COE] appears to be redundant' (RI and GOTL 2004).[16]

The CTF's credibility was further eroded once it began public hearings, which were dominated by senior Indonesian public officials, members of the TNI and former militia commanders. Presenting views that were heavily skewed towards the perspective of the institutions that they represented, these individuals were rarely subjected to rigorous scrutiny by CTF commissioners (Hirst 2008: 26). As Hayner (2011: 64) notes, officials and TNI commanders were effectively granted a public platform to deny particular events and their role in them. Moreover, opportunities for victims to participate in public hearings were highly circumscribed. According to observers, the limited number of victims who were invited to give testimony were treated poorly, often finding themselves in rooms filled with uniformed members of the TNI who ridiculed and intimidated them (Hirst 2008: 32–5).

It was soon after these developments that the CAVR's final report, *Chega!*, was released. *Chega!* generated a new set of debates, which began with the controversy that surrounded its public release. Although it was completed on 31 October 2005 and tabled in the Parliament on 28 November 2005, the report was not made public until early 2006, when it was presented to the Secretary General of the UN. The delay in its public release unleashed a flurry of criticism from NGOs and the media, many of whom suggested that President Gusmão was attempting to suppress the report's findings (see, for example, ICTJ 2005; Amnesty International 2005). One of the suspected reasons for the delay was the fact that although the CAVR was perceived to be consistent with stability imperatives, *Chega!* challenged this perception by arguing that accountability for serious crimes was essential to 'authentic' reconciliation. It suggested that:

> the demand for justice and accountability remains a fundamental issue in the lives of many East Timorese people and a potential obstacle to building a democratic society based on respect for the rule of law and authentic reconciliation between individuals, families, communities and nations.
>
> (CAVR 2005a: Exec Summary, 183)

16 Nonetheless, the COE was established, and its report, which was officially released on 15 July 2005, provided a scathing critique of the Indonesian Ad Hoc Human Rights Court (COE 2005). It recommended that Indonesia should reopen the prosecutions that had been brought before the ad hoc court and that, should it fail to do so within a six-month time frame, the Security Council should create an international criminal tribunal to be located in a third state (COE 2005). However, despite the momentum it generated, the COE report did not lead to any dramatic change of strategy amongst UN Security Council members.

Amongst its many recommendations, *Chega!* proposed that the UN's Serious Crimes Process be continued and that the UN 'be prepared to institute an International Tribunal pursuant to Chapter VII of the UN Charter should other measures be deemed to have failed to deliver a sufficient measure of justice and Indonesia persists in the obstruction of justice' (CAVR 2005a: Part 11, 26). It provided a disturbing account of 'massive, widespread and systematic atrocities' committed by member of the Indonesian security forces during the occupation – including extrajudicial killings, torture, disappearances, sexual violence, and the use of chemical and biological weapons – which it suggested amounted to crimes against humanity (CAVR 2005a: ch 8, 5–6). It also held the Indonesian government and security forces 'primarily responsible and accountable' for the deaths of between 100,000 and 180,000 civilians from hunger and illness that occurred as a direct result of the twenty-four-year occupation (CAVR 2005a: ch 8, 6). *Chega!* also drew attention to a number of uncomfortable and controversial facts about the involvement of the international community in the Indonesian occupation. For instance, it criticised the policies and practices of a number of Western states, including Australia, the US and Britain, for their support of the Indonesian occupation, and urged that a reparations fund be established with contributions from those governments and institutions that had provided military support to Indonesia (CAVR 2005a: ch 11, 35, 42).

Despite their overall enthusiasm for the CAVR, the responses of Western states to *Chega!* showed little support for the report's findings and recommendations. They were not interested in encouraging the report's advocacy of prosecutions and reparations, or endorsing 'truths' that implicated the past actions of the international community. Rather, their responses indicated that they were interested in supporting the CAVR only insofar as it focused on 'local' reconciliation and truth-telling, and continued to bolster the success story narrative and the promotion of their own humanitarian image as part of this.[17] The responses of the Australian government are a case in point. A spokesperson for Australian Foreign Minister Alexander Downer explained that the human rights issues raised in the report were 'essentially issues for East Timor to work through' (Hyland and Murdoch 2006). At the same time, the Australian government was also keen to highlight its humanitarian role in the reconstruction of East Timor, evident in the following response from an official from the Department of Foreign Affairs and Trade (DFAT) to a letter from the Australian Coalition for Transitional Justice in East Timor requesting that the Australian government provide a formal response to *Chega!*:

17 Indeed, Pat Walsh, former adviser to the CAVR, suggests that donors had always been more keen to support the CAVR's reconciliation function as opposed to its truth-seeking work, which may have been because they did not want their own 'dirty linen' hung out to dry (interview with Pat Walsh, Melbourne, 12 December 2011).

> Australia has invested considerable resources in rebuilding East Timor and is widely recognised as a major development assistance partner. Australia remains committed to East Timor and its future as a strong and independent democracy.
>
> (DFAT, in Uniya 2006: 31)

The UN also distanced itself from the *Chega!* recommendations. Although a 2006 UN Secretary General's report devoted six paragraphs to the CAVR report and expressed the 'sincere hope' that it would 'help to prevent the tragic events in Timor-Leste and elsewhere' from recurring (UNSG 2006: 7), the Secretary General was silent on the CAVR's recommendation that the UN itself should debate the report. By restricting his comments to 1999, the Secretary General also failed to acknowledge the crimes against humanity committed during the years prior to 1999 that formed the bulk of the CAVR's findings (Post-CAVR Secretariat 2006), to which, as noted in Chapter 1, Western states had failed to respond.

Not surprisingly, the Indonesian government also denied many of the report's findings. The Indonesian Presidential Spokesman Dino Patti Djalal stated: 'We are unhappy with the report because it contains an untrue and questionable allegation. We also have no idea why the old wounds had to be re-opened' (ANTARA News 2006). General Wiranto said he did not believe that the armed forces or the police were responsible for many of the deaths cited in the report or that they had caused famine in East Timor, stating 'even if there was famine, it may have been because the war made food scarce . . . This is not something intentional caused by the TNI' (BBC News 2006). Indonesia's Defence Minister Juwono Sudarsono also challenged the report's accuracy, and denied that the country had used napalm or deliberately starved citizens:

> This is a war of numbers and data about things that never happened . . . How could we have used napalm against the East Timorese? Back then we didn't even have the capacity to import, let alone make napalm.
>
> (Sudarsono, quoted in Lynch and Nakashima 2006)

The responses of the Indonesian government and those of Western states can be understood as manifestations of what Stanley Cohen refers to as the discourse of 'official denial' (Cohen 2001). As Cohen observes, states routinely hide their responsibility for, or knowledge of, human rights violations, through a range of strategies (Cohen 2001). These may range from literal denial – attacking the reliability, objectivity and credibility of the observer – to more subtle strategies of 'interpretive denial', which involve admitting the raw facts, but denying the interpretive framework place on these events (such as by claiming that responsibility for the events in question do not lie with the state) (Cohen 2001: 105–9). Cohen also concedes that denial may be less the result of a planned and conscious campaign than a process of 'slippage in which uncomfortable knowledge is repressed' (Cohen 1995: 14). In this sense, while the Indonesian government's response to *Chega!* can be seen as a conscious attempt to deny responsibility, it can also be understood, in part, as a product of a 'political need to be innocent of a troubling recognition' (Cohen 2001: 139) in a context in which Indonesian public discourse had long represented East Timor as a 'province delivered from its primordial backwardness by Indonesia's modernizing national culture project' (Kitley 2000: 174). The responses of Western states to *Chega!* can be seen as embodying a discourse of denial common to bystander states that may have indirect responsibility for atrocities. According to Cohen, this discourse, which tends to involve 'selective blindsight' (Cohen 2001: 163), is a product of a combination of national and geopolitical self-interest, direct involvement and collusion in the events in question, and the popular sentiment that 'these are indeed other people's problems'.

Maintaining its reconciliatory stance towards Indonesia, the East Timorese leadership was also critical of *Chega!*, particularly its recommendations. In his 23 January 2006 statement before the UN Security Council, President Gusmão argued that it was more important that East Timor follow the path of 'restorative justice' than pursue prosecutions, by which he meant restoring relations with Indonesia and fostering social harmony:

> I have had to ask myself if it is in our national interest – which must include social harmony – to adopt a process that I am told by some friends will bring justice, and have this process go on for years, possibly setting back the democratic consolidation that is being undertaken in Timor-Leste and Indonesia respectively. The answer that I came to, after wide consultation with the people, was that it would not be.
>
> (Gusmão, in UNSC 2006a: 7)

With regards to reparations, President Gusmão suggested that the international community had already made amends for their mistakes by providing significant development assistance to East Timor since 1999, and argued that demanding reparations would make the new nation seem 'ungrateful' in the eyes of the international community. In a letter, President Gusmão reassured international donors that he did not endorse the report's recommendation for reparations, because of the commitment of the international community to the rebuilding of East Timor. As Gusmão wrote:

> How can we go to the world community, one that was indifferent to our plight for too long, when it did finally help us to achieve independence and made enormous contributions exceeding $1 billion to help us cope with our emergency situation? We still need their help and should not be

> ungrateful for what they have contributed. They are making amends for their mistake.
>
> (Gusmão, in Kingston 2006: 292)

Gusmão's response to the CAVR's recommendations on prosecutions was not surprising. In a context in which, due to international indifference, the East Timorese government was increasingly aware of its inability to hold the Indonesian military to account, it sent a strong signal to Indonesia not to be alarmed. Indeed, for all of their reconciliatory rhetoric, frustrations about the unresponsiveness of the international community continue to be expressed by some members of the East Timorese leadership, such as FRETILIN leader Mari Alkatiri who, from time to time, has called on the international community to establish an international criminal tribunal (see, for example, Gunn and Vltchek 2007; Roughneen 2009). Even Ramos-Horta, who has increasingly promoted a reconciliatory stance, also argued in 2004 that:

> The United Nations were here, from 1999 to 2003, with the massive peacekeeping force. They didn't do that [hold Indonesia to account]. So why should the East Timorese, with our own priorities and concerns, to continue to consolidate peace, reconciliation, creating jobs for our people, reducing poverty – should pretend to be a sort of Don Quixote de la Mancha of justice, in fighting the mighty Indonesian army?
>
> (Ramos-Horta, quoted in Lam 2005)

Gusmão's response to the reparations issue and his concern not to appear 'ungrateful' to the international community can also be understood, in part, as a rational response to the constraints of East Timor's newly won independence. In particular, it recognises that, due to the underdeveloped state of its economy (a consequence of the deleterious impact of years of conflict during the Indonesian occupation and Portuguese colonial neglect), the new nation will be reliant on the aid and assistance of the international donors for many years to come. Although, to some extent, East Timor's economic prospects have been transformed since 2007 due to huge increases in oil and gas revenues from the Timor Sea, a theme to which I return in Chapter 4, it remains the case that the new nation's capacity to influence policy with respect to powerful states and international financial institutions is tenuous. These inequalities continue to be highlighted in the case of negotiations over maritime boundaries in the Timor Sea. Thus, although agreements reached in 2007 between Australia and East Timor increase East Timor's share of revenues from oil and gas fields, they prevent East Timor from seeking delineation of maritime boundaries for fifty years (La'o Hamutuk 2007: 10–11). This may well be depriving East Timor of a much larger share of resources than it currently enjoys. Western states such as Australia, it seems, prefer to provide 'aid', rather than acknowledge that a fair agreement on the Timor Sea could end East Timor's dependence on international aid and secure its development for decades to come (see Grenfell 2004: 46; Cleary 2007: 266; La'o Hamutuk 2007: 10–11). Rather than representing a break with poverty and colonial influence, then, East Timor's independence represents a very constrained form of sovereignty, in which the new nation has joined the 'international community' on vastly unequal terms.

Since East Timor's independence, then, it is clear that stability imperatives have continued to overshadow and distort retributive justice goals. Within the UN, the goal of concluding the Serious Crimes Process and portraying it as a completed success outweighed the demands of those pressing for prosecutions of senior members of the Indonesia military, while the establishment of the bilateral CTF signalled the new East Timorese government's policy of appeasement towards Indonesia in the context of its growing awareness of geopolitical constraints. That the government increasingly distanced itself from the Serious Crimes Process and rejected the CAVR recommendations also suggests that the UN-sponsored transitional justice process, even after independence, was never fully 'owned' by the East Timorese leadership, nor had it responded to their early requests for the international community to take responsibility for prosecuting Indonesian war criminals. In the next section, I discuss some recent transitional justice developments since the 2006 'crisis'. Despite the renewed commitments of both the UN and the East Timorese leadership to 'address the past', their efforts underscore the continuing primacy of stability discourses.

The 'crisis' of 2006 and the unravelling of the East Timor success story

Until early in 2006, the UN and international donors were still promoting East Timor's post-conflict reconstruction as a success story. Indeed, as recently as April 2006, then President of the World Bank Paul Wolfowitz, when visiting East Timor, congratulated the East Timorese people for the 'considerable progress' they had made in the past six-and-a-half years, commenting that 'the bustling markets, the rebuilt schools, the functioning government – and above all, the peace and stability – attest to sensible leadership and sound decisions' (World Bank 2006). Two weeks after this statement, however, the success story began to unravel as the country descended into violence. Precipitated by the government's dismissal of 594 soldiers – around one-third of the military – who had left their barracks complaining of poor pay and conditions and ethnic prejudice, the violence became a catalyst for a range of disaffected groups to express their diverse grievances, and was exacerbated by poverty and unemployment-related frustrations (Kingsbury and Leach 2007: 6; ICG 2006). It also brought to the fore a number of serious issues within the East Timorese government regarding the increasing politicisation of the military and police, the exercise of personal power in political decision-making, and the resurfacing of grievances and ideological differences from the 1970s and 1980s (ICG 2006: 22).[18] By the middle of 2006, the state was 'largely paralysed' (Grenfell 2008: 181). Tens of thousands of people were living in refugee camps in and around Dili, and many houses had been destroyed (ICG 2006).

The tragic events of 2006 also exposed the inadequacy of the 'transition paradigm' (Carothers 2002) that underpinned the UN's state-building agenda (including its transitional justice approach). This paradigm – based on the assumption that international actors could facilitate the establishment of a stable, liberal, democratic state within a two-and-a-half-year period – had depicted East Timor as a *tabula rasa*, and had paid little regard to its specific historical, social and economic conditions and legacies. There is also evidence to suggest that the UN's emphasis on rapid economic liberalisation – a core aspect of its state-building blueprint – was a background factor that contributed to the crisis. For example, as discussed in Chapter 1, it is likely that the free market model of development promoted by international financial institutions in East Timor exacerbated poverty and food insecurity, particularly in rural areas. Indeed, as the World Bank itself observes, poverty increased significantly between 2001 and 2007, with the percentage of the population below the poverty line growing from 36.3 per cent to 49 per cent (World Bank and Directorate of National Statistics 2008: 4–5). Compounding these problems was the artificial 'bubble' created by the UN's presence itself, which had become an attractive draw-card for many people from the rural areas to move to Dili to seek employment opportunities, and had fostered increasing resentment as the mission was scaled back and fewer and fewer jobs were available (Curtain 2006). The focus of international donor activity upon Dili had also promoted an unsustainable expansion of the urban sector that, with UNTAET's departure and as international donor priorities moved elsewhere, led to a 'precipitous economic decline' (Hughes 2009: 141).

Interestingly, following the 2006 crisis, both the UN and the East Timorese political leaderships appeared to demonstrate – at least on the face of it – a greater willingness to 'address the past'. In June 2006, a special Commission of Inquiry (COI), appointed under the auspices of the UN High Commissioner for Human Rights, concluded that the violent events were 'the expression of deep-rooted problems inherent in fragile State institutions and a weak rule of law' (COI 2006: 74). The COI's findings also echoed the concerns raised by East Timorese human rights NGOs about the need for an end to the 'culture of impunity'. A new expanded UN mission – the United Nations

18 Some commentators have suggested that these divisions have long-standing roots in the brief, but brutal, civil war between UDT and FRETILIN in the months of August and September 1975 (see, for example, Aarons 2006b; ICG 2006). I return to these issues in Chapter 4.

Integrated Mission in Timor-Leste (UNMIT) – was announced on 25 August, and was mandated, among other things, to establish a new Serious Crimes Investigation Team (SCIT) to resume investigations into serious crimes cases committed in 1999 that remained outstanding since the closure of the SCIU in 2004, and to strengthen the capacity of domestic institutions to prosecute serious crimes (UNSC 2006b). Another aspect of UNMIT's mandate involved establishing a UN 'solidarity fund' to collect voluntary contributions from member states to fund a 'community restoration program', an initiative that has been widely interpreted as a response to the CAVR's recommendation for a reparations programme (UNSC 2006b: para 11).[19]

The East Timorese leadership's stated willingness to address the past was evident in President Gusmão's televised address on 20 June 2006, just prior to the forced resignation of Prime Minister Mari Alkatiri, in which he referred more than once to *Chega!* Further, during his swearing-in ceremony on 10 July 2006 as the new President, Ramos-Horta referred to the need to learn the lessons of *Chega!* This shift in public position was then bolstered by the release of the final report of the bilateral CTF, *Per Memoriam ad Spem* ('Through Memory to Hope'), which, despite the scepticism of many observers, was not the whitewash that many were anticipating. Handed over to Indonesian President Susilo Bambang Yudhoyono and East Timorese President José Ramos-Horta at a ceremony in Bali on 15 July 2008, the CTF report concurs with many of the CAVR's findings that crimes against humanity did occur in 1999 and that the TNI was principally responsible for those crimes (CTF 2008: ch 8). Moreover, it concludes that these crimes were not an aberration, but resulted from entrenched policies and practices within the Indonesian security sector (CTF 2008: 283; see also Hirst 2009: 6). In addition, although it does not make explicit recommendations for a reparations scheme, it does recommend a number of measures – including the creation of a documentation and conflict resolution centre and the establishment of a commission for 'the disappeared' to recover information about the fate of disappeared persons – that could be seen to constitute 'reparations' in a collective sense (CTF 2008: 300–3; see also Hirst 2009: 28)

A further set of CTF recommendations are aimed at strengthening diplomatic relations, and include the creation of 'peace zones' at the border where visas will not be required, finalising border demarcation issues, and resolving outstanding disputes relating to assets and pensions for former civil servants (CTF 2008: 299–300; see also Hirst 2009: 9–10). Significantly, by not

19 Notably, the UN has preferred the term 'solidarity' to 'reparations' – a term that may perhaps be more palatable to Western states. At this point in time, however, little progress has yet been made towards establishing the Solidarity Fund.

recommending amnesties, clearing names or claiming a 'conclusive truth', and by presenting evidence that could be used to implicate senior Indonesian officials, the CTF report leaves open the possibility of future prosecutions. Given the East Timorese and Indonesian Presidents' explicit endorsement of the CTF, the final report may well have more chance than the CAVR of shifting the approach of both governments to dealing with the past.

The unexpectedly strong CTF report suggests that many observers had underestimated the potential of the CTF commissioners to work with, and to some extent challenge, the narrow terms of reference with which they had been provided, and independently carry out their work. Indeed, despite the politicised appointment process, it appears that over the three-year period of the CTF's operation, staff and commissioners were increasingly driven by a strong sense of pride in their work and a desire to ensure that their results would be credible. The need for the commissioners to negotiate a number of widely divergent understandings of the past had also called for diplomatic skills. Indeed, according to information garnered from an interview with the former East Timor CTF Co-ordinator, over the course of its work, all of the commissioners came to realise that reconciliation could not be achieved immediately, but that a slow process of negotiation and 'reconciling ideas' was required.[20]

Nonetheless, the UN's renewed emphasis on 'addressing the past' gave little attention to the issue of prosecutions. Although investigations into serious crimes cases were reconstituted, the UN Security Council was not wholly committed to prosecutions, as evidenced by the fact that the SCIT was given only investigatory, and not prosecutorial, powers. The SCIT is also precluded from investigating crimes committed prior to 1999 and has even fewer investigative resources than the SCIU (ICTJ 2010: 18). In practice, this has left the East Timorese government, rather than the international community, with the political burden of deciding how to treat over 300 arrest warrants and numerous pending indictments left behind by the previous SCIU, and with the sole responsibility, with its limited resources and capacity, for conducting prosecutions (Rapoza 2006: 534).[21]

Beyond the issue of prosecutions, the commitment to 'addressing the past' on the part of the UN and international donors does not appear to encompass reflection on their own contribution to the 2006 crisis. It does not, for example,

20 Interview with Hugo Fernandes, former East Timor CTF Co-ordinator, Dili, 5 July 2008.

21 Since the closure of the SCIU in 2005, only three serious crimes cases have come before the Dili District Court involving indictees who had returned to East Timor (ICTJ 2010: 21–2). As of February 2010, the UNMIT Serious Crimes Investigating Team (SCIT) had completed 110 investigations into 396 outstanding cases inherited from the previous SCIU and had submitted a number of completed case files with recommendations for indictments to prosecutors; however, the Prosecutor General had not issued any new indictments (see UNSG 2010: para 76; ICTJ 2010: 20).

consider the adequacy of its decision to 'downsize' the UN presence after a mere two-and-a-half-year 'transition' period, and whether the flaws of the Serious Crimes Process had encouraged rather than addressed a 'culture of impunity'. Rather, the fact that most media and political statements have held the East Timorese to be responsible for the resurgence of violence (Stanley 2009: 138; Curtain 2006) suggests that, despite the unravelling of the 'success story', the UN and international donors continued to portray their role as benevolent actors and problem-solvers. This is also evident in the statement of UN Secretary General Kofi Annan soon after the violence, in which he noted that the unrest was particularly painful because the country was a 'child of the international community', whom the UN was determined not to abandon at its critical time of need (UNSC 2006c). Implicit in this analogy and representation of East Timor as child-like is the self-image of the West as a rational and enlightened parent (see Orford 2003: 154). The implication, therefore, is that the renewed violence is the result of inexperienced local actors, rather than any failures on the part of the UN intervention (see Orford 2003: 156).

Hamstrung by geopolitical constraints, the East Timorese government's stated willingness to address the past is also, in practice, highly circumscribed. The leadership's continuing emphasis on 'moving on' is evident in the statements of Indonesian Foreign Minister Hassan Wirayuda and East Timorese Prime Minister Xanana Gusmão in 2008 that they hoped that the CTF report had resolved the case of human rights violations from 1999 (Hirst 2009: 31). It is also reflected in the East Timorese Parliament's repeated postponement of debate on the CAVR and CTF recommendations, and President Horta's decision in 2008 to grant 'pardons' to the vast majority of serious crimes perpetrators convicted through the Special Panels process, issues to which I return in Chapter 4.

The continuing primacy accorded by the East Timorese government to diplomatic relations with Indonesia is perhaps most starkly illustrated by the controversial 'Bere case'. This case, which represented a test of how the political leadership would respond to indicted serious crimes defendants who returned to East Timor, concerned a former leader of the Laksaur militia group in Covalima, and now Indonesian citizen, Martinus Bere, who had been indicted by the SCIU in 2003 for his role in the Suai Church Massacre in 1999 and charged with crimes against humanity. Bere, who had been living openly in West Timor, crossed the border back into East Timor in August 2006 and was recognised by members of his former local community. He was then arrested by the East Timorese police and transferred to Becora prison to await trial. Soon after this, Indonesian Foreign Minister Hassan Wirajuda reportedly demanded the intervention of President Ramos-Horta and Prime Minister Gusmão to release Bere, which occurred on 30 August, the day of the tenth anniversary of the referendum, allegedly in order to ensure that the Indonesian Foreign Minister would participate in the anniversary celebrations (CIGI 2011). In his speech to the nation, Ramos-Horta declared that 'there will be no international tribunal', and asked the UN to disband the Serious Crimes Investigating Team (SCIT) (La'o Hamutuk 2009b). The release of Bere was widely criticised by international and national human rights activists as an abrogation of the Constitution, and resulted in vocal protests in Dili, which highlighted the extent to which the government's handling of the case was out of step with popular opinion. The president of the Court of Appeal released a statement critical of the political interference in the justice system, while opposition parties FRETILIN and the National Unity Party (PUN) introduced a censure motion into Parliament. Although ultimately unsuccessful, the censure prompted a heated day of debate.

In sum, developments since the tragic crisis of 2006 show that the dramatic undoing of East Timor's 'success story' has led to renewed commitments to addressing the past on the part of the East Timorese government, the UN and donor states, but in practice those efforts have been little more than skin deep. The fact that the UN has placed the political burden of dealing with serious crimes prosecutions squarely on the East Timorese government suggests that its institutional interests lie in continuing to retreat from responsibility for these questions and, at the same time, in promoting its benevolent role in East Timor's reconstruction. The East Timorese government's handling of the Bere case, and its calls for the closing down of the serious crimes investigations process, indicate that it has become firmly opposed to a retributive justice agenda.

Conclusion

By tracing the trajectory of transitional justice developments through the UNTAET and post-independence eras, it is possible to see that the UN-sponsored transitional justice process did not transcend either international or national politics, but was deeply enmeshed within both. The Serious Crimes Process and the CAVR were established within a context of conflicting and competing demands in which realist stability goals came to overshadow the legalist principle of 'universal jurisdiction', which denotes that crimes against humanity, war crimes and genocide must be punished wherever they occur. These conflicts reflected the complex policy dilemmas and perceived political imperatives faced by UNTAET, the East Timorese leadership and the UN Security Council: the need to repatriate refugees without antagonising Indonesia; the maintenance of stability along the border with West Timor; the physical redevelopment of the country; and the drive of powerful Western states to maintain Indonesia as a key ally over the pursuit of prosecutions of its military. The full extent of these political interests and conflicting goals was, however, obscured by the UN's narrative of UNTAET as a success story of post-conflict reconstruction. Conscious of its material status as a poor nation with limited political influence on the international stage, and with the knowledge that the principal perpetrators of past violations remain powerful figures in Indonesia, the East Timorese leadership's promotion of a narrative of reconciliation-as-forgiveness was an understandable response to these political pressures.

Since East Timor's independence, the ascendancy of the stability discourse has made the possibility of prosecuting Indonesian perpetrators increasingly remote. The UN Security Council continues to eschew discussions of an international criminal tribunal; the East Timorese leadership's ever more vocal 'forward-looking', anti-prosecution stance reinforces that international indifference, creating difficulties for East Timorese activists seeking to keep this issue alive. Nevertheless, beyond the sensitive issue of prosecutions, the CAVR report and the surprisingly strong CTF report have fostered some unexpected political possibilities. Significantly, the Indonesian President's acceptance of the CTF's findings marks that country's first official recognition of the role its security forces played in the commission of human rights violations in East Timor in 1999. Given that both East Timorese and Indonesian commissioners participated in the CTF, and the explicit endorsement of the CTF's work by the presidents of both nations, it may offer the best hope of shifting their respective government's approaches to dealing with the past.

Further possibilities may emerge following the East Timorese Parliament's belated decision to adopt a Resolution on the CAVR and CTF reports on 14 December 2009, which occurred after repeated delays. The Resolution, which owed much to the advocacy efforts of individual members of Parliament and human rights NGOs, authorised a parliamentary committee to prepare concrete steps to implement the recommendations of the two reports. In response, the committee prepared two draft laws. The first proposes the establishment of an 'Institute for Memory', which would implement agreed recommendations of the CAVR and CTF, including establishing a human rights documentation centre and promoting the search for missing persons, while the second proposes a 'Law of Reparations'[22] to provide a range of symbolic and material reparations to individuals deemed to be 'vulnerable victims'. Although parliamentary debate on these laws has been repeatedly postponed, the fact is that a painfully slow process of negotiation has begun.[23] The CTF report has also provided the basis for the establishment of a Joint Ministerial Commission that is facilitating high-level co-operation between the Indonesian and East Timorese governments, including discussions of the CTF recommendations. While some issues, such as the fate of missing persons, remain off-limits due to their sensitivity, some progress has been made on the less controversial topics of border demarcation, more lenient visa conditions

22 Draft Law Establishing the Public Memory Institute, No II, and the Draft Framework of the National Reparations Program, No II.

23 Both laws were originally scheduled for debate in September 2010. The laws were then delayed for debate until February 2011, and now have been delayed indefinitely.

for East Timorese students studying in Indonesia and pensions for East Timorese who were employed as Indonesian civil servants. The CTF report is also providing an impetus for human rights activists in Indonesia and East Timor to work together, and many have embraced the report as an advocacy tool.

These ongoing developments emphasise that stability discourses, while powerful, are by no means monolithic, and that new, and unforseen, possibilities emerging from the CAVR and CTF reports may be shifting the terrain on which justice struggles are being enacted. Unpredictably, the opportunities that have arisen from the highly controversial CTF are among the most interesting. The fact that these emerging possibilities are specific to the context of East Timor, including the delicate relationship with Indonesia, highlights that the UN-sponsored transitional justice process has been no substitute for, and indeed has been institutionally incapable of engaging with, the difficult national and bilateral political discussions about how to address the violence of the past. These ongoing and sensitive negotiations unsettle the view that transitional justice is a normative and apolitical process that can be introduced and implemented by external actors. They challenge, too, the linear notion of 'transition' that underpinned the UN's transitional justice rhetoric, which suggested that these mechanisms would help to bring about a rupture with the past and foster a new, democratic, order. East Timor's relationship with Indonesia contains no 'rupture' as such, but is inching forward, grounded in past relationships and present realities. It is clear from these developments in East Timor that 'dealing with the past' is a dynamic, fluid and ongoing process, rather than confined to an immediate 'transitional' period. This process continues to be fundamentally shaped and constrained by East Timor's geopolitical realities and the new nation's unequal position within the 'international community'.

Having sketched the broad context in which East Timor's transitional justice mechanisms were established, and unravelling the competing political imperatives that underpinned and disrupted them, the following chapter explores the day-to-day operation of the Serious Crimes Process and the CAVR, in order to consider what forms of 'justice' were possible given in the shadow of these political constraints.

Chapter 3

The Serious Crimes Process and the Commission for Reception, Truth and Reconciliation

Justice possibilities and impossibilities

As in other post-conflict contexts, a key goal of East Timor's transitional justice process was to deliver a measure of justice that would assist both individuals and the nation to come to terms with the past. As we have seen, the Serious Crimes Process was underpinned by a retributive justice narrative that emphasised the importance of establishing individual accountability for the most serious crimes. The prosecution and punishment of individual perpetrators was expected to contribute to a range of other justice goals, including the recognition of victims' experiences of harm, the deterrence of future criminality, and the rebuilding of community trust in legal institutions and processes. By contrast, the CAVR was underpinned by a restorative justice narrative that emphasised community reconciliation and a process of truth-seeking, which was expected to foster the healing of victims and the rebuilding of relationships at the community and national levels.

In this chapter, I unravel some of the country-specific and more universal institutional factors that undermined the ability of the transitional justice mechanisms to accomplish these goals. Some of these constraints were born out of East Timor's unique context – in particular the effects of the 'stability' imperatives discussed in Chapter 2 – while others illustrate some of the general difficulties faced by trials and truth commissions in attempting to accomplish a range of diverse, and at times conflicting, goals. This chapter also sheds light on the inherent inability of the transitional justice mechanisms to attend fully to the demands of justice that are *beyond* the law. Among other issues, I argue that the Serious Crimes Process and, to a lesser extent, the CAVR, were incapable of providing a form of justice that could fully attend to the structural dimensions of East Timor's violence.

This chapter returns, and deepens, the analytical distinction – outlined in Chapter 1 – between 'law' and 'justice'. It considers the factors that impacted on the ability of the transitional justice mechanisms to accomplish their own goals in accordance with the principles of equality, dignity, fairness and transparency that were assumed to be at the core of their work. In addition, it explores some of the constraints intrinsic to trials and truth commissions that compounded the 'gap' between law and justice. These factors demonstrate that the transitional justice process could only incompletely capture what Douzinas (2007: 291) has referred to as 'transcendent' justice, which encompasses legal justice, but is also, necessarily, beyond the law. An exploration of these issues at least partly illuminates why East Timorese survivors are likely to feel dissatisfied with the form of 'justice' provided by the transitional justice process.

The retributive justice possibilities of the Serious Crimes Process

The Serious Crimes Process in East Timor comprised the Serious Crimes Investigations Unit (SCIU), the Defence Lawyers Unit and the Special Panels for Serious Crimes (Special Panels) attached to the Dili District Court. As previously noted, the primary purpose of this process was to prosecute those individuals deemed to be most responsible for 'serious crimes', which were identified as genocide, war crimes and crimes against humanity committed during any time period, and murder, sexual offences and torture committed between 1 January and 25 October 1999.[1] In carrying out its work, the Serious Crimes Process was expected to adhere to the 'universal' standards of 'rule of law', which, as discussed in Chapter 1, the UN Secretary General describes as being at the very heart of the UN's mission (UNSG 2004).

The prosecution and punishment of perpetrators was also implicitly expected to contribute to a range of other justice goals. As in the case of other criminal justice processes, it was assumed that the Serious Crimes Process would provide a form of public recognition to victims' experiences that would assist families to come to terms with the past. Prosecutions, and the creation of an official public record of the conflict through the production of indictments and judgments, were also expected to contribute to the long-term goal of helping to deter future abuses by fostering the community's faith in the rule of law, and thereby to contribute to reconciliation and sustainable peace. These assumptions are made explicit in the Special Panels judgment in the *Joseph Leki* case:

> The objective to prosecute and punish the perpetrators of the serious crimes committed in East Timor in 1999 is to avoid impunity and thereby to promote national reconciliation and the restoration of peace.
> (SPSC 2001)

Similarly, they are evident in two excerpts from the prosecution's opening statement in the *Lolotoe* case:

1 UNTAET Regulations 2000/11 and 2000/15.

> From this record shall future generations know not only what this generation of East Timorese have suffered . . .;
>
> . . . this case will provide a contemporary yardstick and an authoritative and impartial record to which future historians may turn for truth, and future politicians for warning.
>
> (Cited in JSMP 2004a: 26)

At first glance, the Serious Crimes Process appears to have been successful at accomplishing many of its goals. At the time of its conclusion in May 2005, it had brought ninety-five indictments against 391 individuals and had convicted eighty-four defendants (UNSG 2006: para 9). While this record seems impressive, and compares favourably with the pace of prosecutions by other tribunals, including the ICTY, closer investigation reveals another, less positive, story.[2] The most palpable constraint upon the Serious Crimes Process was the Indonesian government's refusal to co-operate with the MOU regarding the exchange of information and the transfer of witnesses. This meant that the Serious Crimes Process was, in effect, able to prosecute only low-level East Timorese militia members, while more than 300 indictees outside the territory of East Timor remained beyond the court's jurisdiction, among then, senior members of the Indonesian military (Cohen 2006: 4).

Indonesian non-co-operation also severely curtailed the version of events that emerged from the trials of the Special Panels. Without evidence or statements from members of the Indonesian military with command responsibility, trials could not explore the relationship between the East Timorese militia and the Indonesian military in detail, including the command structure and funding. This often resulted in a distorted picture of events that was unable to shed light on the military-orchestrated nature of the 1999 violence (JSMP 2004a: 33).

These distortions are reflected in the *Lolotoe* case. This was the second of ten priority cases prosecuted by the SCIU, and the first time that rape was tried as a crime against humanity in East Timor (JSMP 2004a). The case resulted in the conviction of three East Timorese militia members for crimes against humanity, but the Indonesian officer who was originally indicted – the sub-district commander of the armed forces in Lolotoe – could not be prosecuted as he was by then in Indonesia. His absence from the trial also precluded scrutiny of the relationship between the East Timorese militia and the Indonesian military in any depth. Thus, although all defendants argued that they were coerced by Indonesian authorities into their position with the militia, the issue of TNI pressure was primarily discussed in terms of mitigation of

2 Since 1993, the ICTY has indicted 161 persons and tried 121 accused in eighty-six cases (see the website of the ICTY http://www.icty.org/).

sentence, rather than the potential TNI responsibility for the acts in question (JSMP 2004a). In a critical report, the East Timorese court-monitoring organisation, the Judicial Systems Monitoring Programme (JSMP), commented on the general 'injustice' of the *Lolotoe* case:

> If the broad social purpose of the *Lolotoe* trial was to bring those primarily responsible to justice, then it has failed. Although Jhoni Franca, Sabino Leite and José Cardoso were rightly convicted of crimes against humanity, they were low level East Timorese perpetrators and were influenced by the highly coercive environment created by the Indonesian authorities.
> (JSMP 2004a: 33)

Ultimately, then, the inability to bring to trial high-ranking members of the Indonesian military undermined the capacity of the Serious Crimes Process to accomplish its core goal of prosecuting those individuals who were 'most responsible' for serious crimes. The prosecution of a selected number of low-level East Timorese militia members has left the experiences of large numbers of victims unrecognised and, as I discuss further in Chapter 5, has been overwhelmingly perceived by the community as an unfair targeting of the 'little people', instead of those who planned and instigated the violence. These factors may well weaken, rather than bolster, the long-term goal of building community trust in the supposedly 'universal' and 'impartial' criminal justice process.

At a practical, institutional level, chronic resource deficiencies, understaffing and poor management of the Serious Crimes Process had debilitating effects on the quality of criminal justice that could be delivered. Critical areas such as translation, staffing, the public defenders office, witness protection and transport were appallingly neglected.[3] Resources for public outreach were also sorely lacking, which had critical consequences for public perceptions of the Serious Crimes Process and the extent to which victims' experiences could be meaningfully recognised. Thus, although the trials of the Special Panels were open to the public, the courts lacked an external relations capacity, which meant that they were not publicised. According to a 2002 report by JSMP on the Los Palos trial – the first case in which crimes against humanity were prosecuted – no court dates for the trial were publicly listed or otherwise publicised by the court, and there were rarely more than a few East Timorese present in the public gallery (JSMP 2002: 24–5). The only way in which this court-monitoring organisation could ensure it attended the proceedings was to enquire directly of judges and prosecutors. As recently as 2005, four years after the first trials of the Special Panels, JSMP was still calling for a daily hearing schedule to be posted outside the court, to allow the 'public to know

3 For detailed treatment of these issues, see Katzenstein (2003); Cohen (2002); Cohen (2006); Stanley (2009); Burchill (2009); Hirst and Varney (2005); Harper (2005).

that Timor Leste's courts are actually operating publicly and transparently' (JSMP 2005: 17).

Although the SCIU gave more attention than the courts to providing information to the public, its public outreach programme consisted of one staff member who, despite his considerable efforts at disseminating information to the districts, was unable to do this job adequately. Given their workload, investigators also found it impossible to return individually to all those who had given a statement and explain the status of their case. Compounding these problems were the innumerable logistical challenges encountered by SCIU staff attempting to distribute information to the community, including the difficulty of navigating East Timor's terrain to reach those who lived in remote and inaccessible areas – particularly during the rainy season – and the lack of radio and television coverage. Of those cases that were brought to trial, due to issues of geographic isolation, and lack of finances and transportation, victims were often unable to travel to Dili for the trial proceedings. The fact that many victims did not know that the trials were occurring, were unable to participate in them and were not informed of the outcomes had serious consequences for the provision of public recognition to victims, and for building public awareness and confidence in the trials. Local perspectives on these issues are given more detailed consideration in Chapter 5.

Retributive justice possibilities were further restricted by the selective nature of the SCIU's investigations and prosecutorial strategy. Although it could theoretically investigate all serious crimes cases from 1975 until 1999, the SCIU decided to focus its attention on the period of January–October 1999 and, in addition, selected ten 'priority cases' on the basis of number and type of victims, the perceived seriousness and the political significance of the crimes, and the availability of evidence (Hirst and Varney 2005: 7).[4] While the preoccupation with the 1999 period reflected the resource constraints of the SCIU, it was also consistent with the international community's 'blind spot' in relation to the violence of the pre-1999 period. The exclusive focus on the 1999 period had a number of consequences, one of which was that the vast majority of victims' experiences from the pre-1999 period went unrecognised. According to a former SCIU staff member, a related issue was that it did not acknowledge that many East Timorese people believed the violence that had

4 The ten priority cases were: the Liquica Church massacre (6 April 1999); the murders at the house of Manuel Carrascalão (17 April 1999); the Maliana police station (2–8 September 1999); the Lautem case (21 April–25 September 1999); the Lolotoe case (2 May–16 September 1999); the Suai Church massacre (6 September 1999); the attack on Bishop Belo's compound (6 September 1999); the Passabe and Makeleb massacres (September–October 1999); a second case in Lautem (April–September 1999); and other sexual violence cases carried out in various districts (March–September 1999) (Hirst and Varney 2005: 7).

occurred during the twenty-four-year occupation to have been far worse than the violence of 1999.[5]

The overwhelming emphasis on 1999 also meant that little attention was given, during the trials, to the plethora of different roles that individuals played within the coercive context of the Indonesian occupation and the underlying factors that led some to join the militia in 1999. For example, trials were unable to shed light on the way in which individuals were coerced into collaborating with the Indonesian regime. Yet such experiences were common during the twenty-four-year occupation, when the heavily militarised Indonesian state co-opted individuals into its security and administrative apparatus at all levels and developed an intricate system of spies and informers that undermined social bonds (see Robinson 2010; Larke 2009: 654; CAVR 2005a: Part 4). The nature of this system is compellingly documented by Geoffrey Robinson in his recent historical account of the rise of East Timorese militia groups in 1999 (Robinson 2010). Robinson shows how the mobilisation of local people into militia and paramilitary groups was central to Indonesia's counterinsurgency strategy, observing that, from the early years of the occupation, civilians from each village and town were recruited into militia organisations that were designed to assist the armed forces in detecting and combating the 'enemy' (Robinson 2010: 54–6). Most local conscripts and volunteers were grouped into one of two official bodies: *Ratih* (*Rakyat Terlatih*/Trained Populace) and *Hansip* (*Pertahanan Sipil*/Civil Defence). Organised along military lines, they were divided into companies, platoons and teams, and were stationed at military command posts in order to be ready for deployment at short notice (Robinson 2010: 56). Hundreds of individuals, among them boys as young as 12, were also recruited into less formalised units, known as TBO (*Tenaga Bantuan Operasi*/Operational Auxilliaries) and were used as guides in combat missions (Robinson 2010: 56–7). Another military strategy that commenced from the mid-1980s involved the formation of a small number of highly trained paramilitary units, often comprising former FALINTIL guerrillas, which performed important reconnaissance, intelligence and combat roles (Robinson 2010: 73).

Robinson (2010) shows that the mobilisation of militia groups by government and military authorities began with a new vigour in 1998 and that, by early 1999, more than two dozen groups were active. While some of these groups were new, others had existed for many years. Reflecting their close ties to the military, many militia groups adopted military rhetoric and modes of organisation, and were organised into companies or platoons. Further evidence of close military links could be observed in the joint operations and training conducted between TNI officers and the militia, and the fact that militia members were often seen carrying firearms usually available only to the armed

5 Interview with former SCIU staff member, Dili, 24 July 2007.

forces, and wearing new, or nearly new, TNI uniforms (Robinson 2010: 100, 119). Individuals appear to have joined militia groups in 1999 for many different reasons. While some joined more or less willingly, others were recruited directly from criminal gangs involved in gambling rings and protection rackets. Still others were poor, uneducated and unemployed, and were dependent on the patronage of TNI officers. A considerable number too joined the militias under duress, due to the fact that, in each district, a target was established for the number of militia men to be recruited. Those who refused could be subjected to threats and were typically accused of harbouring pro-independence sentiments. Many had their homes burned and their families threatened, and some were killed (Robinson 2010: 101–2).

It was simply not possible to delve into these historical and political complexities during the trials conducted by the Special Panels. The simplifications that resulted from a focus on the violence of 1999, in isolation from the broader historical and political context, are reflected in the Panel judgments. For example, the judgment on Joáo Franca da Silva (alias Jhoni Franca), in the *Lolotoe* case, provides the following statement of facts regarding the actions of the militia: 'In 1999, militia groups operated throughout East Timor. Their goal was to support autonomy with[in] Indonesia' (SPSC 2002: para 97). Similarly, the judgment of the murder trial of Joseph Leki, a 33-year-old farmer from Lalawa Village in Covalima district, begins with the following description of the 'facts of the case':

> In June 1999, the accused joined a Laksaur militia group in his home village. This militia was very active in the Covalima District committing a great number of criminal acts and causing many people to leave their villages and hide in the mountains.
>
> (SPSC 2001: Section D)

At times, defendants sought to contest these boundaries by attempting broader 'explanations' of the reasons for their acts. For example, during the *Lolotoe* trial, one of the accused – 27-year-old Jhoni Franca – attempted a lengthy explanation of the circumstances that brought him to join the militia in 1999 and contended that, under the coercion of the Indonesian military, he had been a mere 'commander of dolls' (in other words, he, and those under his command, had no power):

> I was forced to join the autonomy [to become a member of the pro-autonomy militia] to choose the best way to postpone my death. At that time I didn't join to hurt my nation, my people, which I have lived with for the last 25 years but because of the regime that was in power. At that time I started as a youth of clandestine . . . at that time in 1999 arose the militia in Maliana . . . the militia and the TNI started to carry out operations searching for pro-independence youths. . . . I was a youth and head

> of organising of all the activities of the Clandestine. . . . I was approached by Indonesian intelligence commander Sutrisno. He said to me it is better that you surrender than die. To postpone my death I went . . . I joined, at the same time he knew my background as pro-independence youth . . . I was a commander of dolls and told by the powerful regime if I didn't do these things I would be the first to die.
>
> (SPSC 2002: para 142)

Although in this case the coercive nature of the situation was taken into account by the court's attention to 'mitigating circumstances', the hearings themselves provided only limited possibilities for exploring the historical and political context in which young men like Jhoni Franca came to join the militia. In this sense, then, the trials of the Special Panels provided a very circumscribed record of the facts, which is unlikely to resonate with pre-existing East Timorese understandings of the conflict or to build community trust in the legal process.

The narrow investigations and prosecutorial strategy was further restricted due to the fact that although the Special Panels exercised jurisdiction over the crimes of genocide, war crimes and crimes against humanity, murder, sexual offences and torture,[6] most of the SCIU's initial indictments involved simple murder charges. The effect of this decision was to further divert attention away from the systemic nature of the violence during 1999, including the level of planning and premeditation that underpinned the actions of the Indonesian military (Reiger and Weirda 2006: 18–19). Although, by mid-2001, a more coherent prosecutions strategy was developed, which paid greater attention to compiling evidence for the prosecution of crimes against humanity, the focus remained largely confined to crimes of murder committed on a widespread and systematic basis. This omitted many other serious crimes, such as rape, sexual slavery, torture and forcible transfers across the border to West Timor, unless they were associated with murders (Hirst and Varney 2005: 7; Harris-Rimmer 2010: 84). An important consequence of this was that women's experiences of the conflict often went unrecognised.

What can be observed, then, is that many of the constraints of the Serious Crimes Process reflected the unique circumstances of its establishment: the inability to prosecute senior members of the Indonesian military, the chronic lack of resources, the narrow investigations and prosecutorial strategy, and poor community outreach were a direct consequence of the lack of political and practical support from the UN Security Council in the context of a perceived need to maintain relations with Indonesia. Retributive justice possibilities were further restricted by the challenges of delivering information to the community in the face of inaccessible terrain and poor infrastructure, and the difficulties of gathering evidence.

6 Sections 10.1 and 10.2, UNTAET Regulation 2000/11, 6 March 2000.

Beyond these Timor-specific constrictions, the work of the Serious Crimes Process was also hindered by other factors that are common to criminal trials in the context of transitional justice, namely, the difficulties involved in achieving diverse justice goals. Thus, as previously discussed, the Serious Crimes Process was expected to meet a range of objectives, including the prosecution and punishment of perpetrators and the recognition of victims' experiences, as well as long-term 'nation-building' outcomes such as the deterrence of future criminality and national reconciliation. A further complication was that prosecutions were also expected to benefit the *international* community, for example, by contributing to jurisprudence on crimes against humanity, war crimes and genocide, and restoring the 'universal' values of rule of law that were perceived to have been undermined during the 1999 referendum. Rather than being mutually reinforcing, these goals constituted disparate, and at times conflicting. The end result was that the needs of victims were often overshadowed by other goals that reflected the 'international community' and their 'nation-building' priorities.

Tensions between diverse goals were evident in the SCIU's selection of ten priority cases for investigation. As noted in the Introduction, in the wake of the UN-sponsored referendum, UN officials emphasised that the institution had a 'special responsibility' to undertake prosecutions of violations committed during 1999 which had been committed in direct contravention of a UN Security Council Resolution. Yet, this focus also reflected the fact that it was only in 1999 that the international community's gaze turned to East Timor, after years of complicity in the Indonesian occupation. In addition, these temporal boundaries implicitly served the interests of powerful Western states, in that they diverted attention from the role of the international community in sustaining and benefiting from the twenty-four-year Indonesian occupation (Nevins 2002b: 529–31), thereby contributing to the construction of the UN's image as a benevolent and heroic saviour following the 1999 referendum.

Friction between disparate goals was apparent, too, in the tendency of the Serious Crimes Process to prioritise 'results' over 'process'. Successful prosecutions were prioritised over fostering public awareness of the trials and providing a meaningful form of recognition to victims. This emphasis was a product, in part, of the 'nation-building' orientation of the Serious Crimes Process, which, like other criminal justice processes, equated the achievement of successful prosecutions with goals such as deterrence and strengthening faith in the rule of law. Projecting an image of 'results' also implicitly served the interests of the UN Security Council by helping to construct the Serious Crimes Process as a 'success story', thereby diverting attention away from calls for an international criminal tribunal.

The potential for the interests of victims to be overshadowed by other imperatives was magnified due to the location of the Serious Crimes Process within the broader UN state-building mission; this meant that it was often required to conform to demands and timelines that were beyond its control.

Thus, as noted in the previous chapter, the decision to conclude the Serious Crimes Process was made because the Security Council wanted to end its state-building mission, not because the Special Panels had dealt with all of the available cases (Cohen 2006: 4). This decision meant that no further cases ready to go to trial were progressed after mid-2004, and no new potential indictees were pursued, even in situations in which investigations had been completed and indictments drawn up (Cohen 2006: 4). By the time of its closure, the fifty-five trials completed represented only a small number of the 650 or so indictees who had been investigated by the SCIU (Cohen 2006: 4). The closure of the Serious Crimes Process left many of those who had provided statements confused, and further exacerbated community frustrations with the lack of 'justice.'

In sum, this analysis of reports, trial judgments and interview data shows that a combination of factors, some of which were specific to the East Timor context and others of which are common to all criminal trials, contributed to a Serious Crimes Process that was unable to accomplish many of its retributive justice goals in accordance with the principles of equality, dignity, fairness and transparency that are assumed to lie at the heart of the 'rule of law'. The inability to prosecute Indonesian suspects, the prioritisation of cases from the 1999 period, the lack of resources, the focus on 'results' over 'process' and then the premature closure of that process meant that only low-level East Timorese perpetrators were prosecuted. It also meant that recognition of victims' experiences was restricted and that public awareness of the trials remained low. The difficulties encountered by the Serious Crimes Process in attempting to meet its diverse retributive justice goals illustrates how victims' interests and desires for recognition were often overshadowed by other organisational priorities. Further disrupting the attempts of the Serious Crimes Process to deliver 'justice' was the fact that the very notion of 'justice' as it is understood by criminal justice processes is inherently limited. As I now discuss, the Serious Crimes Process embodied many of the difficulties faced in bridging the gap between the possibilities of criminal law and the demands of justice that are *beyond* the law.

Justice beyond the criminal law

Like other criminal justice processes, the Serious Crimes Process was expected to carry out its work in accordance with the 'due process' requirements of the criminal law. It operated under the assumption that 'justice' was a form of 'settling accounts', which involved prosecuting a one-off crime committed by an individual perpetrator. These factors suggest that even if the Serious Crimes Process had overcome many of the practical and political constraints on its work, it would still have fallen short of providing the form of justice desired by the East Timorese community.

The gap between criminal justice and local expectations of justice was apparent in the circumscribed form of recognition that was provided to victims who took part in trials of the Special Panels. As in other criminal trials, victims had an inherently limited role as witnesses; as one source of evidence amongst many others, their testimony was used to establish the 'facts of the case', and they rarely had the chance to make lengthy contributions to the trial process. That is, there was an inescapable tension between the requirements of the Serious Crimes Process to recognise victims as subjects of the law and the desires of victims to be recognised as individuals, with their own unique life histories and experiences (see also Allen 1999: 10). These tensions, to which I return in Chapter 5, suggest that even if the trials had been more responsive to the needs of individual victims, their approach to victims' testimony would have remained, fundamentally, instrumental.[7]

The strict evidentiary rules of the Serious Crimes Process, which required prosecutors to establish a high level of 'proof' of the elements of each crime and adhere to due process guarantees, further highlight the constricted nature of criminal justice possibilities. Thus, as a former staff member of the SCIU observed, it was difficult to explain to the East Timorese community – many of whom had high expectations that providing a statement would lead to the immediate arrest of a suspect – the slow pace of investigations and prosecutions, and the fact that suspects could be released on a 'technicality'.[8] Another reflection of the narrow conception of justice embodied in the criminal law was the fact that even if the Serious Crimes Process had had more resources available for conducting exhumations, as Blau (2007: 144) notes, its interest was primarily in finding evidence and establishing the cause and manner of death, rather than in identifying bodies, which is often the main concern of victims' families (see also Linton 2001: 212).

The focus of the Serious Crimes Process, like other criminal justice processes, on addressing 'direct' forms of violence committed by individual perpetrators – and its inability to address 'structural' violence – draws further attention to the inherent limitations of criminal justice processes. The preoccupation with questions of individual accountability prevented the Special Panels from fully attending to the broader political and economic structures that contributed to the commission of crimes, including the role played by indirect perpetrators, bystanders and institutions, and the role of international actors in precipitating conflict and abuse. Thus, by locating the origins of atrocity in the acts of the individual accused, the Serious Crimes Process was unable to consider broader questions of responsibility, including the roles of the Indonesian state (for illegally occupying East Timor) and Western states (for their ongoing support and complicity in the occupation).

In effectively reducing East Timor's unique historical, geographic and political context to a series of isolated human rights violations, the Serious

7 For a similar argument in relation to the ICTY, see Haslam (2007).

8 Interview with former SCIU staff member, Dili, July 2008.

Crimes Process was also unable to respond to the chronic, long-term nature of suffering under the Indonesian occupation, and the period of Portuguese colonisation that preceded it. This form of violence, which was manifested in the everyday experiences of poverty, malnutrition and illness, continues to constrict the lives of many East Timorese people, and thus cannot be relegated to the past or addressed by an individualised legal response. Only sustained attention to questions of redistributive justice – to redressing the unequal distribution of economic, social and political power – could hope to bring about substantive changes in the lives of the poor and vulnerable in East Timor. The Serious Crimes Process did not even offer the very limited form of redistribution that is possible through trials, in the form of compensation to individual victims within its jurisdiction. Thus, although the Regulation establishing the Special Panels provided for a 'trust fund' for the 'benefit of victims of crimes within the jurisdiction of the panels, and the families of such victims',[9] such a fund was never established (Harper 2005: 177), presumably because UNTAET did not view it as a priority. As a result, even the limited number of individuals who gained legal recognition as victims did not receive any material assistance to address the ongoing effects of violence in their everyday lives (Stanley 2009: 105).

In sum, the strict rules and narrow criminal law boundaries of the Serious Crimes Process highlight the gulf between the possibilities of criminal processes and the demands of justice. The rules of evidence and the requirements of due process meant that the Serious Crimes Process could only ever have delivered a narrow form of 'criminal justice' to the East Timorese community and provided a circumscribed form of legal recognition to a small number of victims. Moreover, by emphasising specific traumatic events and individualising the origins of the violence, the Serious Crimes Process obscured the social, political and economic structures that made the Indonesian occupation, and the period of Portuguese colonisation that preceded it, an experience of long-term, everyday suffering. The criminal law was also inherently unable to address the effects of structural violence, which continue into the present in the form of poverty and social exclusion. Ultimately, then, the short-term, retributive justice focus of the Serious Crimes Process could only partially respond to the demands of what Douzinas terms 'transcendent justice', which is both within and beyond the law, and perhaps is always an ongoing process.

In the next section, I turn to a discussion of the CAVR, which was intended to move beyond the narrow boundaries of the criminal law and provide a form of 'restorative' justice that was more responsive to the specific needs of victims and the East Timorese community. However, despite the breadth of its mandate, the CAVR was also contextually and institutionally limited in its attempts to bridge the gap between law and justice.

9 UNTAET Regulation 2000/15, section 2.25.

The restorative justice possibilities of the Commission for Reception, Truth and Reconciliation (CAVR)

The CAVR was informed by 'restorative justice' principles, which emphasised the rebuilding of fractured community relations. It was given an expansive mandate, broader than that of many other truth commissions. This mandate included three main functions. The first was to resolve a large number of 'less serious' crimes committed by East Timorese militia members in 1999, including cases of looting, theft, arson and minor assault, through the establishment of an innovative Community Reconciliation Process (CRP), that made use of pre-existing local dispute resolution practices (Figure 3.1).

The establishment of the CRP resonates with what Lars Waldorf (2006) describes as a broader trend towards the embrace of local justice systems in order to apply restorative justice theory in post-conflict contexts. Proponents of local justice systems claim that these mechanisms have greater legitimacy than formal justice systems, which may be devastated after periods of protracted conflict, and also promise 'local ownership, access and efficiency' (Waldorf 2006: 3–4). Aside from East Timor, local justice practices have been utilised in the work of truth and reconciliation commissions in Mozambique

Figure 3.1 A CAVR community reconciliation hearing in progress (CAVR Archives)

and Sierra Leone, while in Rwanda, they have been transformed into a system for resolving serious crimes cases (Waldorf 2006: 3–4).[10] In contrast to the Rwanda case, East Timor's CRP was only mandated to deal with 'less serious crimes', which were defined as 'theft, minor assault, arson (other than that resulting in death or injury), the killing of livestock or destruction of crops'.[11]

The CAVR's second function, more traditionally associated with truth commissions, was to seek and establish the truth about the conflict by documenting 'human rights violations committed by all parties to the political conflict between April 1974 and October 1999' (CAVR 2005a: Exec Summary, 20). Following the conclusion of its research and the CRP, the CAVR was expected to fulfil a third function of preparing a final report on the extent, causes and responsibility for human rights violations, and making recommendations for reforms aimed at preventing the recurrence of violence and responding to the needs of victims (CAVR 2005a: Exec Summary, 18–19).

In fulfilling these functions, the CAVR was expected to accomplish multiple goals. One was to restore victims' dignity and contribute to their healing. Thus the CAVR articulated that it would:

> place victims of human rights violations at the centre of its work and it would create an institution that would be open and responsive to them. As such it would recognise and value their experience. It would also seek practical ways to assist them and would promote their role in nation-building.
>
> (CAVR 2005a: Introduction, 18)

Accordingly, both the truth-seeking process and the CRP aimed to provide opportunities for victims to tell their stories, and to have their dignity affirmed through public recognition of their suffering. In addition, the CAVR established a separate *Acolhimento* (Reception) and Victim Support Unit (VSU), which was responsible for organising a number of national public victims hearings, and co-ordinating a community profile programme, healing workshops and an urgent reparations scheme.

A second goal of the CAVR was to contribute to community reconciliation. By supporting the integration of individuals who had caused harm to their communities in 1999, the CRP aimed to reduce the potential for 'rough justice' within local communities against former militia members and to encourage the reintegration of refugees returning from West Timor, thereby fostering community stability.

10 It is known as *gacaca*, which means 'lawn of small grass', and refers to the place where dispute resolution traditionally took place (Waldorf 2006: 48).

11 UNTAET Regulation No 2001/10, 13 July 2001.

A third goal of the CAVR was to foster national reconciliation. The CAVR – like other truth commissions – was underpinned by what Colvin (2003) terms a 'therapeutic ethic' that stressed the healing power of truth for both individual and nation. The assumed link between individual and national healing meant that victims became emblematic of the healing of the nation; their stories served a wider purpose as sites for the 'transformation of private, individual memory into shared public knowledge' (Humphrey 2003: 172). This link between individual and national healing permeated much of the CAVR's institutional rhetoric. For example, the CAVR described its public hearings as:

> a shared national experience of listening to the voices of victims and confronting the truth and impact of past human rights violations [which] placed ordinary people at the centre of the national debate on healing, reconciliation and justice.
>
> (CAVR 2005a: Exec Summary, 33)

It was also evident in the opening speech of Chairperson of the CAVR Aniceto Guterres to the national public hearing on 'Women and the Conflict', which encouraged women to speak of their experiences and stressed that their stories would be therapeutic to the nation as a whole:

> in telling your stories, sharing them with all the people in our nation, you are helping to create a new culture of peace in our new land so that this violence will never be repeated.
>
> (CAVR 2005b: 9)

Nonetheless, those involved in the establishment and operation of the CAVR did not view storytelling alone as therapeutic. Rather, revealing the truth was understood to be a stepping stone towards the goal of retributive justice. This was evident in UNTAET's early attempts to reassure national human rights NGOs that there would be no amnesty for serious crimes and that, by producing an official record of human rights violations, the CAVR would help to facilitate accountability (La'o Hamutuk 2001).

On the whole, the story of the CAVR's attempts to meet its goals is a much happier one than that of the Serious Crimes Process. During the period of its operation, for example, the CRP programme resolved almost 1,400 cases of minor crimes (CAVR 2005a: Exec Summary, 23). This voluntary programme incorporated elements of the East Timorese local dispute resolution practice known as *nahe biti* (literally, 'spreading the mat'), which typically involves a public meeting between conflicting parties mediated by the community's *adat* (customary) leaders (Babo-Soares 2005). Those who sought to take part in a CRP hearing were required to submit a written statement disclosing any acts they had committed, which was passed on to the Office of the General

Prosecutor, who reviewed it and, provided that the case did not involve a serious crime, it could then proceed through the CRP.

The hearings themselves involved the convening of a Panel, which included CAVR regional commissioners and local leaders (and also was obliged to include women and youth representatives), who would deliberate upon the matter in an open community meeting. During the hearing, Panel members would listen to the perpetrator (known as the 'deponent'), victims and other community members, before deciding on an 'act of reconciliation' that the deponent would be required to complete. This usually involved a form of community service, such as cleaning a school or a church, or repairing a road. On completion of the 'act', deponents received a court-approved notification that they were immune from civil or criminal prosecution for all those acts they had declared during the CRP. Hearings also included a role for traditional elders, and agreements were sealed with binding oaths, and often involved the chewing of betel nut, the sacrificing of a chicken or pig, a symbolic rolling up of the *biti* (mat), and a celebratory feast. As I observed during fieldwork in 2004, hearings often continued late into the night, as community members debated and contested deponents' versions of events, and put forward alternative versions. In this sense, compared to the narrow criminal justice possibilities of the Serious Crimes Process, the CAVR provided opportunities for a much wider range of community members to tell their stories publicly, to participate in resolving community level problems and to have their experiences officially validated.

The CAVR was also successful in documenting victims' experiences of the conflict. Through its widespread statement-taking process, it collected 7,669 statements across all thirteen districts and sixty-five sub-districts of East Timor (CAVR 2005a: Exec Summary, 20). Attempts were also made to collect statements from East Timorese refugees living in West Timor, in order to include perspectives that favoured East Timor's integration with Indonesia. However, according to information from a former CAVR staff member, these efforts were somewhat tokenistic, as only ninety-one statements were collected from the regions of Belu, Soe and Kupang.[12] The CAVR's research unit also conducted over 1,000 interviews with individuals who had held leadership positions at various stages of the conflict (CAVR 2005a: Exec Summary, 20). These testimonies were compiled in the CAVR's final report, *Chega!*

The CAVR's VSU also successfully organised a number of innovative programmes, many of which were aimed at providing recognition to victims' experiences. One prominent programme involved the organisation of national public hearings on issues such as political imprisonment, women and conflict, forced displacement and famine, massacres, the internal political conflict of

12 Interview with former CAVR staff member, Dili, July 2009.

1974–76, self-determination and the international community, and children and the conflict, during which selected community members had the opportunity to give public testimonies (CAVR 2005a: Exec Summary, 32–3).[13] A series of small public hearing books have been published on each of the hearing topics. Another programme – known as the 'community profile programme' – brought communities together for workshops to examine, communally, the history of the conflict from a local perspective, and to map the human rights abuses that had occurred within their village (CAVR 2005a: Exec Summary, 37–8). The VSU also organised a number of 'healing workshops' in Dili and co-ordinated a small urgent reparations fund, which provided one-off payments of US$200 to victims who were deemed to be the 'most vulnerable'.

The CAVR's work was facilitated by an extensive outreach programme that encouraged widespread community participation. CAVR district teams were based in each sub-district for about three months, during which time they provided information about the CAVR's various programmes, took individuals' statements, facilitated community reconciliation hearings and conducted community profile workshops (CAVR 2005a: Exec Summary: 33). Unlike the Serious Crimes Process, the CAVR was strategic in its use of local media to promote its work across the nation, producing its own weekly radio programme *Dalan Ba Dame* ('The Road to Peace'), and broadcasting its national public hearings live on radio and television. These factors, combined with an extensive mandate, a committed and enthusiastic staff, and generous donor funding, enabled the CAVR to become one of East Timor's largest and best-known institutions, in contrast to the dearth of public awareness of the Serious Crimes Process.

Nonetheless, despite its considerable strengths, the work of the CAVR was hindered by a number of factors, many of which were specific to the context of East Timor. One key constraint was the fact that, like that of the Serious Crimes Process, the CAVR was confined to East Timorese participants. This meant that the CRP programme was only able to focus on reconciliation between East Timorese deponents and their communities, and while the truth-seeking process sought to identify and reveal abuses committed by Indonesian actors, it could not compel Indonesian participation (Roosa 2007a: 565). The focus on human rights abuses committed by an occupying power that had already departed from the country was, as Roosa acknowledges, rare for a truth commission, in that these mechanisms are commonly established in the context of a political compromise between forces in a single country (Roosa 2007a: 564–5). According to Roosa, the absence of Indonesian actors had both advantages and disadvantages. On the one hand, 'it allowed the

13 Approximately 124 people spoke at these hearings. A number of public hearings were also organised at the sub-district level at which sixty-five women and 149 men told their stories publicly (CAVR 2005a: Exec Summary, 33).

commission to work with complete freedom, unconstrained by a compromise with elements of the *ancien regime*' (Roosa 2007a: 564–5). It also enabled the writing of a national history based on a collective Timorese memory of suffering and oppression that enjoyed widespread acceptance amongst the general population. On the other hand, the fact that East Timor's former occupiers did not participate in the CAVR potentially reduced the relevance of the Commission's work (Roosa 2007a: 565) by curtailing the nature of the 'truth' that could be revealed, and limiting 'who' could be reconciled. The 'Timor-centric' nature of the CAVR also makes it unlikely that its truth will be widely accepted within Indonesia.

Temporal boundaries placed further obstacles in the way of the CAVR's goals of producing an historical record, fostering community and national reconciliation, and recognising victims' experiences. Thus, although its truth-seeking component explored the period 1974–99, which included the internal political conflict between FRETILIN and UDT in 1974–75, it was unable to consider the continuities between the Portuguese and Indonesian periods of colonisation in any depth. The temporal focus of the CRP – which was confined to the 1999 period – was even narrower, and reflected the fact that a key goal of this process was to foster local-level stability following the violence of the referendum. The 1999 focus precluded an exploration of a much longer history of local conflict and divisions that pre-dated the 1999 conflict, and even the Indonesian occupation. For example, it was unable to address the way in which 1999 conflicts were often a continuation of long-standing cycles of victimisation and revenge, some of which revolved around complex issues of land ownership and distribution (see, for example, Gunter 2007). These pre-existing tensions were exacerbated by the Indonesian occupation, which fostered the increasing militarisation of East Timorese society and created sharp rifts based on the perception that some individuals were benefiting from their alignment with the regime. As I discuss in Chapter 4, many of these rifts continue into present-day East Timor.

As Kammen's work shows, some militia members who participated in the CRP hearings expressed frustrations about these temporal restrictions, suggesting, for example, that it was not possible to discuss their involvement as militia members in relation to 1999 alone, and that their stories needed to begin with 1975 (Kammen 2003: 82). Similarly, as my previous fieldwork shows, some deponents have contended that the CRP did not consider the multifaceted factors that had led to their joining the militia, and their own experiences of victimisation. As one former member of the Mahidi militia group explained:

> The Mahidi [militia group] leaders are still in West Timor and haven't come back. We feel not good that the big people are still free. They are like the root of the tree, we were then branches only . . . When we came back from West Timor we felt that people were suspicious of us, even

> though we were not involved in any crimes . . . We were scared if we didn't join we would have been suspected of supporting the clandestine and killed . . . When we came back [from West Timor] our houses had been destroyed and our things taken. The people had taken the walls of our house off. We had to put it back again. Our buffalo had been stolen, as had our pigs . . . We were also victims of the Mahidi leaders, they beat us, many times, and abused us.
>
> (Kent 2004: 16)

Complicating this issue further was the difficulty of confining CRP discussions to 'less serious' crimes. In theory, CRP hearings were mandated to discuss only matters such as the burning and looting of houses, theft, and cases of minor assault, and if serious crimes allegations were made, the Panel was expected to stop the discussion and refer the matter to the Office of the General Prosecutor. In practice, maintaining this separation proved difficult given that less serious crimes were often committed in the context of more serious crimes, and communities were often interested in discussing the 'whole picture'. Allegations of serious crimes were sometimes made during the CRP hearings in the 'heat of the moment', which could not be taken further by the CAVR, but were passed on to an overburdened and under-resourced Serious Crimes Process, which was unlikely to pursue them.

In addition to its restriction to East Timorese participants, its temporal boundaries, and the difficulty of separating 'less serious' from 'serious crimes', the CAVR was also constrained by the other factors that are common to trials and truth commissions in transitional contexts. For example, like the Serious Crimes Process, the CAVR was expected to accomplish a range of ambitious goals, which entailed mediating a number of diverse interests. These goals, as previously discussed, included restoring victims' dignity by enabling them to tell their stories publicly, contributing to national reconciliation through the production of an historical record of the conflict and fostering local stability through the integration of deponents back into their communities through the CRP. A further complicating factor was that the CAVR was also expected to contribute 'lessons' to the international community based on East Timor's experience. This goal is alluded to in the preface to *Chega!,* where the CAVR Chairperson states:

> The CAVR was required to focus on the past for the sake of the future – both the future of Timor-Leste and the future of the international system which, the Report demonstrates, also has much to learn from the experience of Timor-Leste.
>
> (CAVR 2005a: Preface, 2)

As was the case with the Serious Crimes Process, the difficulties involved in meeting these different goals, and mediating the disparate interests that underpinned them, meant that victim's interests were sometimes overshadowed by other more powerful interests.

In the day-to-day operation of the CAVR, friction between diverse imperatives was manifested in a range of ways. For example, tensions between the goals of recognising victims' experiences and 'nation-building' goals were evident in the way in which the CAVR, like other truth commissions, tended to conflate individual healing with national reconciliation. This meant, for example, that individuals were chosen to participate in the public hearings on the basis of their ability to represent certain 'emblematic' experiences related to the thematic focus of the particular hearing. Victims were encouraged to speak for the good of the 'nation' and their stories were ascribed a national significance. This opened up both possibilities and limitations. On the one hand, it enabled many individuals to have their experiences officially validated. On the other hand, it shaped and constrained the way in which their experiences of harm could be articulated and recognised. For example, as I discuss later in Chapter 5, the CAVR's attempts to 'capture' and document individuals' experiences of harm for the 'nation' were sometimes perceived by survivors as a form of appropriation that did not do 'justice' to their singular experiences.

Tensions between disparate goals were also evident in the CAVR's prioritisation of 'outcomes' over 'process'. As in the case of the Serious Crimes Process, the CAVR's drive towards successful outcomes may have reflected, at least partially, the imperative of portraying an appearance of success to its donors. It also highlights the priority accorded to the CAVR's community stability and nation-building goals over the interests of individual victims. Within the CRP, the preoccupation with results, in the form of successfully concluded hearings, often led to an emphasis on narratives of reconciliation and closure over retribution, unfinished business and *unreconciled* outcomes. The emphasis on the 'collective good' rather than the individual victim was evident in the fact that, although victims could personally decide *not* to accept a deponent, the consent of victims was not required for the successful completion of a CRP hearing. The drive to reintegrate deponents, pursuant to the CAVR's goal of fostering community stability, also meant that the 'acts of reconciliation' that deponents were expected to perform tended to be extremely lenient, and often involved an apology or some form of community service, rather than direct reparation to a victim. The potential for victims' interests to be overshadowed was further exacerbated by pre-existing local power relations within local villages. Thus, as Stanley's work and my own previous fieldwork has shown, some groups – such as women, and those who held little political sway – could be persuaded by local community leaders, family members and the often fiery reconciliatory rhetoric of the CAVR Panel members to 'reconcile' with a deponent rather than request the Panel to impose a heavy sanction (Stanley 2008: 185; Kent 2004).

The drive towards closure within the CRP hearings was also reflected in the level of support provided to victims. Compared to deponents, victims who participated in the CRP hearings were given far less preparation, to the extent that some had little idea of the purpose of the hearing before they took part (Kent 2004). In addition, very little attention was accorded to the issue of victim and witness protection, despite the fact that individuals lived in close proximity to one another. Similar issues emerged in relation to the CAVR's national public hearings. Thus, although victims who spoke publicly about their experiences in these forums were generally accompanied by staff of the CAVR's VSU, and some attempts were made to contact individuals after the hearings to assess their psychological well-being and to provide ongoing support, usually via NGOs and church groups contracted by the CAVR, there were limited resources available for this work.

Underpinning the drive towards successful 'outcomes' was the fact that the CAVR, like all truth commissions, was envisaged as a short-term 'project' with specific designated 'deliverables'. Although, unlike the Serious Crimes Process, the CAVR's work was not constrained by the UN's state-building timetable, it was nonetheless driven by the need to complete its final report and hand it over to the government within a defined period of time. One result of this can be seen in the limited community outreach that has been conducted about the results of the CAVR's programme. Thus, in comparison to the well-resourced CAVR, the post-CAVR Secretariat established to disseminate the final report and conduct community education has very few staff and resources at its disposal, and, at the time of my fieldwork, many individuals who had provided statements had yet to see a copy of *Chega!* Problems specific to East Timor, including high levels of illiteracy, pose additional questions about how best to distribute *Chega!* in a meaningful form. In relation to the CRP programme, very little monitoring has been undertaken, if any, about the extent to which deponents have reoffended, or whether there have been any post-hearing reprisals in local communities following the revelation of sensitive 'truths'. These issues also make the larger point – to which I return in the next section – that there is an inescapable tension between the finality of legal and quasi-legal processes, which attempt to bring about a form of resolution within a defined period of time, and 'justice', which is an ongoing process.

In sum, the CAVR's expansive mandate enabled it to provide a more participatory and accessible form of 'justice' than the Serious Crimes Process. At the same time, a combination of factors, some of which were specific to the East Timor context and some of which were common to truth commissions generally, highlighted the gap between the demands of 'justice' and the possibilities of the CAVR. Temporal boundaries, the exclusion of Indonesian actors, the difficulties in balancing conflicting goals, and the design of CAVR as a short-term 'project' restricted the kinds of experiences of injury that could be recognised.

The next section turns to a discussion of structural violence, a critical 'justice' issue to which I show the CAVR was only partially able to respond.

An exploration of structural violence sheds further light on the possibilities and limitations of truth commissions to respond fully to the demands of 'justice.'

Justice beyond the Truth Commission

In comparison to the criminal law boundaries of the Serious Crimes Process, the CAVR's mandate allowed it to inquire into, and to some extent respond to, structural violence. In addition to documenting individual human rights violations, the CAVR was authorised to explore 'systematic patterns of abuse', including the nature, causes, circumstances, factors and context that led to such violations, and the levels of institutional and individual responsibility for them (CAVR 2005a: Part 2, 7). Moreover, it could consider acts committed by both state and non-state actors (CAVR 2005a: Part 2, 4),[14] and, beyond traditional civil and political rights considerations, it could inquire into violations of the right to self determination, the range of rights relevant to displacement, resettlement and famine, rights violated by acts of rape and other forms of sexual assault/harassment, children's rights, social and economic rights, and reproductive rights.

This broad mandate gave the CAVR scope to explore the extent to which human rights violations were an outgrowth of the systematic violence of the Indonesian regime. It also gave it the capacity to delve into inequalities and discrimination entrenched within East Timorese society and to examine the role of international actors – such as foreign governments – in encouraging the Indonesian invasion and supporting the occupation. The scope of the CAVR's work distinguished it from the work of many other truth commissions. For example, although the South African TRC conducted a number of institutional hearings to explore some of the structural elements of the apartheid regime, it has been criticised for primarily concentrating on the relations between perpetrators and victims, and deflecting attention away from the racially discriminatory nature of the apartheid regime, in which a few benefited at the expense of the majority (see, for example, Mamdani 2001b).

Armed with this expansive mandate, the CAVR's research efforts were able to demonstrate that human rights abuses committed during the twenty-four-year occupation had their roots in institutionalised practices of the Indonesian state that were part of an 'overall strategic purpose' of crushing the resistance movement (CAVR 2005a: Part 7.2, 7). Unlike the Serious Crimes

14 This included members of the Indonesian government (such as members of its security forces, civil defence forces and militia groups), the Portuguese government and its agent, members of East Timorese political parties and the armed resistance movement, members of other states, institutions, groups and individuals who played a role in the political conflict (CAVR 2005a: Part 2, 4).

Process, it was able to show that the formation of the militias in mid-to-late 1998 was the culmination of a much earlier Indonesian military strategy, which involved the extension of its territorial structure down to the village level (CAVR 2005a: Part 4). It demonstrated, too, that, from early in the Indonesian occupation, East Timorese were recruited into ABRI combat battalions, organised into paramilitary groups and civil defence forces, and employed as spies and informants, and showed how these practices led to the extensive militarisation of East Timorese society (CAVR 2005a: Part 4).

The CAVR also attempted to document economic and social rights, although these efforts were somewhat obstructed by the difficulty of accessing statistics from the Indonesian and Portuguese eras.[15] The CAVR established that the Indonesian government's explicit use of education as a propaganda tool, rather than to meet basic learning needs, restricted children's development and future opportunities (CAVR 2005a: Part 7.9, 3). The Indonesian regime's 'resettlement' policies were also scrutinised. The CAVR highlighted, for instance, that these policies led to the permanent relocation of entire villages in areas with poor soils and malarial conditions, which endangered people's health (CAVR 2005a: Part 7.9, 3). These issues were exacerbated by military's deliberate destruction of crops, fruit trees, livestock and food sources, which contributed to dire food shortages and famine conditions in the late 1970s (CAVR 2005a: 7.3, 36). The coffee industry was examined, too, including the way in which coffee prices were manipulated to fund military operations and to benefit military and civilian officials, which reduced farmers' ability to meet their livelihood needs (CAVR 2005a: Part 7.9, 3). In relation to issues such as road-building and government infrastructure, the CAVR found that investment in these areas reflected a bias towards the state's security needs, and occurred at the expense of investment in agriculture, in which the vast majority of East Timorese were employed (CAVR 2005a: Part 7.9, 3–4).

Another way in which the CAVR considered structural violence was by opening up discussion on the brief internal political conflict between FRETILIN and UDT during 1974–75. The CAVR was specifically directed to report on the context, background and historical factors that had led to this conflict, yet, given the highly sensitive nature of these events, this was a challenging task. The CAVR sought to break these silences by documenting East Timor political-party violence through its interview process[16] and, in addition, organised a special public hearing at which key political actors from this period spoke about their role in the internal political conflict, publicly

15 Interview with former CAVR staff member, Dili, 15 June 2009.

16 Nearly 30 per cent of killings of civilians reported to the CAVR during its truth-seeking process were attributed to resistance groups and pro-independence groups, 348 of which related to the period of the internal political conflict between FRETILIN and UDT, following the armed 'coup' by UDT on 11 August 1975 (CAVR: 2005a: Part 3, 43).

accepted responsibility for their actions on behalf of their political parties and expressed regret for the harmful acts that had been committed. The observation by a former CAVR staff member that 'all of Dili was glued to the radio that day' provides an indication of the significance of these events within East Timor's collective imagination, a point to which I return in Chapter 4.[17]

The CAVR also made particular efforts to consider the gendered dimensions of the conflict and post-conflict period, including by encouraging women survivors to participate in its public interviews and hearings. As previously mentioned, a special national public hearing on women and the conflict was organised, which explored women's diverse experiences of violence. To overcome the cultural barriers that make it difficult for women to speak, the CAVR attempted to recruit equal numbers of men and women as statement-takers and victim support staff, and implemented a special six-month research project to document the violation of women's human rights, in co-operation with an East Timorese women's NGO (CAVR 2004c).

As part of its commitment to considering the gendered nature of the conflict, the CAVR devoted special attention to documenting experiences of sexual violence. This included documenting rapes that had occurred in and around victims' homes – acts perpetrated by both Indonesian and East Timorese actors. Through these efforts, the CAVR was able to demonstrate that the conflict had pervaded both the public and private spheres (CAVR 2005a: Part 7.7, 97). The evidence also highlighted the institutional components of sexual violence by showing that rape was used as a specific instrument of the armed conflict for the purpose of humiliating and dehumanising women. For example, *Chega!* notes:

> Institutional practices and formal or informal policy of the Indonesian security forces tolerated and encouraged the rape, sexual torture and sexual humiliation of East Timorese women by members of the Indonesian armed forces and the auxiliary groups under their command and control.
> (CAVR 2005a: Part 7.7, 104)

The experiences of women who had been forced to become 'army mistresses' were also rendered visible by the CAVR. For example, one of the CAVR's public hearing books, entitled *Women and the Conflict*, reproduces the testimony of Beatriz Miranda Guterres, who was forced into three 'marriages' with Indonesian soldiers:

> In 1991 a new Kopassus soldier arrived in Lalerek Mutin. His name was B [name suppressed]. One day, as three friends and I went to the fields,

17 Interview with former CAVR staff member, Dili, July 2009.

> he began following us. He began shooting in our direction when we got there, so we ran back to our house in fear. My friends then started pressuring me into becoming B's wife in order to save myself. I was so ashamed, I stood up and said 'Alright! I will tear myself in two. The lower half I will give to him, but the upper half is for my land, the land of Timor.'
>
> (CAVR 2005b: 25)

The CAVR documented the way in which Beatriz, like many women who became 'army mistresses', was stigmatised by her community for breaking tightly held sexual mores, which did not distinguish between consensual and non-consensual sexual relations (CAVR 2005a: Part 7.7, 97; see also Harris-Rimmer 2008: 90). As Beatriz's testimony recounts: 'People would talk about me and say that I was no good because I had lived with three men' (CAVR 2005b: 26). The CAVR also drew attention to the community complicity in some cases that supported the sacrifice of one or more women to become 'army mistresses' in exchange for collective security (CAVR 2005a: Part 7.7, 99). By making women's experiences of violence visible, and recognising the ongoing shame and discrimination they were suffering, the CAVR acknowledged some uncomfortable truths about local communities – the 'ways in which they stigmatised women and were, thus, complicit in violence against them' (Campbell-Nelson 2003).

In its attempts to unravel a number of difficult and sensitive East Timorese truths, then, the CAVR was able to move well beyond the narrow criminal law boundaries of the Serious Crimes Process. It attempted to encapsulate a more complex truth about the period of the Indonesian occupation that recognised the way in which violence had permeated community structures and relationships, exacerbating pre-existing divisions and forms of discrimination.

At the same time, tackling sensitive issues such as the internal political conflict and violence against women were inescapably difficult tasks. In relation to East Timorese political-party violence, the CAVR report acknowledged its limits in addressing the deep-seated forms of discrimination and marginalisation that prevented people from speaking openly about these issues and notes the 'silence' that continues to surround them:

> Many victims or families of those killed or disappeared have expressed their desire to clear the names of their family members and friends. The lack of recognition of both the violence, the losses suffered by families and the injustice of their treatment has caused the deep suppression of feelings and the isolation of people in this category. Without public recognition that these events occurred, it is difficult for those affected to seek the support they may need.
>
> (CAVR 2005a: Exec Summary, 42)

These difficulties were further compounded by the reluctance of the East Timorese leadership to engage openly with these issues, a theme to which I return in the next chapter.

Similarly, despite the CAVR's efforts to open up discussion of the gendered dimensions of the conflict, fewer women than men took part in the public victims hearings, the CRP hearings and the statement-taking process, which suggests that the CAVR was not always able to overcome the deeply entrenched patriarchal nature of East Timorese society, where, as Stanley observes, women are 'culturally devalued' (Stanley 2009: 117). Thus, as the CAVR report itself acknowledges, some women deferred to male members of their family to recount their experiences, while, in some communities, women did not participate, because they were expected to stay at home and attend to domestic duties rather than to take part in public activities (CAVR 2005a: Introduction, 41–2). Moreover, because fewer women than men were members of formal community organisations, they often lacked public access to information (CAVR 2005a: Introduction, 41–2). Stanley suggests that another related issue was that some women did not feel that their stories were 'worthy' of telling, or faced resistance from husbands or male family members, particularly if the topic was considered to be sensitive (Stanley 2009: 117).

These issues, which limited women's participation and hence undermined the possibility of recognition of their experiences, also surfaced during my fieldwork. One widow I met in Maliana, for example, explained that she had not given her statement to the CAVR because she felt that others had suffered more than she had.[18] Another said that because she was not confident speaking Tetum or Indonesian, she was too *moe* (ashamed/shy) to participate.[19] The difficulties of speaking out were obviously magnified in relation to the issue of sexual violence, due to the stigmatisation and shame associated with these experiences in a deeply conservative and Catholic society (see Harris-Rimmer 2007). Indeed, although the CAVR recorded 853 cases relating to the issue of sexual violence, it was aware that the actual number of these cases was much higher:

> The Commission notes the inevitable conclusion that many victims of sexual violence did not come forward to report them to the Commission. Reasons for under-reporting include death of victims and witnesses (especially for earlier periods of the conflict), victims who may be outside Timor-Leste (especially in West Timor), the painful and very personal nature of the experiences, and the fear of social or family humiliation or rejection if their experiences are known publicly. These strong reasons for under-reporting and the fact that 853 cases of rape and sexual slavery,

18 Interview in Dili, 27 June 2007.
19 Interview in Lautem, 8 August 2007.

> along with evidence from about another 200 interviews were recorded lead the Commission to the finding that the total number of sexual violations is likely to be several times higher than the number of cases reported.
>
> (CAVR 2005a: Part 7.7, 109)

Ultimately, then, despite the CAVR's attempts to discuss a number of difficult and taboo subjects, its efforts in this area were limited. Although it could encourage some individuals to speak about private and sensitive issues, such as violence against women and East Timorese political-party violence, it was unable, given the short-term nature of its programme and the reticence of the political leadership, to impact on the deeply embedded societal attitudes and entrenched structural inequalities that surround these experiences.

Another way in which the CAVR attempted to shed light on the structural dimensions of violence was by documenting the role of international actors in East Timor's conflict. The CAVR undertook substantial research in this area, documenting the ways in which powerful states supported, and benefited from, the Indonesian occupation. *Chega!* shows that billions of dollars in weapons, military equipment and training, economic assistance and diplomatic support were provided to Indonesia during the occupation (CAVR 2005a: Part 7.1). It notes that most nations were prepared to appease Indonesia, which was viewed as a major power in the South-East Asian region, and that key member states of the UN did little to challenge Indonesia's annexation of Timor-Leste or the violent means used to enforce the annexation (CAVR 2005a: Part 7.1, 121). The report suggests that Japan was Indonesia's major investor and had more capacity than other Asian nations to influence policymaking in Jakarta, but it did not use this leverage. Meanwhile, as a permanent member of the Security Council and superpower, the United States had the power and influence to prevent Indonesia's military intervention, but declined to do so. Instead, it consented to the invasion and allowed Indonesia to use its military equipment in the knowledge that this violated US law and would be used to suppress exercise of the right of self-determination (CAVR 2005a: Part 7.1, 122). The Australian government was also found at fault. *Chega!* describes the way in which:

> Australia did not use its international influence to try to block the invasion and spare Timor-Leste its predictable humanitarian consequences. Australia acknowledged the right of self-determination, but undermined it in practice by accommodating Indonesia's designs on the territory and opposing independence, and Fretilin, and giving *de jure* recognition to Indonesia's takeover.
>
> (CAVR 2005a: Part 7.7, 124)

By drawing attention to the complicity of Western states in condoning the Indonesian occupation, and providing recommendations for the establishment of a reparations fund with contributions from governments and institutions who supported the regime, *Chega!* also highlights the consequences of structural violence and the need for amends. In this sense, it expands understandings of justice, by shifting from a retributive and restorative justice emphasis to a reparative and redistributive one.[20]

Nonetheless, the CAVR was able to go only so far in its attempts to focus on the responsibilities of the international community. Although it specifically wrote to the UN Secretary General and a range of governments seeking information about policies during the Indonesian occupation, it did not have the power to compel testimony or written materials from any individuals and thus received no official replies (CAVR 2005a: 7.1, 7). Its efforts to organise a specific public hearing on the theme of 'Self-Determination and the International Community' were similarly frustrated. Thus, although the CAVR invited a number of high-level former officials and ministers to testify at this hearing, including Mochtar Kusumaatmaja (former Indonesian Foreign Minister), Mario Soares (former Portuguese Prime Minister and President), Jimmy Carter (former US President), Gareth Evans (former Australian Foreign Minister), Richard Woolcott (former Australian diplomat and Ambassador to Indonesia) and Ian Martin (former head of UNAMET), all, with the exception of Ian Martin, declined to appear. In the end, invitations were extended to a number of experts who had previously worked on Timor policy in various administrations, who were invited to testify as individuals rather than to defend government policy (CAVR 2004b).[21] The CAVR's efforts to draw attention to international responsibilities were also hindered by the fact that, as noted in Chapter 2, Western states have distanced themselves from the CAVR's recommendations for reparations and have been reluctant to consider their own role in the conflict, suggesting that international actors were only interested in supporting the CAVR insofar as it focused on 'local' reconciliation and truth-telling.

Another factor that interfered with the CAVR's commitment to documenting and responding to structural violence was the legal 'human rights violations' framework that underpinned its truth-seeking work and informed the structure of *Chega!* Like other truth commissions, the CAVR was tasked with collecting information on specific 'human rights violations', and although an open-ended interview format was adopted by statement-takers, which enabled the collection of information on a wide range of experiences, this information was then 'coded' into a series of distinct violations and entered into the CAVR's Human Rights Violations Database (Roosa 2007b: 571–2).

20 As Nevins (2007b) suggests, the CAVR's attention to the role of international actors, and its demands that they pay reparations, is perhaps unique among the recommendations of truth commissions.

21 Those who testified in this category were Ian Martin, Dr Kenneth Chan (former official in the Australian Department of Foreign Affairs), Mr Fransesco Vendrell (former senior official, UN Secretariat) and Gary Gray (former US State Department) (CAVR 2004b).

This process of translation was inevitably reductive: it framed out a great deal of the historical context, and gave priority to specific traumatic 'events' over 'everyday' experiences of violence, and to individual, rather than collective, experiences of harm.[22] The human rights violations framework had the effect of creating a barrier to the recognition of the long-term and chronic nature of individuals' suffering, including daily experiences of fear and intimidation and struggles to feed and clothe children. It also created a binary division between 'victims' and 'perpetrators' which obscured the complexity of individual's roles, including the extent to which people had collaborated with, and resisted, the Indonesian regime at different times. In this sense, then, by attempting to 'capture' individuals' experiences in the language of human rights violations, the CAVR, like other truth commissions, was ultimately incapable of doing full 'justice' to their intricate, fragmented and unique nature, and their continuation into the present.

In addition to being unable to recognise structural violence fully, the CAVR was ultimately unable to accomplish any substantial form of redistributive justice to *respond* to its ongoing effects. The CAVR's conceptualisation of justice was primarily 'restorative', emphasising the rebuilding of community relationships and the healing value of storytelling for both individual and nation. Although it made recommendations for a reparations programme to prioritise the 'most vulnerable' victims (CAVR 2005a: Part 11, 35), its attention to questions of redistributive justice during the life of its programme was minimal. Thus, as previously mentioned, the CAVR did establish a very small urgent reparations programme, through which it provided US$200 grants to those it identified as the 'most vulnerable' victims. However, the small amount of money involved, the fact that only 712 recipients received payments, and that the programme was not widely known or publicised, meant that it had limited impact. Like the Serious Crimes Process, the CAVR was, of course, inherently unable to provide redistributive justice beyond the limited number of 'victims' who fell within its mandate.

As the preceding discussion suggests, although the CAVR was able to move some way beyond the narrow criminal law boundaries of the Serious Crimes Process and attend to the long-term, structural dimensions of violence, and its manifestation in the form of 'everyday' experiences of poverty, hunger and displacement, it was only able to go so far. The silences of the CAVR – many of which reflect the inherent constraints of truth commissions – draw further attention to the limitations of short-term, legal and quasi-legal transitional justice mechanisms. While truth commissions are oriented towards restoration, resolution and categorisation, the demands of justice transcend these parameters and require a response to individuals' unique, personalised, and in many cases ongoing, experiences of violence.

22 Interview with former CAVR staff member, Dili, 18 August 2007.

Conclusion

As this analysis of key documents and interviews suggests, a combination of factors, some of which were specific to the unique context of East Timor and some of which are common to trials and truth commissions, impacted on the capacity of the transitional justice mechanisms to accomplish their own goals. The exclusion of Indonesian perpetrators, narrow temporal boundaries, resource deficiencies and paucity of community outreach restricted the nature of cases that could be prosecuted by the Serious Crimes Process and limited the recognition of victims' experiences. By contrast, the CAVR's broad mandate and significant donor support gave it the capacity to recognise and respond to a wider range of experiences of harm. Yet its work was also constrained by the exclusion of Indonesian actors and its temporal boundaries, which restricted the kinds of experiences that could be recognised.

It is also clear that both the Serious Crimes Process and the CAVR encountered difficulties in seeking to accomplish a range of goals and respond to disparate interests. In the drive to achieve 'nation-building' goals and to demonstrate 'results' to the international community, victims' interests and desires for recognition could easily be overshadowed. These difficulties also reiterate the larger point, made in the previous chapter, that transitional justice processes do not operate 'above' politics, but engage conflicting interests, are constrained by the practical and normative demands of 'state-building', and may play out in ways that benefit the interests of powerful actors, rather than those who have been victimised.

Beyond the context-specific constraints on the ability of transitional justice mechanisms in East Timor to accomplish their own goals, this chapter has also suggested that trials and truth commissions are inherently limited in meeting the demands of justice that are *beyond* the law. That is, the institutional experience of transitional justice in East Timor demonstrates the general difficulties faced in bridging the gap between the concrete and finite form of justice that can be provided by criminal justice processes and truth commissions, and the demands of justice, which transcend the possibilities of the law. In East Timor's case, a key element of 'justice' involves transforming the deep-seated and debilitating experiences of poverty and marginalisation that are the legacy of years of colonisation and occupation. This neither the CAVR nor the Serious Crimes Process was able to address, although the CAVR, with its broad mandate, community-oriented programmes and wide-ranging recommendations, came closest to doing so.

By unravelling the various constraints of the Serious Crimes Process and the CAVR, this chapter has shed further light on the reasons why East Timorese survivors may have been disillusioned with the 'justice' provided by the internationally sponsored transitional justice process. I now complicate the meanings of justice further, by exploring the narratives of justice promoted in the *national* sphere, by East Timor's political elite. These narratives – which invoke collective and forward-looking ideas of social justice and national unity drawn from East Timor's experiences of the resistance struggle – were excluded from the transitional justice process. A consideration of the continuing power of these narratives raises additional questions about the limits of internationally sponsored transitional justice processes in meeting local demands for justice and further unsettles the linear assumptions of 'transition'.

Chapter 4

National unity, collective struggle and the future

The East Timorese leadership's narratives of justice and nation-building

Narratives of justice promoted in the national sphere by the East Timorese political leadership were completely excluded from the formal transitional justice process. As highlighted in Chapter 2, tensions between sections of the UN and the East Timorese leadership pervaded the establishment and operation of the CAVR and the Serious Crimes Process, and neither mechanism was ever fully 'owned' by the national elite. While international transitional justice practitioners emphasised the importance of the rule of law, truth-telling, the rights of individual victims and the need to address the traumatic past, the East Timorese political leadership – in particular, the nation's first President, Xanana Gusmão, and Foreign Minister, José Ramos-Horta – stressed reconciliation-as-forgiveness, and attempted to reorient the justice debate towards collective rather than individual rights, towards social justice rather than retributive justice and towards the future rather than the past. Pragmatic goals underpinned these narratives: the imperative to portray the new nation to the international community as a viable and unified state, and to forge diplomatic relations with Indonesia to ensure future stability.

In this chapter, I delve more deeply into the historical origins and internal 'nation-building' imperatives that informed the East Timorese leadership's approach to justice following the referendum. I show that nationalist understandings of East Timorese identity and history – including ideas and values such as national unity, the centrality of resistance to the Indonesian occupation, sacrifice and liberation – were the basis upon which a new collective identity was being 'imagined' in the new nation state, and were a significant influence on the leadership's vision of 'justice'. The focus of this chapter, then, is on the narratives of an older generation of 'elite' East Timorese political leaders, including the Prime Minister, the President, parliamentarians and others who were intimately involved in East Timor's resistance struggle from the 1970s on. By illuminating the ongoing power of these stories, as well as their internal tensions and exclusions, this chapter sheds further light on the limits of the internationally sponsored transitional justice process in East Timor. In particular, an analysis of these stories helps to develop a nuanced appreciation of the reasons for the political leadership's resistance to the UN's transitional justice agenda, and, as I discuss in the following two chapters, can offer insights into local understandings of justice and survivors' reactions to the transitional justice process.

Narratives of national unity, sacrifice and resistance during the struggle for independence

Scholars have often commented on the powerful sense of national identity possessed by the East Timorese, the origins of which are said to lie in shared experiences of suffering under successive colonial rulers (Anderson 1993; Leach 2008; Babo-Soares 2003). A central aspect of this identity is the belief that the people have the capacity to suffer, to endure, and collectively to overcome great adversity (Traube 2007: 10; see also Babo-Soares 2003; Webster 2007). Thus, as Leach (2008: 145) observes, the story of *funu* (conflict) – of a '450 year "national" resistance struggle against consecutive foreign occupiers' – can be seen as a 'widely endorsed and popular narrative of East Timorese nationalism'. This story is commonly plotted as a progress narrative through which ordinary East Timorese people, collectively portrayed as the 'little people', won their struggle for liberation via acts of determination, unity and heroism, overcoming the oppressiveness of successive colonial occupiers.

Babo-Soares (2003: 21) suggests that, during the period of Indonesian occupation, stories of shared resistance to colonialism were fortified by customary myths recounting the heroism of the ancestors and the widely held belief that the East Timorese adhere to one *hun* (source, origin). Adherence to the Catholic faith (which increased significantly during the Indonesian occupation) gave additional force to these ideas, by linking individual pain to the suffering of Christ and 'arousing a sense of martyrdom in the name of the struggle' (Wise 2004b: 29). Benedict Anderson (1993) also observes that the Catholic Church's decision to use Tetum as the language of the Church in East Timor had profoundly nationalising effects.

Themes of national cohesion were invoked repeatedly in East Timorese nationalist poetry and songs from the mid-1970s, and featured heavily in FRETILIN's independence campaign. FRETILIN evolved from the Social Democratic Association of East Timor (*Associação Social Democrática Timorense*/ASDT), which had formed in May 1974 soon after the overthrow of the fascist Caetano government in Lisbon during Portugal's so-called 'Carnation Revolution'. In contrast to the second major political party formed during this period, UDT, which advocated progressive autonomy oriented towards a federation with Portugal and leading to eventual independence, the more radical ASDT (and later FRETILIN) called for total independence and the rejection of colonialism (Hill 2002: 60; Niner 2009: 22). FRETILIN's philosophy was influenced by Timorese students who had been exposed to radical Maoist and Marxist thought in Portugal (Niner 2009: 22–3). The choice of the name FRETILIN reflected the influence of African nationalist movements in former

Portuguese colonies, among them, the Front for the Liberation of Mozambique (FRELIMO), with which some of the founding members of FRETILIN had strong links (Jolliffe 1978: 63). FRETILIN's campaign drew on the powerful rhetoric of FRELIMO, while its popular education practices drew on the philosophy of the Brazilian educator Paulo Freire.[1]

National unity was a strong FRETILIN philosophy. A united struggle was viewed as a means of countering the regional rivalries encouraged by Portuguese 'divide and rule' policies and of forging a sense of common identity in the rural areas, where many people did not think of themselves as Timorese, but, rather, as belonging to a particular linguistic group (Hill 2002: 76–7). Thus, as FRETILIN's first political programme articulated:

> Our people fell under the domination of a foreign power by virtue of the armed superiority of the colonialist enemy. But this was not the only reason for the loss of our independence. Our forefathers' sentiment for independence was restricted by tribal feuds and by geographical divisions. This fact was able to be exploited by the Portuguese colonialists. Through intrigues and promises the new enemy was easily able to divide us and this helped facilitate our domination . . . We must remember that the DISUNITY of our forefathers caused their defeat. We will not repeat the same error. We will go forward in unity.
>
> (Cited in Hill 2002: 77)

FRETILIN's literacy programme also emphasised the importance of building the nation and promoted the idea of being Timorese. The popular song *Foho Ramelau* ('Mount Ramelau') by the poet Fransisco Borja da Costa, which became the 'revolutionary hymn' of FRETILIN (Jolliffe 1976: 10), conjures up a powerful image of the East Timorese people collectively rising up and casting off their colonial shackles:

> Eh! Mount Ramelau, Mount Ramelau, eh!
> What is higher than your peak?
> What is greater than your majesty?
>
> Why, Timor, is your head forever bowed?
> Why Timor, are your children enslaved?
> Why, Timor, do your children doze like chickens?
> Why, Timor, do your children doze like slaves?

1 Freire's most popular work, *Pedagogy of the Oppressed* (1970), undertook a Marxist class analysis of the relationship between the coloniser and the colonised, and proposed a new educational pedagogy through which people and societies could be 'conscientised' and assisted to overcome their oppression.

Awake! The foot of the mountain is white
Awake! A new sun has risen

Open your eyes! A new sun is over your village
Open your eyes! A new sun is over our land

Awake! Take the reins of your own *kuda* [horse]
Awake! Take command of our own land!
(da Costa 1974, in Jolliffe 1976: 21)

The term *Maubere* was also adopted by FRETILIN as a unifying symbol. Once used as term of contempt for backward, illiterate and poor mountain people under Portuguese rule, *Maubere* was appropriated during the 1970s as a symbol of East Timorese independence, and came to embody a sense of national pride (Jolliffe 1978: 103–5: Hill 2002: 74). These themes are evoked in a poem written by Xanana Gusmão in 1975, the final two stanzas of which read:

MAUBERE People,
Clench your fist,
Shout out loud,
The hour is YOURS, MAUBERE!
And your defiance will bring down
The walls of your own enslavement! . . .

MAUBERE People
Confront and face yourself in the long march of liberation.
Liberate yourself!
BE STRONG! . . . BE MAUBERE!
(Gusmão 1975, in Niner 2000: 35)

The philosophy of *Mauberism* also came to denote East Timor's broader struggle against hunger, illiteracy, poverty and ignorance, and for social justice that was another key strand of the FRETILIN philosophy (Hill 2002: 74). Thus, as the diplomatic representative of FRETILIN, José Ramos-Horta explained in 1975, Mauberism is 'a philosophy which seeks to consider how to get the common people to be literate and free from poverty and other social injustices' (Ramos-Horta, cited in Hill 2002: 74). The FRETILIN programme for economic reconstruction included the creation of co-operatives of production, distribution and consumption, and the 'elimination of the excessive dependency on foreign countries' through diversified agriculture and agrarian reform, including the expropriation of large farms and their distribution to the people to be used within the co-operative system (Hill 2002: 85). This programme actively worked to counter the effects of Portuguese colonial control, which, as noted in the Introduction, had attempted to exploit East Timorese resources by utilising forced labour to produce cash crops for export, including coffee and copra. These colonial practices – which had undermined indigenous capacities for self-sufficiency – indicate that structural violence, in the form of impoverishment, hunger and ill-treatment, had its genesis long before the Indonesian occupation.

Following the replacement of the Caetano regime in Portugal with a government committed to 'progressive autonomy' for the colonies (Taylor 1999: 25), FRETILIN had hopes of a smooth decolonisation process. These hopes, however, were very quickly crushed. By late 1974, the Indonesian government and military had begun to direct a covert destabilisation campaign known as *Operasi Komodo* (Operation Komodo Dragon) against the Portuguese administration, an aspect of which involved the broadcasting of anti-Communist propaganda into East Timor (Niner 2009: 26–8). Then, in the months of August and September 1975, a brief, but brutal, civil conflict between UDT and FRETILIN took place, which claimed the lives of between 1,500 and 3,000 people (CAVR 2005a: 7.2, 8). Sparked by political tensions between the two parties and exploited by the Indonesian government and military, the conflict stemmed from a UDT coup d'etat in August 1975 under the leadership of João Carrascalão. Portuguese authorities fled the territory, and FRETILIN called for a 'general armed insurrection against the traitors of the homeland and for the genuine liberation of the Maubere people' (cited in Niner 2000: 25). FRETILIN won a military victory against UDT and, on 28 November 1975, declared independence in the face of increased Indonesian military operations in the western districts.

East Timor's independence was short-lived. Nine days after FRETILIN's declaration, Indonesia, with the support of UDT and smaller political parties (Apodeti, Kota and Trabhalista), launched Operation Lotus, a massive air and sea invasion on Dili. Western states, including the United States and Australia, acquiesced to the invasion. A puppet provisional government was installed in early 1976, and in May a 'People's Assembly' in Dili (whose members were hand-picked by Indonesia) endorsed an 'Act of Integration' requesting Indonesian President Suharto to formally integrate East Timor into Indonesia (Taylor 1999: 73). As Indonesian troops advanced, thousands of people – including entire villages – fled to the mountains behind FALINTIL, the armed wing of FRETILIN (Niner 2009: 30). Although the UN General Assembly and Security Council condemned the actions of Indonesia, passing Resolutions calling for the withdrawal of its military and for East Timor's right to self-determination to be respected,[2] these calls gradually become more muted.

Until 1979, FRETILIN maintained control over large 'liberated areas' into which the Indonesian army had not penetrated. However, by 1980, the armed resistance had suffered enormous losses; only around 700 FALINTIL fighters

2 See GA Resolution 3485, 12 December 1975 (UN Doc A/RES/3485); SC Resolution 384, 22 December 1975 (UN Doc S/RES/384).

remained alive or active, and the majority of FALINTIL strongholds had been overwhelmed (ICG 2006: 3; World Bank 2008: 5). Thousands of civilians had also lost their lives, some as the result of a devastating famine which was directly linked to the Indonesian regime's resettlement policies, and others from the immensely destructive military campaign known as 'Encirclement and Annihilation', which, from 1977 to 1978, had encircled people in the east of the island on Mt Matebian and killed them with napalm and scatter bombs (Niner 2009: 34–6). Gusmão's message to the United Nations General Assembly in 1982 gives some sense of the magnitude of these losses, while also praising the East Timorese people's capacity to suffer, to endure, and give their lives for the independence struggle:

> This was a painful period for the Maubere People. With their land burnt, their houses destroyed, their possessions plundered, their animals machine-gunned, the Maubere People, in their great and heroic march for the defence of their country, also saw their children, their invalids and their elderly form a human column to be massacred by the constant bombardment and aircraft gunning. But these people were ready to die for their sacred native land!
>
> (Gusmão, 14 October 1982, in Niner 2000: 76)

In the context of this devastation, FRETILIN leaders saw the need for radical restructuring of the movement, and a 'National Conference of the Reorganisation of the Struggle' took place in 1981, which resulted in the appointment of Xanana Gusmão to the leadership of the resistance and the establishment of the National Council for Revolutionary Resistance (*Concelho Revolutionário de Resistência Nacional*/CRRN).[3] From this point, Gusmão began to take tentative steps to decouple the resistance struggle from its exclusive link to FRETILIN and build support for a broader-based movement against the Indonesian occupation. The resistance was no longer linked to a radical plan for Marxist revolution but instead involved a less partisan nationalist movement that emphasised the need for dialogue, negotiation and conciliation. Gusmão also took steps to elevate the role of civilians, also known as the Clandestine Front. Numbering in the thousands, this network was responsible for providing combatants with food, weapons, and ammunition, offering shelter in towns, and facilitating communication between FRETILIN and overseas representatives (World Bank 2008: 5). Women played a crucial role in the Clandestine network, serving as couriers or hiding people, information, or goods, and cooking for the combatants. Meanwhile, overseas representatives – known as the 'Diplomatic Front' – focused on keeping East Timor on the agenda of the UN (World Bank 2008: 5).

3 CRRN was comprised of members of the FRETILIN Central Committee, FALNTIL, and representatives of people living in Indonesian-controlled areas (Niner 2001: 20).

Further restructuring of the resistance movement occurred in 1987 when Gusmão resigned from FRETILIN and formally disconnected it from FALINTIL, transforming the latter into a non-partisan army. Criticising the 'political infantilism of revolutionary Marxism', Gusmão declared that FALINTIL had 'only one noble mission to follow: defence of the Homeland and the maintenance of internal order' (Gusmão, cited in Niner 2009: 113). A year later, in 1988, Gusmão played a leading role in the establishment of the National Council of Maubere Resistance (*Conselho Nacional de Resistência Maubere*/CNRM) – an umbrella organisation that hoped to encompass all political ideologies, and which replaced FRETILIN's Marxist concept of a 'revolutionary' council with the nationalist term *Maubere* (Niner 2000: 24). The movement underwent furthering restructuring in 1998, when the CNRM was transformed into the National Council for Timorese Resistance (*Conselho Nacional de Resistência Timorense*/CNRT), in which the term *Maubere* (which had always been a contentious symbol, given its association with FRETILIN) was replaced with the more unifying term 'Timorese'. At this point, the resistance movement was broadened to include supporters of UDT and the pro-Indonesian integration party Apodeti (Niner 2009: 113). Gusmão increasingly promoted the need to reach out to the Catholic Church and to negotiate with the Indonesians (ICG 2006: 3).

Subtle changes in resistance strategy were also reflected in the increasing links between East Timor and other international causes, such as the anti-apartheid movement in South Africa (Wise 2004a: 169). In September 1994, Gusmão (who by this time had been captured and imprisoned in Indonesia's Cipinang prison) wrote to Nelson Mandela, congratulating him on the end of apartheid and noting that Mandela's election as the first president of a democratic, non-racial South Africa was 'an inspiration to the fight of oppressed people everywhere, the fight of victims of repression, injustice and crimes committed by totalitarian regimes' (Gusmão 1994, in Wise 2004a: 169). In 1997, Mandela visited Gusmão in Cipinang prison, and the two developed a strong bond (Niner 2009: 175; Wise 2004a: 169). It is likely that Gusmão's later views about reconciliation and justice were influenced by the ideas of Mandela, who had explained the South African reconciliation process during their 1997 meeting (Niner 2009: 174–5).

The promotion of national unity continued to be critical during the lead-up to the 1999 referendum, when escalating militia violence (including the Liquica Church massacre in April 1999) threatened to derail the entire process. At this fragile time, Gusmão organised a Peace and Reconciliation Conference in Dare, in June 1999, to which representatives from pro-independence and pro-integration factions were invited, which sought to come up with a comprehensive and peaceful solution.[4] Gusmão's address to

4 This conference, which was known as 'Dare II', began on 25 June 1999, in Jakarta, following the 5 May agreement on the ballot for self-determination. The first Dare meeting had taken place in Baucau at the initiative of Bishop Belo, in 1998 (Niner 2000: 241–2).

the conference underscored the necessity for dialogue and reconciliation rather than confrontation (Niner 2000: 241–2). In an attempt to convince militia leaders to refrain from violence and to assuage their fears about future prosecutions, he offered verbal guarantees of pardons, equal rights and opportunities to all those who had committed crimes against other East Timorese (Niner 2009: 195). These efforts were eventually to be directly contradicted by UNTAET's prosecutorial approach.

As a powerful figure in the resistance movement, Gusmão commanded enormous popular authority during the Indonesian occupation, and has continued to do so during the post-referendum period. As Webster (2007: 583) observes, Gusmão's national unity approach is often portrayed as a means by which an ideologically driven campaign gradually transformed itself into a united political front able to win the support and empathy of the international community. By toning down some of the more radical anti-colonial rhetoric of FRETILIN, and adopting the language of peace, diplomacy and human rights, Gusmão and other East Timorese leaders closely aligned with him – in particular José Ramos-Horta – have been credited with recasting the resistance movement as a self-determination struggle that was more internationally palatable and therefore able to gain critical support (Webster 2007: 583; Wise 2004a: 166–7). As we have seen, however, Gusmão's national unity strategy was also the product of pragmatic necessity. By the end of the 1970s, tens of thousands of East Timorese people, both combatants and civilians, had perished, regardless of their political persuasions, either through direct armed attack or by starvation. In order for the resistance movement to survive, Gusmão had to change the underlying definition of 'national unity' from one of loyalty to a Marxist revolutionary ideology to one of a broad-based nationalist struggle that encompassed Timorese of different political affiliations and included not only an armed element, but also clandestine and diplomatic fronts.

Despite the popularity of Gusmão's version of events, as I discuss later in this chapter, not all political parties endorse this 'CNRT' version of history. FRETILIN, in particular, continues to argue that FRETILIN, not CNRT, represents the 'authentic' voice of the East Timorese resistance (see Leach 2007: 199).

National unity narratives in post-referendum approaches to justice, reconciliation and commemoration

Following the 1999 referendum, the themes of collective struggle and national cohesion remained prominent tropes in many of Gusmão's statements. Thus, in a statement shortly after the referendum, Gusmão emphasised that it was because of national unity that East Timor won its struggle for independence:

> We won the war, not because of military capacity on our part . . . but . . . [the] fundamental political factor for such a victory to come about was National Unity. The civil war divided the Timorese, the ideologies divided the Timorese. And it was only through National Unity with the aim of seeking freedom [and] independence for our Nation, [that] we succeeded in overcoming the enormous and challenging difficulties we encountered in those long years.
>
> (Gusmão 2000, in Babo-Soares 2003: 119)

These themes were echoed in Gusmão's statements on justice and reconciliation. Thus Gusmão's reconciliation narrative stressed the importance of forgiveness, forgetting and moving on, contrasting with the CAVR's version, which promoted the importance of truth-telling for individual and national healing. As I noted in Chapter 2, the leadership's reconciliation vision was driven, in part, by a political judgement that focusing solely on retributive justice would prevent refugees – among them former militia members – from returning to East Timor. This was reinforced by the perceived need to foster stability on the border and strengthen ties with Indonesia, amid a growing consciousness that the international community would not take responsibility for pursuing Indonesian serious crimes perpetrators. However, as I now explore, Gusmão's forward-looking justice agenda also reflected internal nation-building imperatives – in particular, anxieties about building 'national unity' and fostering peace and stability during a formative and chaotic period – which drew upon popular understandings of East Timorese nationalism based in the resistance struggle.

Gusmão's strong reconciliatory stance can be seen as a continuation of his pre-referendum emphasis on dialogue and compromise for the sake of building national unity. To build a consensus for this vision, Gusmão attempted to tap into deep-seated beliefs about the East Timorese people's perceived capacity for suffering and forbearance. Implicit in Gusmão's statements is that forgiveness implies a moral strength and fortitude; suffering is understood as the inevitable consequence of the liberation struggle and, as a result, a preoccupation with vengeance would demean the sacrifices made. These themes are evident in the documentary film about his life, *A Hero's Journey* (see Phan 2006), in which Gusmão implies that there is strength in forgiving and moving on:

> Some people need the perpetrators or the criminals to go to them and say yes, sorry I did a mistake . . . I don't agree too much with this kind of approach. I believe one can be strong enough to say just forget this. I want to live, to close the past.
>
> (Gusmão, interviewed in Phan 2006)

Gusmão also began to argue that a focus on retributive justice would keep people 'trapped in the past':

> When people call for justice they must understand there are no clear lines. Where do you begin? In 1974? In 1999? To take the path of justice there is no beginning and no end, and we all stay stuck in the past.
>
> (Gusmão, quoted in Phan 2006)

Soon after the referendum, Gusmão also promoted a vision of social justice, which emphasised poverty alleviation over prosecutions. The suggestion that addressing socio-economic conditions is more valuable than retributive justice and focusing on the past, and that 'development' is 'real' justice, evokes a vision of the East Timorese state as emerging, liberated, from a shared struggle against oppression. Thus Gusmão's emphasis is on the unified and collective nature of the struggle, and hence collective rights, rather than the recognition of individual victims' experiences.

While Gusmão and Ramos-Horta have been the foremost proponents of a forward-looking reconciliatory stance towards Indonesia, it is fair to say that preoccupations with questions of internal reconciliation and national unity have been shared by other political leaders, even if, at various times, FRETILIN leaders have made strong statements about the need for prosecutions of the Indonesian military (see, for example, FRETILIN 2007). This can be seen in the periodic parliamentary debates about amnesties and pardons that have taken place since the referendum. The first of these debates occurred in the lead-up to independence, in early May 2002, when Gusmão introduced a draft law on amnesty and pardons to the Constituent Assembly, the precursor to the National Parliament (Wilson 2010: 119). Given that it was so close to independence, the Constituent Assembly declined to debate the law, which was reintroduced into Parliament five days after independence (Wilson 2010: 119). Sweeping in its scope, the law proposed an amnesty for all crimes before September 1999 committed by East Timorese who were coerced into joining militia groups, provided that the crimes were not 'violent or bloody'.[5] In addition, it suggested the conferral of an amnesty on all FALINTIL fighters for past criminal conduct, provided that the conduct did not amount to war crimes, crimes against humanity or genocide (Bhuta 2001: 175; Wilson 2010: 119). Despite being passed by the Council of Ministers on 25 May 2002, this law was promptly withdrawn after strong criticism from many sectors, including national and international human rights NGOs, UNTAET and East Timorese lawyers (Bhuta 2001: 175). It was soon followed by another draft law on 'Amnesty and other Clemency Measures', which appeared in 2004, in the lead-up to the anniversary of independence (and around the time of the SCIU's indictment of General Wiranto), the preamble of which stressed the importance of

5 This rather vague term was not defined, but presumably referred to cases of murder.

forgiving even those who have committed so-called 'serious crimes' (Wilson 2010: 118–19).

More recently, in June 2007, in the aftermath of the 2006 crisis and immediately prior to the elections, the Parliament approved the law on 'Truth and Measures of Clemency for Diverse Offences', which included provision for amnesties for crimes committed between April 2006 and April 2007. This was widely regarded as an attempt by the then FRETILIN government to ensure that various members of the political elite who were implicated in the 2006 crisis (including former Minister of the Interior Rogério Lobato, who had been recommended for prosecution) would either be pardoned or their cases abandoned (Wilson 2010: 120; JSMP 2007). However, following a referral by President José Ramos-Horta, the Court of Appeal declared the law unconstitutional (UNMIT 2007: 5). Soon afterwards, on 20 May 2008, the anniversary of Timor-Leste's independence, Ramos-Horta issued a Presidential Decree granting full or partial pardons to ninety-four prisoners, more than half the total prison population (CIGI 2011: 13), including nine former militia members who had been convicted of crimes against humanity related to the 1999 violence. Among those pardoned was Joni Marques, who had been convicted for crimes against humanity in the Los Palos trial and originally given a thirty-three-year prison sentence. By defending his reasons on the grounds of 'fairness', President Ramos-Horta drew upon the popular narrative of the East Timorese as 'little people':

> This militia [has] already served eight years. Can you imagine? There is no Indonesian military on trial or in prison and East Timor, showing great heroism of its judicial system, keeps an idiot, an unfortunate guy, in prison.
>
> (Ramos-Horta, in March 2008)

Another of those pardoned by President Ramos-Horta was former Interior Minister Rogério Lobato who, at that point, had been convicted of distributing weapons to civilians in 2006. This was followed, in July 2008, by the President proposing new legislation that would grant amnesty to the perpetrators of the 2006 violence if they apologised publicly for their actions. Then, in 2009, in the context of the tenth anniversary of East Timor's independence (and in the context of the Martinus Bere controversy discussed in Chapter 2), President Ramos-Horta called for an amnesty for all crimes committed between 1974 and 2009 (ICG 2011a: 16). These calls were reiterated during the President's speech to the nation on 28 November 2011 to mark the thirty-sixth anniversary of FRETILIN's initial proclamation of independence, when the President again articulated his desire for an amnesty law on the basis that this would help to encourage the thousands of East Timorese still living in Indonesia to return to their homeland (Ramos-Horta 2011).

Although no amnesty law has yet been promulgated, the fact that these laws have been 'on the table' since 2002 (Wilson 2010: 118), and that significant numbers of pardons have been granted to convicted perpetrators of serious crimes, indicates the persuasive power of reconciliatory narratives among the political elite. Justified as measures that would promote national reconciliation, particularly between pro-Indonesian and pro-independence supporters, the various iterations of these laws draw on the embedded idea of East Timorese as 'little people', united in the struggle against their oppressors, who should not turn against one another. The ongoing nature of these discussions also calls attention to deep-seated anxieties about the fragility of national cohesion during a chaotic and fraught nation-building period. It suggests, for example, that the leadership remains acutely aware of the multiple roles played by many people during the resistance struggle, and of the deep divisions and resentments amongst the population. These cleavages emerged within the coercive circumstances of the Indonesian occupation, when many had 'collaborated' with the occupiers, and some had committed violence against their fellow East Timorese, not only as militia in 1999, but as members of paramilitary groups, civil defence forces, the military and police. Members of the leadership undoubtedly have a pragmatic awareness, too, of the potential on the part of former East Timorese militia leaders and pro-autonomy supporters who continue to live in West Timor to create instability along the border, and the importance, perhaps, of enlisting their support.[6] The periodic discussions of amnesties and pardons also invoke the spectre of East Timorese 'disunity' during the brief internal conflict between FRETILIN and UDT 1974–75, as well as the crimes committed by the East Timorese leadership during the resistance – issues to which I return later in this chapter.

Despite the political leadership's 'forward-looking' emphasis on reconciliation-as-forgiveness and social justice, the past remains a continuing preoccupation. It is also a contested domain. The leadership has sought to invoke a particular version of the past, one in which the 'heroic' and 'united' struggle against the Indonesian occupation has a central place. This version of the past, which remembers and honours the contribution of 'heroes' and 'martyrs' of the struggle is, I suggest, critical to the forward-looking project of post-referendum identity construction by East Timor's political elites.

Aletta Norval's work on South Africa draws attention to the high stakes involved in the interpretation of the past by national elites, particularly during formative nation-building periods. Drawing on the insights of Benedict Anderson (1983), whose work has been influential in highlighting

6 Estimates suggest that, as of 2010, there were approximately 100,000 East Timorese refugees remaining in West Timor (see ICG 2011a: 3). The ICG also notes that there were some indications that the CNRT government had pushed for repatriation of refugees in advance of the 2012 elections and that Gusãmo's party might well benefit from such movements, due to his outspoken support for returns (ICG 2011a: 11).

the 'imaginings' that shape national communities and command the loyalty of citizens, Norval (1998) shows that these imaginings can be used to reinforce the position of dominant elites and their supporting ideologies. National narratives about the past, she argues, act as 'legitimizing moments for and shape the character of new regimes'. In this sense, these stories do more than 'deal with the past': they represent a struggle for control over the future (Norval 1998: 251). Given that history is intricately linked to power struggles in the present, elites tend to edit out versions of history that reflect poorly on them, and include those that buttress their own political projects. In other words, state-building tends to reinforce selective memories and recognise identities that are essential to a new state's legitimacy, a process that necessarily entails a certain amount of 'collective amnesia' (Anderson, in Norval 1998: 255).

Many of these dynamics can be discerned in East Timor. As Leach (2008: 147) observes, the political leadership's approach to remembering and responding to the past has worked to reinforce political projects of contemporary identity construction. Following the referendum and then independence, the political elite has searched for a 'useable past' (Zamora 1998) to help to build a cohesive national identity. It has sought to construct the Indonesian period as a story of heroic endurance, unity, national liberation, and sacrifice, and to write individuals' painful experiences of suffering and death into the wider story of the march towards freedom. These efforts are evident in the portrayal of the East Timorese people as 'heroes' and 'martyrs', rather than 'victims'. For example, in *A Hero's Journey*, Gusmão says:

> Many people complain and accuse myself and the State of forgetting the suffering of the past, forgetting the sentiments of the victims. I always say that during a liberation struggle we cannot use the term 'victims'; they are all heroes.
>
> (Gusmão, quoted in *A Hero's Journey* 2006)

Similarly, Major Mau Buti – a prominent FALINTIL veteran – has stated: 'We should not talk about victims of war in Timor-Leste. Those who died are not victims of war, but heroes because they won' (Mau Buti, cited in World Bank 2008: 4). Further reference to the heroic past can be found in the key foundational document of the new nation, East Timor's Constitution, the symbolic 'heart' of which contains a 'valorisation of resistance' clause, which 'recognises and sacralises the resistance as the core tradition of the independent state' (Leach 2002: 44). Section 11(1) of the Constitution declares that:

> The Democratic Republic of East Timor acknowledges and values the secular resistance of the Maubere people against foreign domination and the contribution of all those who fought for national independence.
>
> (Constitution of the Democratic Republic of Timor-Leste, section 11(1))

Current official efforts at memorialisation and commemoration also pay tribute to the resistance and, in particular, to the role of the FALINTIL forces. Thus, 20 August is officially designated as 'FALINTIL Day', which commemorates the date of its establishment in 1975. The date of the Indonesian invasion of East Timor, 7 December 1975, is officially remembered as East Timor 'Heroes Day', which has the effect of drawing attention to glory rather than suffering and, as Walsh (2011: 234) observes, deflects attention from the responsibility of the Indonesian government for these events. Both the national heroes cemetery for FALINTIL soldiers in Metinaro and the new Museum of the Resistance give physical expression to the government's desire to 'valorise the resistance' (Leach 2008: 154) rather than remember painful experiences of suffering. By contrast, there are few state-sponsored memorials to remember the violence committed against civilians. By and large, the monuments constructed to remember the massacres against civilians during 1999 – including those in Suai and Liquica – have been initiated by local communities with the assistance of human rights groups (a theme to which I return in Chapter 6). The leadership has been noticeably absent from a number of significant commemoration ceremonies, including the tenth anniversary of the Liquica Church massacre. At the commemorations they have attended, leaders have tended to promote a narrative of reconciliation-as-forgiveness. For example, at a recent commemoration of the Kraras massacre, before an audience of widows dressed in black, Gusmão and Ramos-Horta emphasised the importance of remembering that Indonesians died as well as East Timorese.[7] Needless to say, there are no nationally constructed monuments to remember those who lost their lives during the internal political conflict of 1974–75 between FRETILIN and UDT. Gravestones marking the bodies of UDT victims from this period, in Aileu, remain forlorn and neglected, visited only by family members.

The centrality of resistance identity is equally apparent in current efforts to 'valorise' veterans. Since 2002, a number of commissions have been established to identify and register ex-combatants and cadres of the civilian resistance, for whom some form of recognition would be granted.[8] A law relating to 'Valorisation of the Resistance' was approved in March 2006, which provides for the recognition of veterans who fought for national independence through the provision of medals and certificates, participation in public ceremonies, the right to wear a uniform at ceremonies, funeral honours and burial

7 Personal comment staff member of international NGO, Dili, July 2009.

8 In 2002, President Gusmão established the *Comissão para os Assuntos dos Antigos Combatentes* (Commission on Ex-Combatants) to identify and register ex-combatants of the period 1975–79, and the *Comissão para os Assuntos dos Veteranos das FALINTIL* (Commission on Veterans of FALINTIL) to identify and register FALINTIL veterans during the period 1981–99. A new commission was created in 2004, the *Comissão para Assuntos dos Qadros da Resistência* (Commission on Cadres of the Resistance), to identify and register cadres of the civilian resistance.

in special ceremonies for eligible veterans (Figure 4.1)[9]. While the law as initially drafted provided access to pensions and benefits for a narrow group of beneficiaries based on a combination of vulnerability criteria such as age and disability, loss of parents or husband, combined with time dedicated to the independence struggle, recent amendments to the law suggest a growing emphasis on rewarding years of service and rank.[10] The high priority accorded to veterans by the current leadership is also reflected in the continual raising of pension amounts to the extent that, in 2011, 6 per cent of the state budget was set aside for veterans' benefits (ICG 2011b: 1).

As these post-referendum developments indicate, a national resistance narrative, which portrays the period of Indonesian occupation as a unified and heroic march towards liberation, featured prominently in the political leadership's approaches to questions of justice, reconciliation and commemoration. This story continues to serve a range of pragmatic and symbolic purposes from encouraging refugees to return, focusing the population's energies on the nation's future (including relations with Indonesia) to consolidating the

Figure 4.1 A veterans' medals ceremony (Edith Bowles)

9 Law 3/2006, as amended by Law 9/2009 of 29 July 2009.
10 Interview with staff member international NGO, Dili, East Timor, 16 April 2011.

legitimacy of the leadership itself. The preoccupation with issues of *internal* reconciliation also suggests that the leadership are fully aware of the way in which East Timorese people (including members of the current leadership) were implicated in the violence of the occupation. Importantly, the leadership's emphasis on social justice, collective rights and the remembrance of a triumphal past diverged substantially from the UN's vision of transitional justice, which stressed that nation-building required focusing on the past, prosecuting individual human rights violators and recognising victims' experiences. However, despite the potency of the leadership's ideas of national unity and collective struggle, as I discuss in the next section, tensions surfacing in the post-referendum period suggest that this story is more fragile than it appears at first glance.

Tensions, cleavages and exclusions emerging in the post-referendum period

Cracks in the veneer of national cohesion began to appear soon after the referendum, which made it increasingly clear that without the presence of an immediate 'enemy' it would become more difficult to hold 'the people' together (Federer 2005: 94). Tensions began to emerge, based on competition between FRETILIN and other political parties over the symbolic 'ownership' of the resistance, including debates over which individuals and groups contributed most to the independence struggle (Leach 2007: 193).[11] As the East Timorese anthropologist Dionisio Babo-Soares observed shortly after the referendum:

> There was a new atmosphere of political division, a manifestation of public discontent towards leaders, competition for political recognition, the exchange of verbal insults among political leaders and political opponents, and an apparent breakdown of *unidade nacional*.
>
> (Babo-Soares 2003: 25)

Amid the political complexity of the post-referendum period, the themes of loyalty and contribution to the resistance became a key means by which political groups and individuals sought to claim their legitimacy, prove their 'worth' and compete for recognition in the new nation state. As Babo-Soares writes:

11 There were also ideological differences *within* FRETILIN, which led to the splintering of the party into a number of different groups, all of which claimed to be the 'true' representatives of FRETILIN, including FRETILIN Lu-Olo and Mari Alkatiri, *Partido Nacionalista Timorence* (PNT), the *Associacão Social Democrática Timorense* (ASDT), *Partido Socialista de Timor* (PST) and the *Conselho Popular pela Defesa República Democrática de Timor Leste* (CPD-RDTL) (Babo-Soares 2003: 164–8).

> Whenever differences occurred, each individual group would always refer to the sacrifices they had made in the past for justification, and maintain that those who had contributed to the struggle should be rewarded accordingly, including among other things, with the right to occupy political positions in the new government.
>
> (Babo-Soares 2003: 25)

Amongst the East Timorese leadership, a complex contest developed over particular interpretations of history. Tensions within CNRT – in particular, between those allied with Gusmão and Ramos-Horta, and those allied with FRETILIN leaders – centred around claims to the 'symbolic "ownership" of the resistance, and its national liberation narrative' (Leach 2007: 199). This was a contest between Gusmão's 'divergence to convergence' version of events and FRETILIN's version, which maintained the party's claim to be the 'true' voice of the resistance struggle. These tensions, among others, contributed to the disintegration of CNRT in July 2001.

Competition between FRETILIN and other political parties was also evident in the early debates of the Constituent Assembly (the eighty-eight-member body popularly elected on 30 August 2001 to draft and pass the constitution) over national symbols and commemorations. Being the majority party, FRETILIN was able to control the Assembly's decision-making and shape the Constitution, including by instituting its symbols and days of commemoration as national symbols. Independence day, for example, is celebrated on the 'FRETILIN' independence day of 28 November 1975 as the 'restoration' of independence, rather than 30 August, the day of the 1999 referendum (Leach 2002: 44). The national anthem chosen was *Patria Patria* by Francisco Borja da Costa (who was killed in 1975), which had been played at the initial independence day in 1975. The choice of East Timor's national flag was another contentious issue. The debate about whether to adopt the red, black, white and yellow flag used by FRETILIN in 1975, or the blue, white and green flag of CNRT, was also resolved in favour of the former (Leach 2002: 45). Demands also began to surface for non-FRETILIN political groups – most of which switched sides and supported independence in 1999 – to apologise for their support for integration with Indonesia (Babo-Soares 2003: 128).

The themes of sacrifice and loyalty have also been prominent in a number of election campaigns. In relation to the 2001 Constituent Assembly elections, Tania Hohe (2002: 76) notes that the historical resistance struggle was a detailed feature of many parties' campaigns. The Democratic Party (PD) started election rallies by inviting former resistance fighters onto the stage by their code names. Social Democratic Party (PSD) leaders described their personal connections to the resistance movement and announced the names of family members they had lost (Hohe 2002: 76). FRETILIN went so far as to demand that 'people should not vote for themselves but for the ones that fell in the struggle' (Hohe 2002: 76). These themes were again evident during the 2007 presidential election campaign during which, as Kelly Silva (2008: 256–78) observed, it was common for all of the candidates 'to identify with the population by evoking their own histories of suffering, especially during the Indonesian occupation'. To legitimise their campaigns, speakers at rallies were often chosen because of their former roles as FALINTIL guerrilla fighters (Silva 2008: 256–78).

Tensions around particular versions of history are the backdrop against which many of the political debates about contribution to the resistance have surfaced. In the post-referendum period, accusations of 'mistakes' made in the past, particularly during the internal political conflict of 1974–75, soon became a political 'commodity' with which members of the leadership began to threaten each other and discount each other's claims to legitimacy (Babo-Soares 2003: 174). The counterpart to hero, or nationalist, is, necessarily 'traitor'. Many of the assumptions associated with the label 'traitor', as Kammen (2003: 80) observes, remain powerfully alive for the older generation of East Timorese; it is a narrative that warrants further exploration.

The term 'traitor' is often used in association with the political conflict of 1974–75 between UDT and FRETILIN. According to the CAVR, the highest death toll from this conflict was in the rural areas, where tensions based on long-standing clan feuds and personal grudges, intensified by more recent militant ideological party divisions, exploded into violence (CAVR 2005a: Part 3, 42). Further massacres of UDT and Apodeti prisoners were committed by FRETILIN at its base in Aileu, as the party faced pressure from advancing troops (CAVR 2005a: Part 3, 69).

Additional violence, and new accusations of treachery, emerged after the Indonesian invasion, in particular during first three years of the occupation when FRETILIN retained control over *zonas libertadas* (liberated zones). In late 1976 and 1977, under the strain of the Indonesian military onslaught, FRETILIN faced internal divisions due to differences amongst the leadership about how to continue the struggle in light of the decimation of resistance strongholds and the drastic loss of life. While FRETILIN central committee members maintained a militant position that emphasised mass mobilisation as a vital component of the revolutionary struggle, then President of FRETILIN Francisco Xavier do Amaral argued that the bulk of the population should be allowed to surrender and continue to engage in resistance activities from the towns and villages (CAVR 2005a: Part 3, 77–8). Thousands of combatants and supporters surrendered to the Indonesian army during this period, although to do so was strictly forbidden by the FRETILIN central committee (CAVR 2005a: Part 5, 21–2). FRETILIN began to arrest 'traitors' and 'counter-revolutionaries' within its own ranks, including commanders who encouraged or allowed people to surrender, who were perceived as being opposed to the FRETILIN ideology of revolution (CAVR 2005a: Part 5, 19). Among those arrested was FRETILIN President Amaral himself who, in

September 1977, was publicly 'tried' by an extrajudicial FRETILIN tribunal for planning to negotiate with the Indonesian military, disregarding the struggle and behaving in a 'feudal' manner, and was convicted of treason (Kammen 2003: 80; Niner 2009: 32–3).

Kammen (2003: 81) observes that another permutation of the 'traitor/nationalist' debate emerged during the 1980s, following Gusmão's decision to delink FALINTIL from FRETILIN and establish the CNRM. In particular, FRETILIN members were angered by the shift of decision-making power, and argued that only FRETILIN could command the struggle (Babo-Soares 2003: 140–2). FRETILIN hardliners – including central committee members who were based in Angola and Mozambique – claimed that Gusmão had disregarded the sacrifices made by previous leaders (Babo-Soares 2003: 140–2), and that his strategy of dialogue and compromise was a betrayal of FRETILIN's radical revolutionary philosophy. Many of these debates from the 1970s and 1980s continue to show themselves in post-referendum politics.

As discussed in Chapter 3, the CAVR attempted to air some of these tensions between members of the political elite by holding a special national public hearing on the internal political conflict of 1974–75, during which political leaders publicly accepted responsibility on behalf of their parties for their harmful acts and expressed regret before a packed audience (CAVR 2005a: Exec Summary, 34; see also CAVR 2007). Among those who testified were President Xanana Gusmão, Prime Minister Mari Alkatiri, Foreign Minister José Ramos-Horta, Interior Minister Rogério Lobato, Deputy Speaker of the Parliament and former FRETILIN President Xavier do Amaral, former UDT Secretary General Domingos de Oliveira, and PSD President, and former UDT leader Mario Carrascalão. The five contemporary leaders of East Timor's historic parties also testified on behalf of their parties: Francisco Lu'Olo Guterres (FRETILIN); João Carrascalão (UDT); Clementino dos Reis Amaral (Kota Deputy President); Paulo Freitas (Trabalhista); and Frederico Almeida Santos (Apodeti Pro-Referendum). Invitations to testify were extended to former Apodeti leaders in Indonesia; however, they declined to take part (CAVR 2004b).

Notwithstanding their participation, it was apparent that political leaders had engaged in intensive discussions prior to the hearing to decide on a collective strategy.[12] During the hearings themselves, most leaders were cautious about divulging specific information (including names of those killed and the circumstances in which they were killed) and accepting individual, as opposed to party, responsibility.[13] Some leaders also sought to downplay the extent of

12 Interview with former CAVR staff member, Dili, 18 August 2008.

13 An exception perhaps was João Carrascalão, President of the UDT Party, who accepted personal responsibility for the death of FRETILIN prisoners and whose speech was commented on favourably by some of my interview respondents.

abuses committed by their political party by depicting the violence as a consequence of a 'lack of control' rather than a product of official policy. This narrative was evident in Gusmão's retelling of the story of the massacre of UDT prisoners by FRETILIN in Aileu and Same during 1975:

> Control, I can say . . . there was a lack of control . . . The Aileu massacre, some say that it was the taste for political revenge, but I do not believe it was a party policy, especially because there was already a lack of control . . . I can say that the massacre was not a planned political programme, not a political policy or strategy.
>
> (Gusmão, in CAVR 2007: 33)

Another way in which East Timorese leaders deflected attention from acts of violence committed by their political parties was by writing it into their own particular versions of the story of national liberation. Thus, in his concluding remarks at the public hearing, Gusmão spoke of the 'coming together' of the East Timorese people under the banner of the CNRT that occurred in the aftermath of the internal political conflict, emphasising his narrative of national unity:

> It is true that terrible wrongs were done. We killed others, we were angry with each other. But just as our people have already shown us, we came together under CNRT. We gained much strength when we were able to send our enemy from our land.
>
> (Gusmão, in CAVR 2007: 36)

Mari Alkatiri similarly sought to draw positive, patriotic, lessons from the experience of the internal political conflict by reflecting on 'the capacity of people to make a large sacrifice to gain independence'. He suggested that 'this is a big lesson for us to reflect upon, how can we turn this capacity to make a sacrifice to make development and strengthen peace, strengthen stability and foster peace between all of us' (Alkatiri, in CAVR 2007: 60).

There are striking parallels between the reluctance of East Timorese leaders to publicly acknowledge past violence committed by their political parties, and the attempts by African National Congress (ANC) leaders in South Africa to downplay their responsibilities for violence during the apartheid era in hearings of the TRC. Tom Cleveland (2005), for example, observes that the ANC, including then South African President Thabo Mbeki, attempted to obscure the history of abuses at its Angolan detention camps by subsuming it beneath the triumphal narrative of a new South Africa. Although the TRC made an effort to hear from victims and publicly acknowledge ANC violence, there was little place for these truths within the official nation-building narrative, and the ANC National Executive Committee ultimately sought to block the report's publication in the courts (Cleveland 2005; see also Gready

2011: 41). As in East Timor, during the TRC hearings themselves, ANC leaders were evasive, arguing that abuses were not condoned by the ANC, but were the unavoidable result of a violent struggle.

Cleveland suggests that what appears to have motivated the ANC's approach to these difficult issues was an understandable desire not to place the violence of the apartheid regime on the same moral plane as that of the ANC. Similar motivations may have informed the East Timorese leadership, who, not surprisingly, may have wanted to distinguish their own acts of violence from those committed by the Indonesian regime, and to contextualise the internal political conflict within the confusion, chaos and stress of the impending invasion. Nonetheless, as in South Africa, the failure to engage with these issues in any depth has left little space for the acknowledgement of a more complex truth and, arguably, has inflicted further violence on victims by failing to acknowledge the reality of their experiences. Until efforts are made to address these difficult, complex issues – for example in the form of fact-finding to identify the circumstances of those who were killed and their bodies, and the rehabilitation of the reputations of those who have been accused as traitors – there is likely to remain an acute sense of 'unfinished business' for the many ordinary people implicated in these events, who remain stigmatised and ostracised.[14]

The sensitivities surrounding the issue of East Timorese political party violence do not appear to have diminished with time. Indeed, the continuing power of long-standing ideological splits and grievances from the 1970s and 1980s was brought to the fore during the 2006 crisis, which, as the International Crisis Groups notes, can be partly attributed to 'ten people [members of the East Timorese elite] who have a shared history going back 30 years' (ICG 2006: 1). Anxieties about these issues also appear to have informed the leadership's ongoing desire to promote amnesties and clemencies for East Timorese perpetrators. Thus, as some observers have noted, a level of jitteriness is evident amongst former members of the East Timorese resistance movement now in key leadership positions about the spotlight being put on atrocities they committed during the Indonesian occupation (see, for example, King's College 2003: para 274). In a context in which a number of members of the current leadership have 'dirty hands', there is thus a collective vested interest in not opening up discussion of these difficult truths.[15]

In addition to political frictions, the centrality of the resistance struggle to elite conceptions of nationhood has also had the effect of excluding certain

14 FRETILIN did make some initial efforts to consider the issue of FRETILIN abuses against party members, including by announcing the establishment of a 'Unity and Tolerance Commission', in 2000, to conduct research on FRETILIN 'errors' over the previous twenty-four years and to rehabilitate the names of those condemned as 'traitors' (FRETILIN 2000); however, this commission never got off the ground.

15 Interview with East Timorese NGO leader, Dili, 2 July 2009.

individuals and groups from claims to legitimacy and hence recognition – namely, those who are deemed not to have contributed to the struggle. The implication is that those who collaborated with the Indonesian regime or who did not make sacrifices for the liberation struggle have been in some way privileged – particularly in an economic sense – over those who demonstrated loyalty to the resistance (Silva 2008: 167). Tensions and anxieties have surfaced as groups and individuals seek to contest these labels and prove their own 'worth' by seeking to demonstrate their loyalty to the resistance.

One key issue of contention concerns the respective roles of East Timorese who remained in the country during the Indonesian occupation and those who left to go abroad. As scholars and observers have noted, arguments are often made that those who remained in East Timor contributed more to the resistance struggle than those who left to lead the 'good life' (see, for example, Babo-Soares 2003; Silva 2008; Crockford 2007). These tensions were accentuated during the UNTAET period when those who were able to speak English and Portuguese were prioritised for jobs within the UN (Babo-Soares 2003: 155). Divisions are also evident amongst those who remained in East Timor during the occupation. There are perceptions that, through their 'collaboration' with the Indonesian military in the past, certain individuals or groups had access to education or civil service employment, in contrast to those who actively resisted through clandestine activities or by joining the armed resistance. Similar resentments have been evident in other post-conflict contexts, including South Africa, where some ex-ANC combatants have expressed opinions that those who played no role in the anti-apartheid struggle or who were actively opposed to it have benefited in the new South Africa, while some white South Africans have resented the extent to which fellow whites who left the country to avoid conscription during the apartheid era have had access to better work opportunities and education (Gear 2002: 19–20).

Similar debates have surfaced in relation to the role of youth. Timorese who came of age in the 1990s and who generally spent a number of years in the Indonesian education system are sometimes referred to disparagingly by members of the older political elite. For example, Mari Alkatiri has referred to the 'young' generation of East Timorese (by which he refers to those now in their late 30s) who were educated in Indonesia as *sarjana supermee* ('*supermee* graduates' – named after a popular brand of Indonesian instant noodle). Young people have been further excluded from constructions of national identity by virtue of the decision to introduce Portuguese, along with Tetum, as the official languages of the state. The majority of young people were schooled in Indonesian and thus do not speak Portuguese, which makes it difficult for them to take up positions in the civil service or the government. Similarly in relation to commemorations of the past, Leach observes that there are few state-sponsored memorials to reflect the contribution of young people to the resistance struggle (Leach 2008: 158). For example, although planning is now under way, at the time of writing there remains no national monument to commemorate those young people who were killed during the 1991 Santa Cruz massacre.[16] Indeed, the government initially suggested that 12 November should not be a holiday at all, and that the best way in which to honour those who had died was to 'work hard' on that day.[17] In a context in which their contributions to the struggle are downplayed, the younger generation has been cautious not to overstate their resistance credentials and to give due acknowledgement to the role of their elders. This is reflected in parliamentary debates, in which younger parliamentarians often defer to their elders in relation to critical policy issues, due to their status as former resistance figures, and in doing so tend to get embroiled in the rivalries and cleavages of the older generation.[18] Moreover, the fact that many young people have been reluctant to register for the veterans' process, even though those who had leadership roles in organisations such as RENETIL[19] are eligible to do so, suggests that they are conscious that they are perceived as privileged (see Kent 2006).

Those who consider themselves to be 'victims' or *povu ki'ik* (small people/ ordinary people), rather than heroes, also perceive themselves to be marginalised by the centrality of the resistance movement to constructions of national identity. Thus it became apparent during my fieldwork that many of my respondents had not been eligible to register for the veterans' process, given its restriction to individuals (or in cases of death, their family members) who had held identified positions of responsibility within the formal resistance structures, excluding those who were rank-and-file 'members', those who merely assisted the resistance movement from time to time and those who were not active in the resistance movement at all. In addition, many of those who had been active in the 'Clandestine movement' were not entitled to receive pensions, due to the fact that only time spent 'full-time' in the resistance counts towards eligibility and members of the Clandestine generally combined their activities with other work (see World Bank 2008: 23). Strong views were also expressed by a number of respondents that civilians who had not been involved in the resistance movement, but who nonetheless suffered human rights violations during the Indonesian occupation, should be considered 'victims' rather than heroes and duly acknowledged as such. These perceptions – which suggest that Gusmão's attempts to label the East Timorese people collectively as 'heroes' has not been wholly successful – are explored further in Chapters 5 and 6.

Not surprisingly, women's experiences have been particularly marginalised by the centrality accorded to the resistance in constructions of national identity. As Niner (2011: 428–9) observes, a form of 'militarised masculinity' is privileged in present-day East Timor, a product of the militarisation of East

16 Interview with member of the 12 November Committee, Dili, 2 July 2009.

17 Comment by staff member international NGO, Dili, 15 July 2008.

18 Interview with NGO leader, Dili, 2 July 2009.

19 *Resistência Nacional dos Estudantes de Timor Leste/* (National East Timorese Students Resistance) (RENETIL) was a non-partisan student resistance group established in 1988.

Timorese society during the long years of the occupation and the male-dominated nature of the resistance movement itself. Reflections of this can be seen in the relegation of East Timorese women to the domestic sphere in the post-conflict period and the valorisation of male contributions to the resistance struggle, such as bearing arms, over women's diverse roles as couriers, cooks and nurses. Very few women were eligible to register as veterans of the armed resistance, as the majority had not carried weapons. While women had played active roles in the Clandestine movement, the fact that they had not usually held particular ranks within the leadership structure also excluded many from recognition through the civilian veterans' process.

Women are further marginalised due to the patriarchal nature of local-level structures such as the family. For instance, there is evidence to suggest that, in some cases, widows eligible to receive veterans' pensions on behalf of their husbands have been pressured to relinquish their payments to male members of their families.[20] In addition, women who experienced rape and sexual violence during the occupation (often because of their participation in the resistance struggle or that of a family member) and those were forced to become 'mistresses' to Indonesian army officers are often accused by their local communities of 'disloyalty'. These ironies have been pointed out by the prominent women's rights leader, Maria Domingues-Alves, who has rhetorically asked, 'Why is it that men who are tortured by the military forces are seen as heroes, whereas women who are tortured (including rape) are seen as traitors?' (Domingues-Alves, in Harris-Rimmer 2010: 125). In this context, Harris-Rimmer (2008: 124) has observed that East Timorese women have taken pains to point out that those who bore children to Indonesian army officers remained loyal to the independence movement. She points to a statement to the UN Security Council by the East Timorese women's network *Rede Feto:*

> We know that colonialism leaves vestiges where it passes; the same thing has happened in East Timor where many children have been left without a father. Children have often been born as a result of rape but the mothers have raised the children to oppose the Indonesian administration and become part of the resistance.
>
> (*Rede Feto*, in Harris-Rimmer 2010: 124)

Tensions amongst the political elite, and debates over who contributed the most to the resistance struggle, were some of the background factors that contributed to the 'crisis' of 2006 that followed Prime Minister Alkatiri's dismissal of around one-third of East Timor's military in response to the submission of a petition alleging discrimination in the armed forces. One of the most troubling aspects of the crisis was its manifestation in conflicts

20 Interview with staff member international NGO, Dili, July 2009.

between groups of young men who described themselves as *Lorosa'e* (easterners) and those who described themselves as *Loromunu* (westerners). These divisions, which were exploited by East Timorese political parties and leaders with long-standing rivalries, became salient due to the popular association of resistance fighters with the eastern regions of East Timor (where FALINTIL had been more sustainable because it was further from the Indonesian border). Thus the dismissed soldiers all described themselves as *Loromunu*, and complained that they had been discriminated against and labelled as 'untrustworthy' because they were perceived not to have fought as hard in the resistance as *Lorosa'e* (easterners) (1CG 2006). Clashes between *Lorosa'e* and *Loromunu* gangs in 2006 resulted in the killing of more than thirty people, the burning and looting of thousands of houses and the displacement of around 140,000 people (ICG 2006: 21). The 2006 violence illuminated how attempting to establish the resistance to the Indonesian occupation as the primary basis for a postcolonial national identity has the potential to be, as Brown (2009: 158) puts it, 'dangerously divisive'.

By comparison, the 'development' and social justice agenda promoted in particular by Prime Minister Gusmão and President Ramos-Horta appears to offer a more inclusive nation-building vision, one that avoids competition over a perceived sense of contribution to the resistance in favour of 'social justice' for all. The hope perhaps is that calls for retribution will be replaced by a sense of national purpose in overcoming poverty and developing the economy (Bhuta 2001: 174). The social justice vision seems to offer a broad conceptualisation of justice – one that moves beyond the narrow legal preoccupations of the transitional justice mechanisms – and considers questions of structural violence and redistribution. Given East Timor's position as one of the poorest states in the world, which, in 2010, ranked 120 out of 169 countries in the UNDP Human Development Index (UNDP 2010), this emphasis on development also has popular resonance.

However, it has become increasingly evident in the post-independence era that there is a vast gap between the rhetoric of 'social justice for all' and the reality. Under the first FRETILIN government, development centred around the establishment of state institutions, fostering private sector investment as the 'engine for growth', and encouraging a 'lean, effective, accountable and transparent civil service', themes that were reflected in East Timor's National Development Plan (National Planning Commission 2002: 28–9). This approach, which largely followed World Bank and IMF prescriptions, was highly constrained and centralised, and had the effect of marginalising many among the rural population. When the AMP government[21] came to power

21 At the 2007 elections, no one party gained enough votes to govern outright. Instead, Xanana Gusmão formed a coalition government called the Alliance of the Parliamentary Majority (AMP), comprising his own party, the CNRT, plus ASDT, PSD, PD and UNDERTIM.

in 2007, headed by Xanana Gusmão, it signalled a radically different development approach, one that aimed at rapidly boosting rates of investment in infrastructure and human resources and improving the living conditions of the population. This policy, facilitated by the huge increases in oil and gas revenues from the Timor Sea, permitted the amount allocated to government spending to increase tenfold from US$68.5 million in 2002–03 to $687.1 million in 2009, and then to double again by 2011 to $1.5 billion (Goldstone 2012).

In the context of this rapid rise in the new nation's economic fortunes, the AMP government's approach to development has both raised expectations amongst the population and exacerbated real and perceived experiences of inequality. Thus, as the East Timorese NGO La'o Hamutuk (2011) observes, much of the government's expenditure is being channelled into contracts for large-scale infrastructure projects, while, in 2012, only 6.3 per cent of state expenditures will go to education and 2.9 per cent to health. Another key facet of government spending has shifted to the provision of benefits and pensions to different interest groups, in particular those who, in the wake of the 2006 crisis, are perceived as being a political threat or danger to national security. Among those who have benefited are 'Petitioners' (the group of sacked army officers, some of whom later joined with a group of 'rebels' from the western parts of the country led by Alfredo Reinardo), families of police officers killed by the military during the crisis, people who were internally displaced during the crisis and, as previously discussed, veterans. These payments, which have been justified on the grounds of the need for political and social stabilisation, appear to have had little impact upon poverty reduction (Goldstone 2012). This is partly because funds have tended to remain concentrated in Dili, which, as the site of the most widespread and sustained violence of 2006 and 2007, has been the geographic focus of the government's monetary distribution efforts (Goldstone 2012). Tensions have begun to emerge amongst those who feel they have been excluded from state assistance and recognition, an issue that is especially acute given the crippling poverty affecting much of the rural population. What can be observed is that a form of identity politics is emerging, through which different groups are attempting to claim recognition and resources from the state. The implications of the emerging competition between different interest groups, particularly in relation to advocacy for victims' rights, are taken up in Chapter 6.

The leadership's responses to *Chega!*

The leadership's responses to the CAVR's report, *Chega!*, at once reflected the potency of national unity narratives and their underlying frictions. The statements of Gusmão and Ramos-Horta in particular have evinced an ongoing desire to promote a 'forward-looking' vision of social justice and reconciliation-as-forgiveness, in contrast to the *Chega!* emphasis on individual suffering, retributive justice and reparations. Competing narratives are also evident in the CAVR's emphasis on the recognition of victims, and the leadership's preference for promoting the acknowledgement of 'heroes' and 'martyrs'.

The political leadership's responses to *Chega!*, and in particular those in the executive, can best be described as lukewarm, although there have been variations. On tabling the report to the Parliament in November 2005, Gusmão, as President, criticised the 'grandiose idealism' of the CAVR commissioners and argued that the CAVR's recommendations, particularly those relating to prosecutions and reparations, might be used to 'manipulate our people's state of mind' (Gusmão 2005b). He suggested that the pursuit of criminal justice would not 'take into account the situation of political and social chaos that could easily erupt if we decided to bring to court every crime committed since 1975 or even 1974' (Gusmão 2005b). Reflecting his continuing preoccupation with questions of 'national unity' in the fragile post-independence period, Gusmão expressed concerns about the potential 'wild justice' or 'revenge' that could emerge if crimes were prosecuted in the courts. 'Let us imagine', he said, 'the culture of persecution that we would be sowing into Timor-Leste.' It would make people 'rise up against each other' and the East Timorese would be portrayed as 'brutal, violent and bloodthirsty people' (Gusmão 2005b). Rather than retributive justice, Gusmão stressed that true 'justice' was the self-determination of the East Timorese people:

> I must say that, upon learning about the contents of the Report, I concluded that both Prime Minister Ramos-Horta and myself were right when we said that the best justice, the true justice, was the recognition by the international community of the right to self-determination and independence the people of Timor-Leste have! . . . The goal was to Liberate our Homeland because only with a liberated Homeland, could all the people enjoy better living conditions as the product of their rights. And this goal was much too important for us to consider individual sacrifices.
>
> (Gusmão 2005b)

Gusmão and Ramos-Horta have also been critical of the CAVR's recommendations for reparations. As discussed in Chapter 2, a key reason for this is pragmatic: both leaders have been reluctant to press the international community for reparations due to a desire to not to appear 'ungrateful' for the aid and assistance they have received. Gusmão and Ramos-Horta's responses have also drawn on the continuing power of resistance narratives, with their emphasis on 'heroism' rather than 'victimhood'. Thus both leaders have reiterated their concerns about the difficulties of defining victims in a context in which so many people have suffered, and have opposed the concept of reparations on the grounds that it could help to foster a 'victim' mentality that does not recognise the 'heroism' of the East Timorese people. As Ramos-Horta put it:

> The East Timorese government does not believe that we should consider compensation for the victims because there are tens of thousands of people who were, in one way or another, affected by the violence either directly or indirectly. There are those who died by the thousands and those who are still considered 'disappeared.' It would be a mind-boggling endeavour to try to identify each individual who claims to have been a survivor of victimisation during this period of 24 years.
>
> (Ramos-Horta, cited in Asia Society 2006)

Similarly, as Gusmão argued:

> In times of sacrifice we rose to be heroes. Today, in times of peace, we are regarded as victims! Our people, the heroic and forsaken people of Timor-Leste, do not deserve to be treated with so blatant a disrespect.
>
> (Gusmão 2005a)

Rather than a reparations programme, in the view of Gusmão and Ramos-Horta, the best contribution to those who have suffered would be the provision of economic development and better services to people. For Gusmão:

> We can best honor that struggle and these sacrifices by building a better democracy here, improving governance and providing better services to the people.
>
> (Gusmão, in Kingston 2006: 282)

In contrast to their lack of support for the *Chega!* recommendations, the political leadership appears to have become more prepared to acknowledge the contribution of the report as a national history, particularly following the 2006 crisis. At his 10 July 2006 swearing in as Prime Minister, José Ramos-Horta suggested that it was necessary to undergo a 'deeper reflection about our collective experiences of the years 1974–1999', and acknowledged that 'the extensive CAVR report is an encyclopaedia of our history, both rich in teachings and suffering. We must utilise its great teachings to better understand today's crisis and to help prevent future crises' (Ramos-Horta 2006). Gusmão's speech at the swearing in of members of the government, in 2007, similarly referenced *Chega!* when he acknowledged that 'we cannot ignore the lessons of the past in order to understand the current crisis, and protect the future' (Gusmão 2007).

To some extent, these positive reactions underscore the extent to which *Chega!* resonates with a pre-existing 'CNRT' narrative of the past. Thus, as Webster (2007: 582–3) observes, *Chega!* plots 'an oppressed people continually fighting for their freedom and being punished for it, until they finally triumph', and analyses the resistance movement as moving from 'divergence to convergence', which reflects Gusmão's national unity narrative. Yet *Chega!*

also draws attention to 'difficult' issues – including the internal political conflict and violence against women – and focuses on ordinary people's experiences of suffering rather than narratives of heroism. In this sense, *Chega!* departs at critical points from both CNRT's and FRETILIN's narratives of the past and attempts to challenge and broaden their preferred constructions of nationhood.

Questions remain about whether some of these more 'difficult' memories, and less 'heroic' stories, will be acknowledged in any official version of the past, or whether, and how, they will be used as fodder to fuel ongoing political tensions. Reflecting a continuing desire to minimise the extent of violence during the internal political conflict, then Prime Minister Mari Alkatiri contested the CAVR's findings on these issues. While acknowledging that FRETILIN committed 'errors' and 'excesses', he stated that 'It's an absolute lie that there were 3,000 killed in the civil war. A few hundred died in Ermera and Maubisse, a few tens in Dili and isolated killings in other areas' (Lusa 2005). He charged that the inflated casualty figures had been influenced by 'some foreigners' interviewed by the CAVR (Lusa 2005). On the whole, however, it is fair to say that there has been remarkably little national-level discussion or debate about the *Chega!* version of history, which may indicate that *Chega!* is largely viewed as irrelevant to current debates amongst the leadership about the past. Where *Chega!* has been taken up by the political leadership it has been when this has served their interests, for example as a clarion call for national unity in the wake of the 2006 crisis.

As of late 2011, the fate of the *Chega!* report and recommendations remains far from clear. During 2009 and 2010, three 'National Consensus Dialogues' were facilitated by the retired Norwegian Catholic Bishop Gunnar Stalsaat on the theme of 'Truth, Justice and Reconciliation', which aimed to provide members of Parliament and the government the opportunity to discuss openly, and in a non-partisan fashion, how best to implement the recommendations of the CAVR and the CTF. The dialogues, however, achieved very little consensus. Indeed, during the first dialogue, President Ramos-Horta removed the entire CNRT party[22] for a whole day and, during the discussions, Gusmão referred to those calling for prosecutions as 'troublemakers', shut down the discussion of reparations,[23] and the issue of 'amnesty' for serious crimes was once again raised. Moreover, as noted in Chapter 2, parliamentary discussion of two draft laws establishing an Institute for Memory to implement the recommendations from the CAVR and CTF reports and a National Reparations Programme, has been delayed indefinitely. Key issues of contention revolve around whether the Institute should be located within the

22 CNRT here refers to the *Congresso Nacional da Reconstrução de Timor* (National Congress for Timorese Reconstruction). Founded by Xanana Gusmão in 2007 as a new political party, it very cleverly uses the same acronym as the earlier umbrella resistance body.

23 Interview with staff member of international NGO, Dili, 1 February 2010.

government or external to it, and whether it would 'reopen old wounds' (including the issue of violence committed by the resistance movement), or implement a 'foreigner-driven agenda'.[24] According to close observers of the debate, a number of MPs have also expressed fierce opposition to a reparations programme, on the basis that outstanding issues relating to veterans' payments need to be resolved first, and that reparations may benefit those who were 'anti-independence' or who did not contribute to the resistance struggle.[25] This opposition indicates that the resistance narrative, and its constituent tensions regarding who is 'deserving' of recognition and assistance from the state, remains as potent as ever.

The status of *Chega!* as a historical record remains similarly ambiguous, and there is ongoing uncertainty about which truths will be formally acknowledged and what meanings will be assigned to them. For example, although the current Minister for Education has formally acknowledged the importance of integrating *Chega!* into the school curriculum, there continues to be nervousness about progressing this agenda without further guidance from the political leadership as to what constitutes the 'official' view of history. As one staff member of the Education Department bluntly put it: 'We can't talk about people in the past until we know who is a hero. If they're dead, we don't know whether they're a hero or traitor.'[26]

The leadership's ambivalent responses to *Chega*! and the ongoing debates that are occurring about the significance of the past, the nature of national identity and the meanings of 'justice' further unsettle the assumptions that transitional justice processes can operate 'above' the national political sphere and have the capacity to draw a clear line between the conflict and post-conflict period. Instead, they suggest that the leadership is reinterpreting the transitional justice process by referencing, explicitly or implicitly, pre-existing preoccupations and disputes, many of which date back to the early 1970s, and precede the Indonesian occupation.

Conclusion

Nationalist narratives of East Timorese identity and history, which evoke historical themes such as national unity, the centrality of the resistance, collective sacrifice, endurance and liberation, remain powerfully alive and continue to inform the East Timorese leadership's approach to nation-building, 'justice' and reconciliation. The continuing salience of these themes points to underlying anxieties amongst the leadership about their capacity to maintain national unity during the fragile, fluid period of post-1999 nation-building. They suggest too, that the political leadership has a pragmatic

24 Personal comment, staff member international NGO, Dili, April 2011.
25 Personal comment, staff member international NGO, Dili, April 2011.
26 Comment reported by staff member international NGO, Dili, July 2008.

awareness of the limits of prosecutions for dealing with the intricacies of past violence, including its chronic, debilitating effects upon many of the population and the fact that large numbers of East Timorese were implicated in this violence. Moreover, they are only too aware of the acts and reprisals committed by their own political parties and the new nation's proximity to Indonesia. Amid the fragmentation and uncertainty of the post-referendum period, when there was a perceived breakdown of national unity, heroic stories were viewed as a means of binding together 'the people' based on a shared past and perceived solidarity, and imagining a new postcolonial national identity. The leadership's attempts to redefine justice as 'social justice', emphasising collective rights over individual rights, are evidence of their desire to institute a triumphal and unified nation-building vision.

Like the transitional justice narratives promoted by the international community, the leadership's nation-building narratives are built upon their own self-interested categories of inclusion and exclusion, which have their own inherent contradictions and speak to current relations of power. Thus, as we have seen, notions of sacrifice and contribution to the resistance have emerged as key categories through which claims for political legitimacy and recognition are being negotiated in the new nation state, and the basis upon which the 'worthiness' of political parties, groups and individuals is assessed. Given its potential to exclude those perceived not to have made sacrifices for the resistance – among them 'traitors', 'collaborators', returned diasporans, women and young people – the resistance narrative holds the capacity to divide as much as unite.

The persistence and potency of themes of resistance and national unity tests the value of short-term, internationally sponsored, transitional justice processes as nation-building exercises. The extent to which the transitional justice narratives directed from the international sphere – with their emphasis on the recognition of individual rights and human rights violations – will provide a sufficient enough basis on which to forge a new national imaginary remains uncertain. Although the political leadership appears to have endorsed some aspects of the *Chega!* version of history, arguably this is because they resonate with a pre-existing national story of East Timorese suffering at the hands of Indonesian oppressors and serve current political preoccupations, such as the need for 'unity' in the wake of the 2006 crisis. The continuing reluctance to acknowledge some of the more 'difficult' truths of *Chega!*, including those relating to the internal political conflict and women's experiences of violence, suggests that *Chega!'s* status as an 'agreed to' truth remains far from settled. In fact, it is being marginalised within pre-existing political debates about the meaning of the past. These developments suggest that international narratives of retributive justice and reconciliation have been largely overshadowed by pre-existing political conflicts between national elites, although, as I discuss in the next chapter, there is some resonance between the content of *Chega!* and *local* narratives. The dynamic and unsettled nature of these developments points to the inadequacy of metaphors such as 'transition' and 'coming to terms with the past' to describe the trajectory of East Timor's nation-building process, suggesting that it is continuity, rather than rupture, that best describes these ongoing discussions about the meaning of the past.

In the next two chapters, I turn from the 'official' narratives of justice and nation-building promoted by actors within the international and national spheres to the 'local' narratives of East Timorese survivors. In Chapter 5, I explore the highly personalised forms of justice that East Timorese survivors have sought through participating in the transitional justice process, some of which resonated with the underlying objectives of these mechanisms, while others diverged from them.

Chapter 5

Local narratives of (in)justice

Recognition, retribution and economic assistance

> I have just driven the five hours from Dili to Los Palos, in the eastern tip of the island, along the winding coast road. In contrast to the heated debates in Dili over the recent *indultos* [pardons] granted by President Ramos-Horta to 94 convicted militia members (including Joni Marques and other members of the *Tim Alpha* militia group) the discussions of these issues here are surprisingly muted. Maleve agrees to take me to the *suco* of Leuro on the back of his motorbike, which is where, according to sources in Dili, a number of *Tim Alpha* members come from, and have recently returned following their release from prison. Expertly navigating the rough, pot-holed roads, Maleve deposits me in the small, shady *suco* an hour or so later. Maria, whose child had been killed by a *Tim Alpha* member, agrees to speak to me. As we sit in her tiny bamboo house, with its uneven, dirt floor, Maria does not focus on the fact that the militia have not served their full custodial sentence. Rather, she tells me that she is *laran moras* (sick inside/upset) because the state has 'looked after' the interests of the militia [by releasing them from jail] before her own. 'Who is going to provide food for us? The state doesn't think about us, they only think about Joni and the others.'
>
> (Field diary entry July 2008)

I began this book by describing two encounters with survivors that evoked a profound sense of disillusionment with the lack of 'results' from the transitional justice process. In their different ways, the frustrations expressed by José in Liquica and two widows in Covalima illustrate the divergence between the official claims made for East Timor's transitional justice process and the grounded expression of disenchantment with its achievements. The vignette above suggests, further, that local understandings of justice may differ from prevailing criminal justice understandings of this concept. In this chapter, I draw closely on my fieldwork to explore, and begin to account for, some of the meanings contained within survivors' desires for 'results'. In particular, this chapter is informed by the views of survivors who participated in the transitional justice process, and some community leaders, from the districts of Liquica, Covalima and Lautem, and, as much as possible, presents these views in their own words. While some survivors are educated and live in district capitals, the majority come from rural backgrounds, have low levels of literacy and education, and have limited access to basic services. And even though local narratives are diverse, and evolving, I nonetheless suggest that some common themes can be identified.

In Chapter 1, I discussed scholarship that has shed light on the multiple reasons people have for participating in transitional justice processes, some of which may have very little to do with the official aims and objectives of trials and truth commissions. These studies have also shown that survivors may invoke notions of justice that diverge significantly from the legal understandings of this concept. Building on these insights, this chapter explores the diverse and often highly personalised forms of justice that East Timorese survivors have sought through participating in the transitional justice process. In so doing, I draw on Merry's concept of 'vernacularisation' in assessing how concepts of 'justice' promoted by the official transitional justice process that are compatible with local justice ideologies may find more resonance with survivors than those that do not (Merry 2009). Merry's work – and that of other anthropologists (see, for example, Shaw 2007) – also highlights that human rights concepts (including transitional justice ideas) are rarely adopted in 'whole cloth' (Merry 2009: 4), but are redefined in specific contexts in accordance with local value systems. Attending to the multiple narratives of justice circulating in the local sphere also helps to bring the inherent limitations of law more sharply into focus. In particular, it illuminates that recourse to legal (and quasi-legal) mechanisms alone may be insufficient to meet fully survivors' historically and culturally situated, and ongoing, demands for 'justice'.

Customary beliefs and local justice practices in East Timor

Anthropological scholarship provides important insights into East Timorese belief systems and customary dispute resolution practices from the pre-colonial period to modern times. As in other post-conflict contexts such as Afghanistan, Uganda, Rwanda and Sierra Leone, East Timor is a society characterised by legal pluralism, in which informal 'indigenous' practices of peacemaking and dispute resolution continue to exist alongside the formal legal system (see Waldorf 2006: 10–11; MacGinty 2008). Rather than being a stable body of fixed rules, local dispute resolution practices are fluid and evolving, and have undergone constant change in response to the effects of modernisation and colonialism. Nonetheless, a number of common features can be identified amongst these practices in East Timor, which, as Hohe and Nixon identify, remain surprisingly resilient in present-day society, although they are less prevalent amongst educated and urbanised sections of the population (Hohe and Nixon 2003: 57).

Before discussing customary dispute resolution practices, it is important to make the general point that these practices are strongly linked to deeply held beliefs that the spirit world is as real and as present as the physical world (Robins 2010: 49). Many East Timorese believe that, for life to be sustained, there must be good relations between the secular world of the living and the spirit world of the ancestors. Spirits are believed to exercise a fundamental role over the lives of the living and to exert a powerful influence over social conduct (Hohe and Nixon 2003: 16; Nixon 2008: 318). *Adat* (custom) refers to the 'order' or set of rules that is prescribed and inherited from the ancestors (Hohe and Nixon 2003: 16).[1] Transgressing these rules is perceived as contravening this order, and likely to have disturbed the spirit world, leading to an 'imbalance'. These forms of trespass, which can encompass acts from violating kinship and marriage relations to committing murder, may invoke the wrath of the ancestors, which could potentially lead to sickness, death or natural disaster (Nixon 2008: 317; Babo-Soares 2005: 22).[2]

In a context in which the spirit world is perceived to have significant power, Hohe and Nixon explain that customary norms are concerned primarily with the 'replacement of values, to re-establish their correct exchange and restore the socio-cosmic order' (Hohe and Nixon 2003: 18). Because these rules are unwritten, certain members of society – often referred to as *Lian Nian* (literally, the owner of the words) – have to be 'in contact' with the spirit world in order to interpret the 'will' of the ancestors, to reveal transgression from the order, to define punishment and hence to speak law (Hohe and Nixon 2003: 17). Wrongdoing is perceived as a community, rather than an individual, problem, and 'justice' is largely understood as a collective, restorative practice aimed at returning to a harmonious society and satisfying the ancestors (Nixon 2008: 328).

In terms of local dispute resolution practices, since colonial times the most serious acts of wrongdoing, such as murder, have been referred to the official authorities (Hohe and Nixon 2003: 19). Many other problems, however, continue to be resolved through local and informal processes of dispute resolution, sometimes referred to as *nahe biti* (literally, stretching the mat). *Nahe biti* is widely practised in East Timor, albeit in many different forms and, as noted in Chapter 4, revolves around the idea of meeting and discussion in order to reach consensus among opposing parties (Babo-Soares 2005: 15). The process generally starts with a report of the issue to the village or hamlet

1 *Adat* is the Indonesian word for customs or belief systems, and is still commonly used in East Timor.

2 East Timorese researcher Josh Trindade even suggests that some Timorese interpreted the 2006 crisis as a form of ancestral punishment of the nation for relying too heavily on modern or imported values, which caused an imbalance between the real world and the cosmic realm (Trindade 2011: 12).

chiefs by the heads of the families, or the family of the victim.[3] A meeting is then set up to resolve the conflict as soon as possible, and takes place in a communal area where a symbolic woven mat *(biti bo'ot)* is unfolded. Apart from the families involved in the dispute, the *Lian Nian*, along with other authorities of the community, come together to participate in the resolution of the problem, which is sealed with some form of binding oath.

The aim of the *nahe biti* process is not only to achieve swift resolution of a community dispute, but also to re-establish the social order of the community. Fundamental to this process is the acknowledgement of the 'source' of the dispute that generated the conflict in the first place, which may go back years and even generations (McWilliam 2007b: 77; Nixon 2008: 232). Until this is achieved, it is likely that bad relations and acrimony between conflicting parties will continue to fester and be passed down to subsequent generations (McWilliam 2007b: 77). Elizabeth Traube, who has conducted extensive research amongst the Mambai ethnic group, also observes that local dispute resolution practices stress the importance of 'making public the fault that is to be redressed,' which leads to an emphasis on public confessions (Traube 2007: 19). This emphasis is reflected in the views of Traube's informants about the kind of process that would be required to reintegrate former militia members into the community in the post-referendum period. As Traube writes:

> In describing the process they envisioned, many people emphasised the confessional over the evidentiary or punitive stages. Those responsible, people reiterated, needed to make a public declaration of *what* they had done (destruction of property or the more serious crime of murder), and just as importantly, *why* they had done it.
>
> (Traube 2007: 19)

Shaming and compensation are other important aspects of the *nahe biti* process, both of which are linked to the restoration of balance that is understood to be essential for the survival of the society. In order to ensure that the grievance is resolved, the perpetrator must be publicly shamed, and the reputation of the victim's family must be restored – their shame 'covered' – through the payment of appropriate compensation (Hohe and Nixon 2003: 18–21). Thus, as the anthropologist David Mearns explains, 'Justice is never simply a matter of punishment but rather of compensation for the victim and the victim's family whose honour had been damaged by the crime or offence' (Mearns 2002: 43). In this sense, unlike the process of restitution in the Western sense, compensation has a symbolic transformative power in the East Timor

3 However, before getting to this point there has generally been an attempt by the elders of the two families to resolve the problem (Grenfell 2006: 317).

context, and is informed by the cultural code of reciprocity or exchange (Traube 2007; Silva 2008). Through the public shaming of wrongdoers and the payment of compensation, values are restored, and 'harmony' in both the spirit world and the community is re-established (Hohe and Nixon 2003: 18). This community 'harmony', however, should not be romanticised. Indeed, Graydon (2005: 68) makes the salient observation that just as the 'official' law can often privilege the needs and interests of dominant groups, customary East Timorese dispute resolution practices may entrench powerful social groups at the expense of more vulnerable members of a community, including women, ethnic and religious minorities, and poor and less influential families (Graydon 2005: 68). In this sense, the 'harmony' that is restored serves to reinforce the existing 'local order' within local communities, which tends to be deeply conservative and patriarchal, and favours particular powerful families (see Grenfell et al 2009: 102; de Araujo 2005: 13).

The spirit world also exerts a powerful influence on East Timorese attitudes to the dead. Proper care of the dead is a matter of great concern to the East Timorese and, as Robins (2010: 11) observes, death rituals often combine elements of both animist and Catholic traditions. The church ritual requires a mass to be conducted, followed by the taking of flowers to the cemetery for the first and second weeks after the death, again after six months, and then after one year (Robins 2010: 11). Animist rituals are also essential to facilitate the safe travel of the soul of the dead to the sacred world (Robins 2010: 11). The spirit must be led to rest after death, through burial or the offering of sacrifices, so that it will not torment the living. This is even more important if someone has died a 'bad' or unnatural death, because it is believed that the spirit may seek vengeance on the family and whole community. In these cases, the importance of dispatching the dead becomes a community issue, and not just an issue for the family (Robins 2010: 11–12). If appropriate rituals cannot be conducted – for example when a body is not recovered – the dead may be condemned to become a 'wandering ghost', unable to enter the spirit world (Field 2004: 207–8; Rawnsley 2004). As the anthropologist van Gennep explains:

> Like children who have not been baptized, named, or initiated, persons for whom funeral rites are not performed are condemned to a pitiable existence, since they are never able to enter the world of the dead or to become incorporated into the society established there.
>
> (van Gennep, in Field 2004: 207)

The performance of burial rituals, then, is important both for the sake of the dead themselves as well as for the restoration of the social order of the living.

Having sketched a basic outline of East Timorese customary belief systems, I now turn to an exploration of survivors' expectations of the transitional justice process. As will become evident, customary beliefs continue to exert a strong influence on survivors' understandings of justice and their responses to the 'official' transitional justice mechanisms. These belief systems are not absolute, however, and intersect with other influences, including personal experiences of violence, national resistance narratives and socio-economic conditions, to inform survivors' diverse conceptions of justice.

Truth-telling: symbolic recognition and a stepping stone to practical results

Survivors' views about telling their stories and the importance of establishing a historical record about the violent past suggest, on the face of it, a high level of resonance between the official goals of the CAVR and local narratives. Almost all those I spoke with were overwhelmingly positive about the idea of an official 'story about the conflict'.[4] At the same time, during my fieldwork, in mid-2007 and again in mid-2008, very few respondents had actually seen the truth commission report, or heard about it, let alone read it. Their views, then, were based on the 'idea' of an official history, rather than *Chega!* itself.

The production of an official record of the Indonesian period was valued as a means to cultivate a distinctive national identity, forged out of collective experiences of suffering and a sense of shared history. One respondent, for example, explained that *Chega!* could help people to appreciate that 'people in the West [of the country] suffered and people in the East also suffered'.[5] Another explained, 'If we don't know the story we don't know how our foundations were built. We don't know where our nation has come from'.[6] Central to *Chega!*'s legitimacy was the perception that it had included the stories of the *povu ki'ik* (ordinary people) in the broader story of the liberation of the nation. Thus, as Silvino, in Liquica, stated, it is important to establish that it was not just the 'big' people, but also the 'small' people who participated in the struggle. As another respondent put it, 'The *Chega!* story is true because it comes directly from witnesses, not only [from] the leaders'.[7] In this sense, then, the idea of an official, national history was seen as a way in which to recognise the contribution of so-called 'ordinary people' to the resistance struggle. *Chega!* was also valued for its educative or forward-looking function. As Maria, in Covalima, explained:

4 This finding differs from that of Robins (2010), who found that families of missing persons did not place a value on *Chega!* One of the reasons for this may be because my study focuses on individuals who had participated in the transitional justice process, while Robins' study does not.

5 Interview in Suai, Covalima, 29 May 2007.

6 Interview in Suai, Covalima, 30 May 2007.

7 Ibid.

> *Chega!* is important for the new generation. Our nation was formed by struggle. If there is conflict in the future people can understand the struggle. It can be an example for the new generation, so that the same things can't happen again.[8]

Or, as another survivor put it:

> It's important to have the story. From 1975 to 1999 so many people died. FRETILIN killed, Indonesians killed. In the future the children will know that FRETILIN killed how many, Indonesia killed how many, and why they killed . . . so that the children can follow this . . . If we just tell them these things they won't listen but if we have a book they will follow.[9]

Maria and Pedro's comments are indicative of the strong views held by respondents that a history of the conflict should serve the pedagogical function of educating future generations in order to ensure that historical mistakes were not forgotten or repeated.

Beyond their beliefs in the power of an official, public history, survivors who participated in a CAVR public hearing, or had their testimonies documented for inclusion in *Chega!*, generally welcomed this opportunity. Many were motivated by a desire for public recognition of their experiences by their family, local community and the political leadership. Thus, as Gracilda put it:

> When we spoke it was broadcast through the radio, television. We spoke about how our husbands died . . . So our children could see this. Not just how my children can understand but so my family can understand my experiences and how we became independent . . . So that the State, all people can see . . . It's important that the big people hear us victims speak. This is how we got independence. We didn't buy independence like buying a buffalo or horse. We bought it with our bodies.[10]

Storytelling was also understood as a means of discharging a moral duty to the dead. Angelo of Los Palos, for example, had spoken publicly for the first time, at the CAVR's hearing on 'Massacres', about surviving a forced march and execution of prisoners by FRETILIN in 1976, in Lautem district, during which his father, brother and five friends were executed. Although eventually he escaped, FRETILIN soldiers returned to the village and massacred a further

8 Interview in Suai, Covalima, 29 May 2007.

9 Interview in Kamanasa, Covalima, 31 May 2007.

10 Interview in Poros, Lautem, 6 August, 2007.

thirty-seven people, including his entire extended family. Angelo's desire to speak at a CAVR public hearing had arisen from a sense of obligation to his dead family members, to ensure that his family's name would be remembered in an official record public record of the past: 'If I didn't speak, my family's name would be lost, so I wanted to go.'[11]

Given East Timor's recent emergence from a long history of colonisation, during which freedom of expression was denied, it is not surprising that strong sentiments were expressed about the power of speaking out about past experiences and the importance of a national record of the conflict. These opinions can also be seen, perhaps, as highlighting a widespread hope for a more peaceful, prosperous and just future, and the restoration of a peace that many believe was shattered by the long years of conflict and oppression. Popular support for *Chega!* is also reinforced by the report's resonance with the widely endorsed national resistance narrative, which invokes collective experiences of suffering, fortitude and liberation against consecutive colonial occupiers. It suggests, too, a link to customary beliefs that emphasise the importance of revealing the 'source' of the conflict in order to end bad relations and acrimony, and to restore the good name of the ancestors. Arguably, then, because of the resonance of *Chega!* with pre-existing value systems and hence the ease of its translation into the vernacular, the overarching narrative in the CAVR report gained popular acceptance among interviewees.

Yet, in spite of their willingness to share their experiences, many survivors did not view the symbolic recognition of their experiences as the ultimate purpose of storytelling. Thus those who spoke at a CAVR public hearing generally articulated a desire to feel more than 'listened to'. As Maria from Lautem put it:

> The government needs to do something, not just listen to us. They should provide us with something . . . We tell our story, but when I speak about these things it impacts on me again . . . My suffering is very heavy. From my feet to my head I feel bad again.[12]

Similarly, as Fransisco, of Suai, stated:

> I felt unsatisfied with the hearings because the politicians who came listened with their mouths only but not with their *laran* [insides]. The President and Prime Minister came. They said our cases are not important, development is important. When I heard this I felt *laran moras* [sick/troubled inside].[13]

11 Interview in Los Palos, Lautem, 7 August 2007.
12 Ibid.
13 Interview in Suai, Covalima, 30 May 2007.

These views are an indication that survivors did not fully embrace the CAVR's therapeutic ethic, with its invocation of the healing power of truth for the individual and nation. That is, storytelling was not experienced as intrinsically healing, as many hoped that speaking of their experiences would lead to other, more 'practical', results, such as the public shaming and punishment of perpetrators, the recovery of bodies, economic assistance and the restoration of survivors' status in their communities.

Another related theme that emerged from interviews was that some survivors who participated in a CAVR public hearing had hoped for a 'direct' encounter with the perpetrator, often in order to establish facts that could lead to the recovery of bodies and to establish 'who was right and who was wrong'.[14] These hopes were reflected in the views expressed by Esmeralda, who had been raped during the 1999 post-referendum violence in Suai, and who spoke at a CAVR public hearing. Esmeralda emphasised the need to speak directly to the man who raped her: 'I want to talk to the perpetrator. Maybe he thinks that I have lied.'[15] For Esmeralda, a key requirement of justice was the need for a 'public discussion between the victim and perpetrator in the tribunal'. She had participated in the CAVR hearing under an erroneous assumption that she would be able to confront her rapist: 'I wanted to speak at the public meeting because I thought the *pelaku* (perpetrator) would be there, but he wasn't. I thought I would be able to meet my *pelaku*.'[16] Similar themes pervaded the comments of Kristina, from Liquica, a former member of the East Timorese women's organisation OMT (*Organisação da Mulher Timorense*/National Women's Organisation),[17] who had spoken at a district level hearing about her experiences of being arrested and detained by FRETILIN in the early 1980s, under suspicion of being a 'collaborator'. Kristina, like Esmeralda, had hoped for a face-to-face encounter with her perpetrator. She also desired a specific apology from the FRETILIN leadership:

> When I spoke I felt *fuan kanek* [broken-hearted] . . . I wanted a response from the government. I wanted to speak directly to those who punished me. I wanted to meet them . . . At the time I spoke I wanted a result but I haven't got a result. . . . We spoke with broken hearts, with tears, but they only know how to take our information. We don't yet have the truth because there is no response from the perpetrators.[18]

14 Interview in Salele, Covalima, 1 June 2007.
15 Interview in Salele, Covalima, 2 June 2007.
16 Ibid.
17 OMT was connected to CNRT.
18 Interview in Liquica, 28 July 2001.

Echoes of customary belief systems can be heard in Kristina and Esmeralda's desire to confront their perpetrator face-to-face in order to have them acknowledge their transgressions. These customary beliefs call for full disclosure of acts and the public 'shaming' of wrongdoers, to ensure that the wrong is fully resolved and that acrimony is not passed down to the next generation.

Expectations of discussions with perpetrators were, of course, foreclosed by the constraints of the CAVR's mandate itself. The fact that the national public hearings were designed to provide victims with an opportunity to tell their stories publicly, and to have them affirmed, but without perpetrators being present, precluded victims from hearing perpetrators' versions of events, receiving direct acknowledgement and apology, or learning the specific facts about the deaths of loved ones. These constraints exacerbated survivors' frustrations with the lack of 'results' from telling their stories.

Survivors' frustrations may well also be exacerbated by the lack of information they have received about *Chega!* At the time of fieldwork, many of those who had taken part in the CAVR's truth-seeking process had not yet seen a copy. The high levels of illiteracy in East Timor had created further obstacles for the distribution of *Chega!* – a 2,000-page document – in a meaningful form. These constraints had contributed to a widespread view that information provided to the CAVR disappeared into a 'black hole'. Indeed, a common question raised during my interviews with survivors was: 'What has happened to our information?' Thus, as Maria put it:

> The *audiensia* (public hearing) had an impact because we could tell our stories, but we have not had any results from the process. The good impact is that they have taken our information. But I want them to come and explain where our information has gone. Otherwise we feel *laran susar* (worried inside) without a response.[19]

Overall, the perceived lack of 'results' led some interviewees to be critical of the CAVR for being a short-term 'project' and to conclude that it was not concerned with victims' welfare.

Thus, although survivors emphasised the value of telling their stories and the writing of an official, public history, which suggests some important resonances between official and local narratives of justice, the fact that storytelling was generally not understood as the 'end goal' points to some significant differences. For many survivors, recounting their stories was not experienced as an intrinsically therapeutic process, but was seen as a means towards achieving other, more practical, results, such as material assistance, the recovery of the bodies of the missing, and prosecutions. In the next section, I unsettle the assumed link between storytelling and therapy further by

19 Interview in Salele, Covalima, 1 June 2007.

exploring some of the anxieties of survivors who spoke publicly about 'difficult' truths. These anxieties throw light on the inherent restrictions of the CAVR's form of recognition.

Ambivalence, hesitancy and the limits of CAVR recognition

While most survivors who participated in the CAVR's public hearings had done so willingly, this was not the case for all. As discussed in Chapter 3, some women did not participate in the CAVR because they believed their experiences were not important, because they were *moe* (ashamed/shy), or because they were expected to attend to domestic duties. For the small number of women who spoke publically about the sensitive issue of sexual abuse, the desire to tell their stories was mingled with a sense of 'shyness' or shame. This ambivalence was expressed by Gracilda, in Lautem, who had spoken at a public hearing about her experiences of being sexually abused by the Indonesian military following the capture and disappearance of her husband – a former primary school teacher and leader in the Clandestine movement. She described her hesitancy about speaking out:

> At the time I spoke at the public hearing in Dili I felt *moe* [ashamed/ shy]. I thought of my body, my family who died, my husband who had died. When they asked me to speak I knew I should speak because in the past I was sad. We have independence now so we have to tell our stories. We are women, we should not have been threatened the way we were. The big people asked us to speak and we were happy to speak.[20]

Importantly, Gracilda's account of her husband's disappearance following his interrogation by Indonesian military at the local military post, which is reproduced in the CAVR's public hearing book on political imprisonment, places her suffering in the context of the resistance struggle. She suggests that bringing up her child to resist the Indonesian military was an act of patriotism and a way of continuing her husband's legacy:

> When I arrived home my husband said to me, 'My wife, I will go and face Military Post 641. I believe I will not return. I have only one child. May this child replace me. It may be that after I am gone you will be made the sex-slave of the Military Battalion 641. But be strong and patient. All of this is happening because of the political conflict, and so that we can free ourselves from the oppressor. If we do not return, record our stories, because the time will come when everyone will ask about us. May you be

20 Interview in Poros, Lautem, 6 August 2007.

> our witness that we struggled for the liberation of our nation.' After saying this, my husband was taken to Military Post 641 in Lalua Lopo.
>
> (CAVR 2005d: 43)

Another interviewee, Mariana, from Muapitine, in Lautem, had experienced years of sexual abuse following the death of her husband in 1983. Mariana spoke at a CAVR public hearing about the horrific massacre in her village, in which five men, including her husband, had been killed during a publicly organised *festa* (celebration/party) by the Indonesian military in 1983 in which the community was forced to participate. Like Gracilda, she also sought to link her suffering to the liberation struggle, and did so by recounting the last words of her husband to her as 'Kiss my hand and go and look after our children. I want to have descendants' (CAVR 2005c: 45). Mariana and Gracilda's testimonies show that one way for women to navigate speaking out about their experiences of sexual violence – which continue to be stigmatised, shameful and excluded from official narratives of national identity – was to situate these experiences within the broader context of their husbands' involvement in the liberation struggle, thereby linking their suffering to the nation's struggle.

Ambivalence and hesitancy also pervaded the comments of those who had testified about violence committed by East Timorese political parties during the 1970s and 1980s. I encountered a number of survivors who had spoken about these experiences and, through conversations with them, gained a deeper appreciation of the unresolved and 'unspeakable' nature of these issues. One such survivor, Angelo, whose experiences I described earlier, alluded to the stigma attached to speaking publicly about the issue of FRETILIN violence: 'Before the CAVR hearing, I had not even spoken of these things to my own children.'[21] During a conversation with Angelo's son, after the interview, I was told that Angelo had still not talked to his children about these events, and had refused to allow them to watch the video-recording of his testimony. According to his son, this was because he did not want the children to 'beat up' those he named as responsible for the massacre. Angelo's reluctance to speak to his children also suggests the significance of customary belief systems in that, because the 'source' of the dispute has not yet been fully acknowledged and atoned for, the bad relations and enmity may be passed down to the next generation.

A further complication for Angelo, and other victims of East Timorese political-party violence, is that many of those suspected of ordering, or committing, the acts in question remain present in the country, and some are now members of the political elite. This means that, while they have experienced shame and unease about speaking out, telling their stories has also

21 Interview in Los Palos, Lautem, 8 August 2007.

fostered hopes of acknowledgement by the leadership. Angelo, for example, had hoped for public recognition and an apology from the FRETILIN leadership in order to restore his family's name:

> When we spoke at the CAVR I felt I wanted to cry, I felt *laran susar*. It was good that people from other nations came and listened to me. Timorese people also came, Parliamentarians came. But until now we don't have any result. They killed so many of my family, they need to ask for sorry. I ask those who ordered these things to happen to ask for sorry, they need to declare this.[22]

Angelo had also hoped that speaking out about his experiences would yield information from the leadership that would lead to the recovery of the bodies of his family members:

> We still don't have their bodies. The state needs to help us find them. I want to speak directly to FRETILIN and ask them to look for our family's bodies. The CAVR has made a book. But I want to speak to the President of the Republic of Timor-Leste.[23]

Another victim of FRETILIN violence was João, from Los Palos, who gave testimony at a CAVR public hearing about his experiences in 1979. João had been held prisoner by FRETILIN for six months and interrogated. His brother, a FRETILIN regional commander, had been killed due to accusations of being a 'traitor', and the whereabouts of his body remained unknown. Like Angelo, João expressed deep ambivalence about speaking about these issues. He had agreed to take part in the public hearing because he believed it could help him find information about the location of his brother's body and he had hoped to recover his brother's remains in order to give him a proper burial. Following the hearing, the widow of João's deceased brother has been writing regularly to Xanana Gusmão to request assistance in identifying the place where he was killed and exhuming his body. João explained that, for him, 'justice' was to know the truth and have the body of his younger brother recovered.[24]

Angelo and João's comments evoke the anxieties of those accused of being 'traitors' or 'collaborators', and their desire to rehabilitate their family's name by having this label formally revoked by the leadership. There was, however, no possibility of this kind of rehabilitation by way of the CAVR's public hearing process. As previously discussed, during the public hearing on the

22 Ibid.
23 Ibid.
24 Interview in Los Palos, Lautem, 9 August 2007.

internal political conflict, political leaders did not divulge specific information regarding the names of those killed and the places where they were killed, nor did they take direct responsibility for this violence. For João and Angelo, the leadership's continuing silence about these issues means that their suffering continues to reverberate and that their acute need to recover the bodies of their family members, in order to provide some form of resolution and conduct the appropriate burial rites, remains unaddressed.

For victims of East Timorese political-party violence and sexual violence, then, truth-telling has been painful and difficult, and has afforded little change to the liminal status they occupy. While the CAVR has attempted to include stories of East Timorese political-party violence within the broader story of the nation, the labels of 'collaborator' and 'traitor' – which provide a counterpoint to the term 'hero' – continue to play a powerful role in popular conceptions of national identity. Similarly, the recognition of women's experiences of sexual violence remains circumscribed by the precarious and stigmatised position they continue to occupy within a deeply conservative, patriarchal and Catholic society.

Another group that did not always wholeheartedly embrace the truth-telling opportunity was comprised of self-described activists or members of the formal resistance movement. During my field research, it became clear that many activists did not wish to regard themselves as victims, and the association of victimhood with passivity and a lack of agency was implicit in their accounts about why they chose not to participate in the CAVR. Edilmiro, for example, a former staff member of the CAVR, suggested that although he had been imprisoned and tortured by Kopassus from 1991 to 1994, he did not consider himself a victim because he had been a member of the Clandestine movement:

> About my case, I feel that we needed independence. Justice for me means getting independence. Cases are different. I was involved in the Clandestine. Everyone was victim. Because I went to prison my objective was clear. It was to get independence.[25]

At times, self-described activists did participate in the CAVR's public hearings, but sought to contest the CAVR's categorisation of them as victims. For example, Simplisio Celestino de Deus, who spoke at the Public Hearing on 'Massacres', began his testimony by stating:

> The first thing I want to say is that I do not see myself as a victim. I see myself as a combatant who struggled and who, fired by patriotism, succeeded in liberating our land.
>
> (CAVR 2005c: 50)

25 Interview in Liquica, 29 July 2007.

For East Timorese activists, victims are often deemed to be 'other people' – widows, orphans, those disabled because of the war, those in more economically vulnerable positions than themselves and those who did not have opportunities to study abroad. These findings resonate with research in other contexts, including Fiona Ross's work on South Africa, which explored why many individuals involved in the anti-apartheid struggle did not participate in the Truth and Reconciliation Commission. Ross writes:

> activists did not make statements because they felt that the Commission's ideals ran counter to those that had provided impetus for the struggle. Ideas about collective action and the greater good that had informed their mobilisation seemed subverted in the Commission's insistence of the primacy of the individual.
>
> (Ross 2003a: 158)

Even those who did seek to be publicly identified as 'victims' were not always pleased with the way in which their experiences of violence were recognised by the CAVR. As discussed in Chapter 3, one effect of the legal human rights violations framework, which underpinned the CAVR's work, was to reduce the complex, highly personalised and long-term nature of individuals' suffering the experience of a particular 'direct' human rights violation, for example torture, sexual assault or imprisonment. The testimonies of individuals who spoke publicly were also shaped to conform to the specific themes of the CAVR public hearings and were endowed with a broader 'nation-building' purpose. These constraints led some survivors to express frustration about the form of recognition they had received. Francisco, for example, who spoke at the CAVR Public Hearing on 'Famine', expressed the view that the CAVR had omitted large swathes of his story from the public hearing book:

> When I went to speak in Dili it was about the famine. In the book they only wrote about my experiences with the famine. But when they came to take my testimony I gave information about a lot more than this. I spoke about my life in the jungle, my capture, my imprisonment.[26]

Gracilda, a widow from Lautem who, as discussed earlier, had spoken at a CAVR public hearing about the forced disappearance of her husband in the early 1980s, was acutely aware of the impossibility of ever rendering into words her highly personalised, long-term, experiences of suffering:

26 Interview in Los Palos, Lautem, 9 August 2007.

> I went to speak to the big people but only I can know my suffering. They can't understand this. And you can write as much as you like, 100 pages even, and still you won't know my suffering.[27]

The views of both self-described activists and victims point to the limits of recognition on the basis of victimhood and the inherent constraints of the 'human rights violations framework' that underpinned the CAVR's work. They illuminate the way in which victims tend to be portrayed in human rights literature as passive – 'the locus of inflicted power' – rather than as active agents (Ross 2003a: 76). This portrayal was constricting in that it prevented individuals from ascribing their own personal meanings to their experiences. In addition, the CAVR's framework was unable to do 'justice' to the ideals of collective struggle and liberation that had motivated many individuals to become involved in the resistance movement.

The community reconciliation process: a tentative and conditional acceptance

Respondents rarely raised community reconciliation as a hoped-for 'result' from the transitional justice process. Nonetheless, when prompted to discuss the CAVR's CRP, those who had participated in this process expressed views that appeared to resonate with the formal goals of the CAVR, at least initially. One of the reasons for this is perhaps because, as discussed in Chapter 3, the CRP, which was designed to reintegrate local perpetrators responsible for so-called 'less serious crimes' committed during the 1999 referendum period, built upon pre-existing customary dispute resolution practices. Indeed, in some areas, communities had already conducted their own local conciliation and reintegration processes for returning refugees without any UNTAET or CAVR involvement. This was particularly evident in the district of Covalima, where, due to their proximity to the West Timor border, local communities had been forced to grapple with the reintegration of returnees soon after the referendum, long before the CAVR commenced its CRP. In these cases, the CRP hearings had provided a familiar method with which to consolidate these earlier processes. In other cases, communities had been unable to conduct their own *nahe biti* processes for returning refugees due to a lack of funds; in these cases, the CAVR had provided much-needed resources for the purchase of food for ceremonial feasts.

Given their location at the *suco* (village) and *aldeia* (hamlet) level and their flexible format, the CAVR's community reconciliation hearings enabled the participation of a far wider array of community members than the public victims' hearings. Many respondents had taken part in a CRP hearing in their local community and most endorsed them as an appropriate way in which to

27 Interview in Poros, Lautem, 6 August 2007.

resolve less serious matters. In this sense, then, community attitudes appeared to accord with the distinction made in the transitional justice process between serious and less serious crimes. As a male community leader in Covalima put it: 'If there are small problems they can be resolved in the *suco*, through the *nahe biti*, but big problems must be the priority. They need to follow the law of the nation.'[28] Similarly, as Maria, whose husband was killed during the 1999 post-referendum violence, explained: 'About burning houses, destroying things, we can *nahe biti*. But not for murder, because I have lost something big. We can make a house, we can replace our things, but we can't replace a person.'[29] Some community leaders expressed disappointment that the CRP process had ended prematurely, when there remained many former militia who were still willing to participate. As a *Chefe de Suco* in Lautem explained: 'We still need reconciliation. Many are still in West Timor. Many want to come back. The CRP can open the door to them.'[30]

Despite this apparent resonance between official goals and local expectations, satisfaction with the CRP process appeared to be contingent on a range of factors. One of these was the extent to which community members believed that deponents had told the 'whole truth', which in some cases was doubted (see also Larke 2009). Lino, for example, a *Chefe de Suco* in Covalima, suggested that he did not believe that deponents had told the whole truth:

> There were many victims at the *nahe biti bo'ot* [CRP hearing]. But because we were family we said the problem had already passed. Victims and militia are family . . . We gave peace and shook hands at the end. The militia who spoke said they didn't do anything wrong. To my observation some spoke the truth, others didn't . . . Victims were not satisfied with the process because even those who did do wrong said they didn't.[31]

Similar frustrations about the lack of 'truthfulness' were voiced during my 2004 study of the CRP, including by a young widow in Los Palos, whose husband Virgilio was killed in 1999:

> When 'Aze' [the deponent] came to speak at the CAVR I went to hear him. He said he didn't know who killed Virgilio. But I said to him 'you were a big person in the *Tim Alpha* [militia] how can you have not known?' He didn't speak the truth. If the CAVR comes here again there is no point, we don't get any result.
>
> (Cited in Kent 2004: 25)

28 Interview in Suai, Covalima, 29 May 2007.

29 Ibid.

30 Interview in Titilari, Lautem, 10 August 2007.

31 Interview in Beco, Covalima, 30 May 2007.

Such statements suggest a link to customary ideas of justice, discussed earlier, which stress the centrality of acknowledging the 'source' of the conflict and declaring past transgressions, in order to end the cycle of vengeance and to restore the status of the wronged parties. In many cases, aspirations to learn the whole truth were also foreclosed by the CRP's mandate, which was focused on the 1999 time period, was restricted to 'less serious' crimes and could only consider reconciliation between those present in the territory of East Timor. Another limitation was that, unlike the customary *nahe biti* process, victims did not receive direct compensation through the CRP hearings. The frustrations arising from these constraints suggest the extent to which the CRP left many issues unresolved.

The fact that more serious perpetrators have evaded punishment through the Serious Crimes Process has further exacerbated community frustrations with the CRP process. That only those perceived to have been the 'small fish' have been required to atone for their acts has fostered considerable scepticism of the reconciliation project. Thus, as one individual put it: 'The CAVR has a good programme, but people are asking what is its *rohan* [end point]?'[32] As another stated: 'Reconciliation can have value, or not have value. It does not have value if it's just a story. It has value if it leads to justice.'[33] In this context, the 'peace' delivered by the CAVR is perceived to be fragile and tenuous. As Ermegildo, in Suai, put it:

> The CAVR did help to create peace but the serious crimes have not been resolved. New problems can arise, because of what happened in the past. Victims now wait for the results . . . If those who committed serious crimes do not have their crimes resolved, they can commit them again. Or, victims can become perpetrators.[34]

Those who were victims of 'serious crimes', in the form of torture, loss of family members during the conflict and rape, often actively resisted the CAVR's philosophy of community reconciliation and peace. Some of these individuals did not attend the CRP hearings, or did not participate 'wholeheartedly'. As Rosa, in Suai, explained: 'I didn't participate in the *nahe biti* because I lost my husband. I don't want peace because I still don't have justice.'[35] Francisco, whose mother was killed in the 1999 violence, was similarly critical:

32 Interview in Beco, Covalima, 31 May 2007.
33 Ibid.
34 Ibid.
35 Interview in Salele, Covalima, 1 June 2007.

> Reconciliation is not a road to justice. They are 100 kilometres apart. Reconciliation is not important. It just increases people's thinking, their stress, because it does not lead to justice.[36]

Hermina explained that she continued to have her own individual feelings about the deponents and to 'think badly of them', despite participating in a CRP hearing. Regina, who lost her husband in 1999, suggested that she only participated in the CRP because 'people might think I don't want peace if I don't'. In this sense, then, Hermina and Regina – who had participated in the CRP because they had also been victims of a 'less serious crime' – appeared actively to resist the CAVR's goals of reconciliation and peace, which were perceived as undermining the gravity and ongoing nature of their pain.

Regina's comments also allude to the extent to which there could be an element of pressure involved in gaining people's participation in the CRP process, either from community leaders or from CAVR staff. As discussed in Chapter 3, pre-existing power relations in local villages and the fiery reconciliatory rhetoric of CAVR commissioners could sometimes influence individuals to reconcile with a deponent rather than to request a heavy sanction. These experiences also suggest that, far from being the sites of cohesion, the CRP hearings – like the *nahe biti* process on which they were based – could reinforce pre-existing power relationships within local communities. Ben Larke (2009), former adviser to the CRP, has also noted this to be the case, suggesting that the CRP hearings sometimes became a basis for local leaders to re-establish the 'local order of things' that had been disrupted during the Indonesian occupation through a process of public shaming:

> The social fissures that were the legacy of the Indonesian occupation, and resultant power vacuum on its departure, represented a significant challenge to community politics. Such a public event [as the CRP] which called to account those who had strayed from the path and held them up in a public shaming exercise, demonstrated the resurrection of past community-based hierarchies of power.
>
> (Larke 2009: 679)

As previously noted, this 'local order' is male-dominated and tends to uphold the position of particular powerful families.

The question of *who* was being asked to reconcile was also raised during interviews. Many respondents were acutely aware that reconciliation was being expected of local communities rather than the political elite. Expectations placed upon local communities to air events honestly and reconcile with one another were juxtaposed with the leadership's secrecy and unwillingness to

36 Interview in Suai, Covalima, 2 June 2007

take responsibility for their acts. As one interviewee asked: 'Why should we have reconciliation out in the open while the leaders do theirs in hotels, behind closed doors? They should be out in the open too.'[37] Another stated:

> If we really want justice and reconciliation then the leadership needs to take responsibility for their actions. We can't just have reconciliation at the *baze* [community level] only. The leaders need to get together and work out their own problems. This will have an impact on the people.[38]

These issues were particularly salient given that a new community 'dialogue' process had been initiated following the 2006 'crisis' to respond to a spate of house burnings and conflicts between easterners and westerners. Some interviewees had begun to greet these dialogues with a sense of weariness and as a replacement for more substantive 'results': 'reconciliation as a substitute for justice; dialogue instead of meaningfully addressing problems or taking action' (Larke 2009: 674). Community reconciliation was also perceived by some as a means of diverting attention away from the responsibilities of the political leadership for the events of 2006. Although local attitudes about the crisis could reflect particular political-party allegiances, and hence mirror the divisions amongst their political leaders, there was nonetheless a more general view expressed that the 'big people' collectively had to sort out their grievances, many of which were perceived to have a basis in the internal political conflict of 1974–75.

Despite their awareness of the limitations of the CRP processes, there were cases in which individuals and local communities worked creatively to navigate the hearings and to extend their boundaries to pursue their own personal goals. For example, individuals who were not necessarily committed to the official goals of the CRP sometimes viewed the hearings as useful arenas for furthering their efforts to gain 'facts' that might be relevant to the recovery of bodies, or future prosecutions, or as a means to clear their family's name in relation to a pre-existing dispute (see also Kent 2004). This was evident in an interview I conducted in 2004 with a young widow in Ermera. Although she was disappointed with the lack of 'results' from the CAVR in the form of practical material assistance and prosecutions, this young woman explained that the CRP had been useful to some extent because it had helped her to identify witnesses who saw her husband being killed. She hoped that this would lead to a prosecution one day (Kent 2004). Such comments also allude to the extent to which, despite the restriction of the CRP mandate to 'less serious crimes', CRP discussions could range into the territory of more serious crimes as accusations were made in the heat of the moment.

37 Interview in Liquica, 28 June 2007.

38 Interview in Suai, Covalima, 7 June 2007.

The creative use of the CRP process by survivors, local leaders and other community members to pursue specific local agendas was also evident in the CRP hearing conducted in a small *aldeia* in Lautem.[39] In this case, the impetus for a hearing came from villagers and the *Chefe de Aldeia* who wanted to 'clarify' facts surrounding the 1999 murder of a father of seven, 'Gil', allegedly by *Tim Alfa* militia members from a neighbouring *aldeia*. While the CAVR staff explained to the community that they could not run hearings for serious crimes, they nevertheless agreed that a hearing could be organised in this community to discuss a less serious issue that related to the burning of a house and minor assault in 1999 by members of the neighbouring *aldeia*. The CAVR then gained the consent to participate of three deponents who were suspected by the *aldeia* of involvement in the murder as well as these less serious crimes issues. Despite the attempts of the CAVR commissioners and Panel members to confine the discussion to the less serious crimes, Gil's family, and the local community, used this hearing to challenge one of the deponents – 'Ze' – about the extent of his knowledge about the murder (see Kent 2004). The hearing thus served as a means of exposing and chastising 'Ze' in a context in which the public shaming of perpetrators and the restoration of the reputation of the victim's family is an important aspect of customary understandings of justice.

On the whole, then, it appears that the CRP was accepted by respondents because it offered a familiar method of resolving community-level disputes. In this sense, its work could be translated into the vernacular. At the same time, the fact that many survivors hoped for more than the symbolic recognition of their experiences of suffering in the form of compensation for their losses, learning the 'whole truth' and the prosecution of serious crimes perpetrators is indicative of the tenuous and conditional nature of this acceptance, and points to the differences between the CRP and customary dispute resolution processes.

Justice as trials, declarations and punishment

The need for prosecutions and punishment was a strong theme in local accounts of justice, suggesting, on the face of it, a high level of support for the concepts of rule of law and retributive justice promoted by the Serious Crimes Process (if not actually delivered in practice). Yet, digging a little deeper, it was apparent that there were some significant differences between international and local retribution narratives. This suggests that, as Tim Kelsall (2009: 16) has argued in the context of Sierra Leone, it should not be assumed that local desires for retribution can be conflated with wholesale endorsement of the norms and practices of criminal justice.

39 Interviews in Somocho, Lautem, 6–7 August 2007.

On the face of it, there appeared to be a general consensus that perpetrators of murder and rape needed to be tried in an official public forum, and severely punished, generally by sending them to jail. While customary means of resolving cases involving serious offences may have been acceptable in *avo nia tempo* (their grandparent's time), some respondents explained, they were no longer acceptable today. As Ana Maria, whose husband had been killed in 1999, stated:

> Formal justice is important. Because when someone commits a crime we cannot feel good about this, our *laran moras* [sickness/ worry] will still be there until he goes to jail. If he gets a punishment I will feel calm. Otherwise, if he doesn't I could commit a crime against him.[40]

Salvador, a *Chefe de Suco* in Liquica, similarly remarked:

> The *nahe biti* is for small crimes, like beating. Killing has to go through the tribunal, and to jail. In our culture in the past we could resolve this in our community, but now we have a change in our state. In *avo nia tempo* [our grandparent's time] we could resolve according to *adat* [custom]. But now we have a state.[41]

Many respondents stressed that in the absence of prosecutions, people will continue to harbour vengeance against one another, passing it down to the next generation and perpetuating a cycle of violence. As Ermegildo, a community leader in Covalima, stated: 'If those who committed serious crimes do not have their crimes resolved they can commit them again, or victims can become perpetrators.'[42] Prosecutions were viewed by respondents as important to provide satisfaction to individual victims, to teach perpetrators a lesson, and for their broader contribution to nation-building by ending a cycle of vengeance. Thus, as one male survivor stated: 'It's important for justice to go ahead, otherwise Timor cannot go ahead . . . With justice our thinking can reduce, our anger can reduce and our nation can become peaceful.'[43] Another key component of justice as understood by survivors appeared to revolve around the need for perpetrators to publicly 'declare' what they did and to ask for forgiveness. As Esmeralda put it:

> Justice is very important for us because of our children's future and our grandchildren. For me, I have received many violations. But I want that

40 Interview in Liquica, 25 June 2007.
41 Interview in Muapitine, Lautem, 10 August 2007.
42 Interview in Matai, Covalima, 1 June 2007.
43 Interview in Suai, Covalima, 31 May 2007.

> they can't do it again to our children. Justice means if I kill someone, someone needs to bring us together to discuss. And if they have wronged, they have to go to jail. There has to be a discussion between the victim and perpetrator in the tribunal.[44]

Similarly, as Regina in Dili explained:

> Justice means to take people to the tribunal to find out whether they are right or wrong. It's not up to the family members to decide, it's up to the tribunal to give a sentence. The perpetrator needs to explain what happened, to declare what happened, to tell the truth.[45]

The importance attached to ideas of public explanation and declaration suggests that there is more to local expectations of justice than prosecutions alone. Echoes of customary justice concepts that emphasise the need for public acknowledgement of wrongdoing in order to shame the perpetrator, re-establish the status of the wronged party, rehabilitate family names and end long-standing cycles of vengeance can be heard. In the absence of such public shaming, there can remain a perception that the 'wrong' has not been fully resolved and that the victims' family remains in a position of weakness. Aspirations for public declaration and explanations would be unlikely to be met however, through the rigid trial procedures and rules of evidence of a criminal justice process, which inevitably treat victims as one source of evidence among many, limit the way in which stories can be told, and circumscribe opportunities for face-to-face discussions between victims and suspects.

Discussions about *who* should be prosecuted also revealed diverse opinions. At one level, there was a broad consensus that the 'big fish' – namely, senior members of the Indonesian military – should be prosecuted. The inability of the Serious Crimes Process to fulfil its own mandate by holding to account those 'most responsible' has undoubtedly contributed to the acute sense of 'injustice' felt by many respondents. As Justino, from Lautem, put it: 'People are not *puas* [satisfied] because only those who carried guns, not those who made the orders, are in jail. Justice is still not *los* [right].'[46] Similarly, Maria, in Suai, eloquently expressed the view that 'justice has fallen in the middle'.[47] Understandably, popular desires for the trial and punishment of members of the Indonesian military reflect the importance of making *visible* the gravity of Indonesian violence and contesting the official Indonesian narrative that its twenty-four-year governance of the territory had been benevolent.

44 Interview in Salele, Covalima, 1 June 2007.
45 Interview in Dili, 27 June 2007.
46 Interview in Titilari, Lautem, 6 August 2007.
47 Interview in Suai, Covalima, 4 June 2007.

Beyond these views about the 'big fish', a range of opinions were expressed about whether prosecutions were required for the many East Timorese militia members who carried out violent acts in 1999. Some were adamant that trials should be held for all those who were involved in organising or committing serious crimes, such as murder or rape. Thus, as Rosa put it, trials are needed for 'those with blood on their hands' and 'blood on their mouths'.[48] Similar views were expressed by a *Chefe de Suco* in Liquica, who spoke of his satisfaction that a local militia leader involved in a murder had been imprisoned, although this was tinged with an awareness that many others remain beyond the reach of the law:

> If he didn't go to jail we would not be happy. But he has gone, even for a month or a few days, it's important, because he has to go to jail . . . He has killed, he has destroyed. He got justice . . . But there are still many others in Atambua [in West Timor]. We still wait for the others to come back.[49]

Others, however, did not appear to believe that prosecutions were necessary for East Timorese militia members who were sometimes referred to as 'little people' or 'stupid people' who had been coerced into committing violent acts. For example, José from Liquica suggested that he could forgive the East Timorese militia member who struck him with a machete during the 1999 Liquica church massacre, but not those who ordered the violence:

> The militia hit me with a *katana* [machete] but behind them were the Indonesian military . . . Some of the militia have come back [from West Timor]. I don't feel bad towards them because the military made them do it – they gave them money, food . . . I have forgiven the militia but I want the person who gave the support, the guns, to go to justice. They have to go to the tribunal.[50]

A *Chefe de Suco* in Covalima also alluded to the sensitivities that would be involved in prosecuting lower-level militia members in his village, given the strength of family ties:

48 Interview in Maucatar, Covalima, 28 May 2007.

49 Interview in Metagou, Liquica, 3 July 2007. Interestingly, even though this militia member had only served five years of his murder sentence, the views of this *Chefe de Suco* suggest that the symbolic public shaming he had received through his trial, conviction and imprisonment had been enough to constitute 'justice' in this particular case.

50 Interview in Liquica, 2 July 2007.

> In my opinion it was not the small people who committed the crimes. Maybe the government wants to take the process ahead, but we don't want this in our *suco* . . . they are our family.[51]

The issue of 'justice' in relation to 'pre-1999' violence was also raised by some respondents, including violence committed by East Timorese political parties during the internal political conflict of 1974–75 and throughout the Indonesian occupation, although there was similarly little consensus on what should be done about these cases. Kristina, for example, from Liquica, who, as previously discussed, had been imprisoned by FRETILIN in the 1980s as a suspected 'collaborator', was adamant that she wanted her captors to be formally punished:

> They need to explain what they did, otherwise we will continue to *odi malu* [harbour vengeance] . . . They need to be punished otherwise I don't want to make peace with them . . . I still wait. My children now have children but I still wait for justice.[52]

Despite her emphasis on punishment, Kristina's reference to the need for 'explanation' suggests a link to the importance, within customary dispute resolution practices, for the 'whole story' to be told. As discussed above, this would be unlikely to be achieved through the narrow parameters of the criminal law.

Others were more willing to accept violence instigated by East Timorese political parties, and suggested that much of this occurred as a 'consequence of the conflict'. Inacio in Lautem remarked, for example, that:

> For the pre 1999 issues I think we don't need justice. Because this means that Timorese will also need to face justice as well, including the Prime Minister and President, because everyone committed crimes. Then who will build this nation?[53]

Similarly, as a *Chefe de Suco* in Lautem said: 'If we have justice for all of this [the pre-1999 crimes] there will be a big confusion. We need to say it was a consequence of the war.'[54]

The fact that diverse opinions were expressed about the prosecution of East Timorese actors underscores the close-knit nature of communities, where bonds of dependency are high, and where 'victims' and 'perpetrators' may

51 Interview in Beco, Covalima, 7 June 2007.

52 Interview in Liquica, 28 July 2007.

53 Interview in Muapitine, Lautem, 10 August 2007.

54 Interview in Muapitine, Lautem 9 August 2007.

often be related. In this context, strategies of accommodation and reconciliation may be a practical necessity. It suggests, too, that, like their political leaders, some community members perceive that, within the coercive context of the Indonesian occupation, people had often 'collaborated' in order to survive and, as members of civil defence units, the Indonesian intelligence, political parties, the Indonesian military and police, and, more recently, as militia members in 1999, they had sometimes been implicated in violence. In this sense, they evince a complex awareness of what Primo Levi has termed the 'gray zone': 'a morally ambiguous space of mutual betrayal and complicity with the enemy' where people are 'engaged in a "desperate, covert and continuous struggle" to survive' (Levi, in Scheper Hughes and Bourgois 2004: 10). These understandings contrast with the notions of criminal justice promoted by the Serious Crimes Process, which emphasised the agency and responsibility of individual actors and produced bifurcated positions of 'victim' and 'perpetrator'. Traces of the national resistance narrative – in which the East Timorese people are referred to as the 'little people', who should not turn against one another – can also be heard, suggesting that this narrative continues to exert a potent influence on many survivors' ideas of justice.

The Serious Crimes Process as a continuation of *injustice*

The limits of criminal justice processes in meeting survivors' situated understandings of justice has shown itself in many of the above stories; it was even more obvious in two encounters I had with individuals who had experienced the successful trial of a perpetrator by the Special Panels. In the first encounter, I met with 'Isabel' in the hills behind Liquica, whose husband had been killed during the post-referendum violence by a member of the East Timorese *Besi Merah Putih* (Red and White Iron) militia group. Although the perpetrator of this crime had been prosecuted and imprisoned, he had been jailed for only five years before being released. During my conversation with Isabel, it soon became apparent that material preoccupations, rather than the length of the perpetrator's sentence, were her foremost priorities. Isabel expressed disappointment that the criminal justice process had not had any practical outcomes:

> It was *los* [right] that he [the perpetrator] went to jail. But he came out and he has a wife and children, but I am still alone . . . The state needs to think about me. Who is going to look after our day-to-day lives?[55]

As a widow with children, living in a remote rural area, Isabel continues to occupy a marginalised status in her community. Struggling to find enough

55 Interview in Lauhata, Liquica, 27 July 2007.

money to buy food and to pay for her children's education, her house, which had been burnt during the 1999 violence, had still not been repaired. Compounding Isabel's frustration was the fact that she had received no formal information about the trial outcome, or the eventual release of the perpetrator, which she knew about only because community leaders informed her: 'We didn't know when he went to jail and we didn't know when he was released. We feel that the trial, the imprisonment, was secret, it was not public.'[56] Isabel's comments suggest, then, that, rather than delivering 'justice', the Serious Crimes Process has been experienced as a continuation of injustice and marginalisation.

In the second encounter, I met with 'Maria' in Leuro, Lautem. This meeting – described at the beginning of this chapter – provided another indication of the way in which the Serious Crimes Process has not been able to meet the material needs of survivors. Maria's lament that the state has considered the interests of Joni Marques and other militia leaders before her own suggests that she was less concerned with the fact that the murderer of her child had not completed his custodial sentence than that the government (or the Serious Crimes Process) had not attended to her material needs.[57] Maria's reluctance to criticise the recent presidential *indultos* (pardons) may also have reflected her delicate family situation, due to the fact that the murderer of her child was related to her husband's family. Like other rural East Timorese, Maria's family lives in a close-knit community, where bonds of dependency are high, and where victims and perpetrators are often related; this often makes the need for 'reconciliation' a practical necessity.

In addition to illuminating the inherent constraints of criminal justice in addressing ongoing experiences of poverty, the experience of Isabel in particular illustrates many of the practical constraints on the Serious Crimes Process discussed in Chapter 3, among them the lack of attention to community outreach. These restrictions were also reflected in the frustrations of other respondents with the lack of feedback that they had been provided about the progress of their case, and the fact that evidence, including victims' remains, had not been returned. Regina, for example, had been interviewed a number of times by investigators from the SCIU regarding her husband's death in 1999 during the Maliana police station massacre. She expressed her anger that the SCIU had yet to return several items of her husband's clothing, which she had provided as evidence:

> They [serious crimes investigators] should not promise things and then not deliver. They closed without telling us. They need to explain this to us and to give me back my husband's things. We lose time if they keep

56 Ibid.
57 Interview in Leuro, Lautem, 14 June 2008.

> coming and explaining to us why they can't arrest people . . . These things are our *heranca* [heritage/ legacy].[58]

Regina also spoke of feeling that she had been treated like a 'project' by the SCIU:

> They [serious crimes investigators] keep coming and asking the same questions, taking the same data. We feel they have just come and taken our information and put it in a cabinet to make their final report. We feel like a 'project'.[59]

The term 'project' – which was also used by some survivors in relation to the CAVR – has particularly derogatory connotations in the East Timor context, where it is associated with Indonesian economic development projects, in which corrupt Indonesian officials pocketed resources intended for local communities. The choice of this term also suggests that many survivors felt that they had been treated in instrumentalist terms, rather than as individuals with unique experiences and needs. It highlights, too, the inevitable tensions that exist between victims' desires for recognition and the restrictions of transitional justice processes, which will always use victims' testimonies for a broader purpose.

Rui, in Suai, expressed anger that the SCIU had taken so long to return the remains of his brother after autopsy. By the time these remains were returned, it was too late to bury his brother at the site of the new memorial along with others who had been killed during the Suai church massacre:

> In 2004, the *malae* [foreigners/SCIU staff] came and said we are going to bring your brother's bones back. I said I would not receive this. I was angry because they had the remains for a year and a half. I asked whether I was going to receive them 'empty' [ie, with no assistance for a burial] . . . I ran to the Church and spoke to the priest, but they had already closed the cement of the monument [of the Suai Church memorial] so I couldn't put the remains there. So I then agreed to receive the body but only when the *malae* agreed to provide me with money for a separate monument because he could not be buried in Suai . . . But if I had more money I would make a better monument.[60]

In another highly unusual case that I encountered, the SCIU had somehow 'lost' the remains of a young man, whose body had been exhumed from a site

58 Interview in Dili, 27 June 2007.
59 Ibid.
60 Interview in Beco, Covalima, 8 June 2007.

near Liquica. The father of the victim, 'João', had not been informed about the exhumation from the SCIU, but had heard about it from others in the community. Some years afterwards, the remains had still not been returned, having been misplaced. This was continuing to cause anguish as it meant that customary burial rituals could not be undertaken.

The anger and distress expressed by Rui and João provide another example of the way in which the Serious Crimes Process could be experienced as a continuation of injustice. These cases show that the customary obligations of families to the *matebian* (the ancestors/ghosts of the dead) could clash with the requirements of the SCIU, for example in relation to the length of time needed to conduct autopsies. Rui's response to the staff of the SCIU – his request to them for material assistance to buy cement to build his own memorial – highlights his creative and assertive attempts to extend the boundaries of the criminal law to meet his personal need to bury his brother in accordance with the demands of custom. In João's case, however, the incompetence of the SCIU means that these customary obligations remain unfulfilled, condemning the dead child to become a 'wandering ghost'.

Tensions between the requirements of formal criminal justice processes and survivors' responsibilities to the dead have also arisen in relation to requests by the SCIT to exhume bodies. Some survivors have expressed reluctance to exhume the remains of their loved ones, for whom, ten years on from the referendum, burial rites have been conducted. These issues emerged during a discussion with Regina, in Lautem, who, in 2008, had been offered $50 by the SCIU to allow the exhumation of her husband's remains, who had been killed in 1999. These funds – which were presumably to enable the reburial of the body following autopsy – were 'not enough' according to Regina, 'because we have followed *adat* (custom) already, we can't just dig it up'.[61] At the same time, Regina continues to demand 'justice' from the Serious Crimes Process, in the form of prosecution of her husband's perpetrator, again highlighting the disconnection between local expectations and the limits and requirements of the law.

The observations of Rui, Regina and Isabel reinforce the argument that, while perhaps meeting the procedural requirements of prosecutions – for example the rules of evidence, the burden of proof, and imprisonment and punishment for those convicted – criminal justice processes will nevertheless be unable to fully recognise survivors' unique demands for justice, as this is variously understood within their singular experiences. That is, even if the Serious Crimes Process had been able to prosecute a larger number of cases (including Indonesian perpetrators) and had been more responsive to the needs of victims, for example by providing regular feedback on the progress of their case, survivors' expectations of justice may well exceed the type of

61 Interview in Somocho, Lautem, 1 July 2008.

justice that is possible through the criminal law alone. Such 'justice' might include the restoration of status and reputation through the 'declarations' and public shaming of perpetrators and the recovery of bodies in order to fulfil responsibilities to the dead (which are also essential for the reconstitution of everyday life). As I now discuss in more detail, it might also include providing material assistance to help to establish economic security for the family and better educational opportunities for survivors' children.

Material assistance

Survivors' aspirations for economic assistance highlight further dissonance between official and local understandings of justice. As already alluded to, the desire for the state to *tau matan ba* (look after) people, by providing financial assistance, was often viewed to be as important as retributive justice, and indeed the two hopes were often expressed simultaneously. Thus, as Rosa put it:

> Assistance is not justice but it's important because we lost our husbands. Because the justice process is very long the government needs to look after us. We need food, assistance for our children's schooling. This would make us feel *kmaan* [lighter] but we still need justice.[62]

Similar views were expressed by a community leader in Covalima, who explained:

> When they are going to do a justice process they have to look at people's lives – whether they are hungry, whether they have clean water. This needs to happen first. Then, if justice is slow people can wait.[63]

There are strong parallels between the hopes expressed by East Timorese survivors for economic assistance and research conducted in other post-conflict contexts (see Robins 2009 on Nepal; Shaw 2005 and 2007 on Sierra Leone; Colvin 2003 on South Africa; Lambourne 2009 on Sierra Leone, East Timor and Rwanda). Echoing Rosalind Shaw's findings regarding survivors' responses to the Sierra Leone truth commission (see Shaw 2003: 201), it became clear, during interviews, that many East Timorese survivors had expectations that telling their stories to the CAVR or the Serious Crimes Process would help to connect them to resources that would enable them to rebuild their lives. The fact that economic assistance had not been forthcoming was perceived as emblematic of a failure of international and national decision-makers to truly

62 Interview in Maucatar, Covalima, 28 May 2007.
63 Interview in Maucatar, Covalima, 29 May 2007.

listen, and respond to, their ongoing experiences of hardship. While local desires for economic assistance allude, in part, to the centrality of compensation within customary dispute resolution practices, they have a particular resonance in a context in which, as I discuss below, there is endemic poverty, increasing wealth disparity and a widely held perception that the *povu ki'ik* have been forgotten by the nation's leaders.

For many respondents, economic assistance was understood as an essential form of public recognition of victims' experiences of suffering. This was often connected to a belief that they were 'owed' something from the state for their years of sacrifice and struggle during the occupation. These views were reflected in the statements of a number of respondents that the *ema bo'ot* (big people) – the elite Dili politicians – had neglected the *povu ki'ik* (small people), among them widows, orphans and ordinary civilians who had not played formal roles in the resistance, but who had nonetheless made sacrifices for the nation. As Gracilda explained:

> In the past FALINTIL said 'if we come in to the village from the *ai laran* [jungle] you will eat before us, because you helped us.' We were their legs, their voices, their eyes. We assisted them. But now they have been assisted first . . . At independence they promised us that we widows and orphans will eat before them. But it has been nine years already and they have received roofing iron and money . . . We have many widows here. It's our right to receive, because we were all involved in the war . . . If we didn't have victims we wouldn't have the state. But the big people go ahead as always – they have houses, cars, they are all complete – but we victims go backwards as always.[64]

Similarly, as Margadida put it:

> The government needs to *tau matan ba ami* [look after us], to look at what has been destroyed, to open their eyes. We think a lot about this. The government has not opened their eyes. If the government gives some assistance it will help to *taka kanek* [close our wounds]. The government has not recognised us, for seven years.[65]

Gracilda and Margadida's comments embody the widely held view that the government had forgotten the sacrifices of the *povu ki'ik* and the difficult conditions in which they lived. The leadership – who now had *cadeira* (chairs/positions) – thought only about themselves, it was argued, and failed to recognise the contribution of the *povu ki'ik* to the independence struggle. This

64 Interview in Poros, Lautem, 6 August 2007.
65 Interview in Beco, Covalima, 9 June 2007.

belief was exacerbated by the perception of some that pro-independence supporters continued to suffer, while those who had collaborated with the Indonesian regime, including by working for the civil service, had prospered. Thus, as Justino, a community leader in Lautem, put it:

> I was involved in the Clandestine and didn't get a good education. I feel angry at the pro-autonomy leaders. They got an education. The government now has put pro-autonomy [supporters] in the government. The pro-autonomy [supporters] have got scholarships. Not us . . . I gave my youth to the war, not to love or play . . . I also want to go to school. This is not justice.[66]

Such comments link aspirations for economic assistance with popular understandings of national identity that revolve around the need for those who contributed to the resistance struggle to be recognised. As discussed in Chapter 4, there are popular beliefs that 'sacrifice' for the resistance movement is the grounds on which legitimacy and recognition may be claimed in the new nation state. The anthropologist Elizabeth Traube has coined the term 'unpaid wages' to describe the popular narrative that those who purchased the nation 'not with silver or gold, but with the blood of the people' need to be repaid for their sacrifices (Traube 2007: 10). At its narrowest, the narrative of unpaid wages – which invokes customary beliefs about reciprocity and exchange – revolves around the view that those who suffered and sacrificed for independence should be recompensed, and that former 'collaborators' should be made to pay (Traube 2007: 21). At its broadest, it encompasses a more inclusive category of *povu ki'ik* (small people), including widows, orphans, young people and others who were not involved in formal politics, but who nonetheless are perceived to have made sacrifices for the nation and to have been abandoned by the nation's leaders (Traube 2007: 21). Echoes of the narrow and more inclusive versions of the 'unpaid wages' narrative could be heard in many survivors' comments.

Frustrations with the lack of economic assistance have no doubt been compounded by the government's approach to development. As discussed in Chapter 4, the recent provision of cash payments and pensions to selected groups, including veterans, internally displaced people and petitioners, has fostered resentments amongst those who feel they have missed out, including the rural poor.[67] These resentments are not without basis as, according to the UNDP's most recent Human Development Report, despite increases in

66 Interview in Titilari, Lautem, 8 June 2008.

67 Although the government has introduced a range of schemes to address poverty, including a 'support allowance' to meet the basic needs of the elderly and the disabled, and a *Bolsa de Mae* ('mother's pocket') to provide a monthly payment to the neediest female-headed households, the amounts provided pale in comparison to the payments being provided to veterans.

revenue from the Timor Sea oil and gas fields, poverty levels remain high amongst much of the population, with a third of households relying exclusively on subsistence agriculture and most households regularly experiencing food shortages in a given year (UNDP 2011: 19). There are indications, too, that the 'crisis' of 2006 has made life even harder for rural communities, by leading to a rise in the price of goods, making it harder to buy and sell goods, and disrupting local services, including transport and education (see Grenfell et al 2009: 70). Compounding these problems are the increasing wealth disparities between the rural and urban areas (UNDP 2011: 7). Currently, Dili is the only district that has a population belonging overwhelmingly (71 per cent) in the highest wealth quintile, with only 0.4 per cent belonging in the poorest quintile. By contrast, the largest percentage of the rural population belong in the lowest wealth quintile (24.6 per cent) and the smallest in the highest quintile (8.7 per cent) (National Statistics Directorate 2010).

During interviews, the long-term, chronic aspects of suffering were often stressed over the acute human rights violations that survivors had experienced. Gracilda made it clear that the forced disappearance of her husband in 1983 at the hands of the Indonesian military was only the beginning of a long period of hardship, fear and intimidation that she endured, during which she was repeatedly sexually abused:

> Men were killed straight away, but our bodies were the Javanese rights . . . We thought about dying. If they just killed us we would not feel anything . . . They used to come and look for us all the time. This is also *todan* [heavy] . . . Men did not experience these things. We did not have rights because we were women.[68]

Many survivors also sought to emphasise that their past suffering has ongoing consequences that continue to shape and constrict their present lives. As Francisco put it:

> When the CAVR came to take my information I wanted to tell about my suffering, because for twenty-four years I suffered for independence. But I still suffer because I can't work. I can't provide for my children's schooling. I am still injured from being beaten in the past . . . When we spoke about our experiences I felt a bit lighter because I had broadcast my experiences. But after we spoke we still suffer. The simple people are still living very badly. Some of us don't even have shoes. How can the government do a programme to look after the victims who really suffered? I can't help my child to go to university. My children will just become slaves.[69]

68 Interview in Poros, Lautem, 6 August 2007.
69 Interview in Legore, Covalima, 31 May 2007.

Appeals by survivors for practical, material needs – for children to have better lives and to reap the benefits of the liberation struggle – once again illuminate the dislocation between formal legal processes designed to prosecute perpetrators in courts of law and justice as it is understood by interviewees. No transitional justice process focused entirely on retributive justice and restorative justice could ever hope to address the long-term structural dimensions of violence that are evident in ongoing poverty, exclusion and limited opportunities. In this sense, survivors resist the assumptions guiding the CAVR and Serious Crimes Process, and shared by the East Timorese political elite, that the violence of the occupation is an historical artefact, stressing that their suffering cannot just be spoken about and then left behind because it continues to reverberate in the present. The importance that respondents accorded to practical needs speaks of *injustice* that can be understood as an experience of 'lack, incompleteness or disorder' (Douzinas 2000: 332) in the form of continuing marginalisation, oppression and poverty. Their views give further weight to the argument that, for many East Timorese survivors, justice is an ongoing process that entails both addressing the past and, equally as important, transforming the present and the future.

Conclusion: elusive justice

That survivors have not simply accepted or rejected the transitional justice process, but interacted with it in a range of complex ways, reveals how a number of different narratives of justice circulate within the local sphere, drawing upon, and contesting, official transitional justice narratives. Close attention to the stories of survivors shows how their demands for justice are at once highly personalised, and historically and culturally situated. For many survivors, 'justice' not only requires the need to address the past and transform the present and future, but also involves responsibilities to the ancestors and to the generations not yet born. Justice at the local level may variously mean the need for perpetrators to 'declare' their guilt and be formally punished in order to restore the status of the wronged party, the need to establish the 'truth' in order to recover bodies to properly care for the dead, the need for suffering to be formally recognised and for transformation of the material circumstances of the *povu ki'ik* and their children. It may also embody the more general hopes for an end to violence and for the restoration of morality and humanity that many believe have been shattered by years of conflict. Conversely, the widespread view that *injustice* continues – embodied in survivors' feelings of frustration and disappointment with the lack of practical 'results' – can be understood best, perhaps, as an expression of 'lack' that is experienced as social exclusion, inequality and poverty (Douzinas 2000: 332). While underscoring the significance of legal forms of recognition, narratives of justice and injustice circulating in the local sphere also call attention to the limits of the law in responding to calls for justice, which transcend the retributive and restorative justice possibilities of trials and truth commissions.

This chapter, then, has shed further light on the tension between law and justice, by showing that recourse to forms of legal (and quasi-legal) mechanisms alone are unlikely to meet East Timorese survivors' demands for justice. In the following chapter, I reflect more deeply on how communities and survivors themselves are working to 'remake the world', outside the formal transitional justice process, and the nation-building attempts of the national leadership. In particular, I explore the significance of local memory practices, which, I suggest, reveal how the process of reconstituting everyday life and pursuing 'justice' in the wake of the conflict is at once intensely personal and openly political.

Chapter 6

Local memory practices and the emerging politics of victims' rights

> In the sleepy town of Liquica, about half an hour's drive along the coast from Dili, stands a small white monument of an angel. Tucked behind the church, in the garden beside the priest's residence, she stands in the shade of frangipani and magnolia trees, with hands joined in prayer. One Sunday afternoon, Ana Maria takes me there on the back of her small motorbike. She points out the places where as many as sixty people were cut down by machetes, axes and swords and shot, alongside the priest's residence, as they ran to escape the church where they had been sheltering from the *Besih Merah Putih* [Red and White Iron] militia group. Maria then explains how the Liquica community got together with the help of a women's organisation, raised the funds for the monument by collecting small contributions from local families, carrying the stone and cement for its construction.
>
> Unlike some others I have seen, the Liquica monument is not built in a large, square militaristic style; it is small, human sized, suggesting fragility rather than grand martyrdom. Tucked away as it is in the garden, far from the street, it seems a place for quiet personal reflection, rather than ostentatious public grief. The well maintained church yard stands in stark contrast to the dilapidated and half-finished official government memorial a few hundred metres down the road that faces the District Administration offices.
>
> (Field diary entry July 2007)

In this chapter, I look more deeply at narratives of justice that are circulating in the local sphere by reflecting on the myriad of *unofficial* memory practices that have been taking place since the referendum, within the realm of the family, and at the district, *suco* (village) and *aldeia* (hamlet) levels. I suggest that these practices – which include the reburial of remains of loved ones and the construction of memorials, the commemoration of massacres, and the establishment of victims' support groups – can be understood as rituals for reconstructing everyday life (see Das 2007) and pursuing highly personalised forms of justice in the wake of years of conflict (Booth 2001: 777). I argue that some local memory practices can be seen, too, as political struggles for recognition from the state by those who perceive themselves to be excluded from the official nation-building process (see Humphrey and Valverde 2007).

This chapter also charts the emergence of a fragile and tentative politics of victims' rights, and discusses some of its possibilities and limitations. In particular, I raise concerns that the current campaign for victims' reparations is unfolding in a broader context of impoverishment and identity politics in which a range of different groups are competing for state resources and official recognition. In this context, there is a potential for conflicts to emerge between different *kinds* of victims, and between victims and other marginalised groups, as they compete for recognition of their unique claims. At the same time, a politics of victims' rights, while still in its infancy, is a positive sign that some victims are participating in a conversation about the meaning of the past and of justice. This has the potential to disclose previously unrecognised experiences of harm, and may lead, at the national level, to the broadening and deepening of current nation-building narratives and the emergence of more locally grounded conceptions of 'justice'.

Local memory practices: remaking the world

After the 1999 referendum, and long before the establishment of the official transitional justice process, a myriad of unofficial local practices of remembering and commemorating the violence of the twenty-four-year Indonesian occupation began developing across East Timor. In the realm of the extended family, reburials of those who had died during the occupation, whose bodies had been previously lost or interred in shallow bush graves, began to take place, in order to lay to rest their spirits (McWilliam 2007a; Field 2004). Reports have also emerged of families making ritual visits to nearby mountains to collect human bones, which are presumed to belong to loved ones, in order to bury them in an appropriate place (Robins 2010: 24). In a context in which *adat* (custom) still plays a strong role in the lives of many East Timorese people, these reburial rituals serve an important function of helping families to fulfil long-delayed obligations to the dead, in order to restore balance in the worlds of the spirits and the living. In cases in which a body cannot be recovered and the appropriate rituals cannot be performed, families experience acute anguish. Nonetheless, alternative rituals can sometimes be performed using a substitute body. This may occur following a dream by a family member during which they are visited by the spirit of the deceased who communicates the circumstances of death and requests a proper burial (Robins 2010: 4). Robins (2010: 12), for example, describes a ceremony in which the body of the dead is replaced with another object, often a stone. Families will go to the place where the person is believed to have been killed and collect a stone, which is then buried in a coffin as if it were the body of the dead. The spirit of the dead is presumed to enter the stone and thus is prevented from becoming a 'wandering ghost'.

The departure of the Indonesian military also led to a resurgence of cultural practices such as the rebuilding of *uma luliks* (sacred houses), many of which were destroyed during the Indonesian invasion and occupation, or burned during the post-referendum violence (Brown 2009: 153; McWilliam 2005: 28; Field 2004: 283). As anthropologists have documented, *uma luliks* serve an important function in the maintenance of the social and moral order of East Timorese society, acting as a 'ritualised focus for the articulation of social relations and exchange amongst "house" members' (McWilliam 2005: 28). Through the reconstruction of *uma luliks* and the carrying out of rituals for their sanctification, families are working to appropriately honour the dead, including the spirits of those whose remains lie abandoned in unknown places, to reconstitute fractured family relationship and to return order to the world of the living (Brown 2009: 154).

Beyond the realm of the extended family, a number of public memory practices, including the construction of memorials and commemorations of massacres, have also been taking place at the district, *suco* and *aldeia* levels. These local memorials stand in stark contrast to the dearth of official national monuments to commemorate civilians who died during the Indonesian occupation (see Leach 2008: 158). Like reburial practices and the rebuilding of *uma luliks*, memorials and commemorations provide a way for families to ensure that their obligations to the dead are carried out, particularly in places where bodies have not been recovered. These practices also demonstrate that acts of remembrance have a collective, public dimension. That is, they show that memories of the past transcend the private realm and become part of the culture, tradition and identity of communities (see, for example, Czarnota 2001: 119; Halbwachs 1980).

In the district of Covalima, two memorials have been constructed by the local community to commemorate the Suai Church massacre that occurred on 6 September 1999, the day after the announcement of the results of the referendum. The first is a formal 'Western-style' monument made of marble, upon which are inscribed the names of those who were killed during the massacre, including the names of three priests. Built by the people of the district, the monument also had financial support from the East Timorese government, the UN's SCIU, and the governments of the United Kingdom and Ireland (Leach, 2008: 155). The second is a more informal 'circle of stones' situated close to the church, marking the spot where Indonesian military and East Timorese militia brought the hacked and mutilated bodies of those who had been killed, to be burned in an attempt to render them unidentifiable. The stones were collected by families of victims and on each stone is inscribed the name of a loved one. Unlike the roped-off 'formal' memorial, the circle of stones is inclusive, accessible and without hierarchy (Rawnsley 2004: 10–11) (Figure 6.1).

In the district of Liquica, members of the local community completed the construction of a small 'Angel' monument in 2006, at the site of the Liquica church massacre of 6 April 1999, where as many as sixty people were killed by the *Besih Merah Putih* (BMP/Red and White Iron) militia group while they were seeking refuge in the church. Constructed with financial assistance from a key women's NGO, *Fokupers* (Women's Communication Forum), the United Nations Development Programme (UNDP) and the government of Japan, the small statue was inaugurated with a ceremony involving the blessing of stones to put the souls of the dead to rest, including those of the many bodies that have never been recovered after being taken away from the massacre site. On 6 April each year, members of the Liquica community organise a mass and then lay wreaths of flowers there in memory of their loved ones. As the extract from my field notes at the beginning of this chapter suggests, this monument is particularly moving due to its unassuming size and position.

Figure 6.1 Liquica Angel Monument (Lia Kent)

Local memory practices are also taking place at the *suco* level. In the remote mountain *suco* of Maununu, Ainaro, a monument – painted in the colours of the East Timor flag – has been constructed to remember the massacre committed by members of the *Mahidi* militia group on 23 September 1999. Village commemorations are not confined to the 1999 events and, in 2008, a ceremony was organised in Kraras, Viqueque district, to remember a series of brutal killings that occurred in 1983 to quash local uprisings against the Indonesian military, which resulted in the deaths of up to 300 people, mostly men (CAVR 2005a: Part 7.2, 168–9). Similarly, in Muapitine, Lautem, a small monument has been constructed of stone and cement to commemorate the organised killing of five members of the village in 1983 (Figure 6.2). This was a particularly brutal event, in which villagers were ordered by the local Indonesian military command to kill five prisoners from their own community who were suspected of being members of FALINTIL. The killings took place with *katanas* (machetes) during a specially organised public *festa* (party), which local villagers were instructed to attend. Completed in 2006, one panel of the monument lists the names of the five men who were killed and, on a separate panel, a painting visually represents the scene. The killers are depicted as having 'no choice' but to conduct these acts: members of the Indonesian military stand behind them, guns pointed at their heads. A third panel inscribes the names of all villagers who died or 'disappeared' during the Indonesian occupation period. Interestingly, and somewhat controversially within the *suco*, this list also includes names of a number of villagers presumed to have been killed by members of the FALINTIL resistance.[1] Given the way in which this massacre involved the whole community, either as participants or as observers, the monument can be seen as a particularly important act of collective solidarity.

The work of Veena Das and Arthur Kleinman, discussed in Chapter 1, helps to shed light on the way in which everyday activities such as these help to 'remake a world' in the wake of protracted conflict (Das and Kleinman 2001; see also Das 2003; Das 2007). Das suggests that, rather than occurring through 'grand gestures in the realm of the transcendent', the reconstruction of everyday life takes place through a 'descent into the ordinary' (Das 2007: 7). Engagement in 'ordinary' activities, Das and Kleinman (2001: 1–2) write, is an achievement in itself for those who have had their lives severely disrupted; it provides a stand against the destruction of bonds of trust between communities and families shattered by conflict. The work of James Booth also draws attention to the way in which local memory practices can be understood as the pursuit of a locally grounded form of 'justice'. Justice, Booth suggests, is in part a 'duty to remember' the past and to honour the dead (Booth 2001: 777). Unlike legal justice, acts of 'memory justice' do not seek to make a break with

1 Interviews in Muapitine, Lautem, 6–8 August 2007.

Figure 6.2 Muapitine Monument (Lia Kent)

the past, but endeavour to remain faithful to the dead by keeping the memory of the past alive.

Accordingly, by constructing memorials, engaging in reburial practices and rebuilding *uma luliks*, individuals and communities in East Timor are seeking to remake the social order by pursuing locally grounded forms of 'justice'. Local memory practices are oriented both to the spirit world and to the world of the living. In a context in which there are powerful beliefs about the importance of respecting ancestors and ensuring that the ghosts of the dead rest, these practices provide a culturally resonant way for family members, including those who have been unable to locate the remains of loved ones, to restore balance in the worlds of the living and the dead. Given the way in which the years of occupation and conflict imbued everyday East Timorese social relations with suspicion and ambiguity at the community and family levels, memorials, commemorations and reburial practices also provide a way in which to reconstitute fractured family and community relationships and integrate the past into the everyday life of the present. Those involved in local memory practices also articulate a desire to transmit memories to the next generation. Thus, just as many survivors have embraced the symbolism of *Chega!* because of its educative potential for their children and grandchildren, local memory practices are seen as a way in which to educate the younger generation as part of a 'struggle against forgetting', to ensure that historical atrocities are not repeated. Thus, as Gracilda from Lautem stressed: 'We can't have any more suffering like ours. It should stop with us.'[2] This emphasis on transmission evokes, too, the importance of fidelity to the dead and respect for the ancestors; it is also through transmission that young people are seen to gain the necessary knowledge of their lineage and, consequently, a sense of their place in history. While these narratives are, at one level, 'restorative', they also reflect the desire to keep the memory of the past alive. In doing so, they resist the idea of closure and resolution; they refuse to let the 'past become the historical past, the past perfect' (Booth 2001: 788).

This is not to idealise local memory practices. Just as national elites reconstruct and shape memories based on the needs of the present, so too do local memory practices. Thus, as Katherine Verdery has observed in the post-Yugoslav context, reburials and commemorative practices may serve 'not just to *reaffirm* community but also to *narrow* and *bound* it' (Verdery 1999: 108). In this sense, attending to who organises and participates in local memory practices can reveal a lot about who is included and who is excluded from the society that is being remade. Like local practices of customary dispute resolution, some commemorations may seek to reinstate and reinforce the 'local order of things', including the power of existing community leaders. Local acts of remembrance may also intersect with, replicate and unsettle national and international narratives in different ways. There are times, for example, when these practices seek to inscribe local struggles into the national struggle of heroism and sacrifice; they should not simply be seen, then, as

2 Interview in Poros, Lautem, 6 August 2007.

counter-hegemonic stories that always challenge, resist and broaden official narratives (Dwyer and Santikarma 2006: 210).

Some past traumatic events have now become iconic symbols of nationalism. One such event is the Santa Cruz massacre (or Dili massacre) of 1991, during which hundreds of mostly young people were killed by Indonesian military officers during a demonstration against the occupation at the Santa Cruz Cemetery in Dili. As Crockford observes, this massacre has come to represent an archetype of youth resistance, heroism and martyrdom that is 'synonymous with the struggle for self-determination, inscribed in collective memory as a revolutionary moment in which "incorruptible" youth appeared as heroic protagonists' (Crockford 2007: 95). The ongoing symbolic significance of this massacre is indicated by the way in which it has been interwoven with struggles of the present and other local narratives in a range of ways. The 12 November Committee, for example, an organisation comprising survivors and family members of those killed during the 1991 Santa Cruz massacre describes as one of its key goals to 'transfer the spirit of nationalism', thus linking to struggles for victims and their families with the nationalist struggle.[3] Similarly, a media conference organised by the Association of Ex-Political Prisoners (ASSEPOL) in July 2008 offered solidarity to student demonstrators who were arrested by the East Timorese Police (PNTL) and UNPOL for protests against the current government. ASSEPOL spoke as ex-prisoners and citizens of the resistance, responsible for the 'edification of the nation', drawing a link between the principles of the student movement of the past and the ongoing student struggles for rule of law and democracy in independent East Timor (see Tempo Seminal 2008). In Lautem, the Santa Cruz massacre has been integrated into commemorations of a local massacre. Each year, commemorations are held at the site of a 1984 massacre and young people organise a 'long march' to the site to place candles to commemorate the dead. Yet rather than being tied to the specific date of this massacre, the march is held on 12 November, the date of the Santa Cruz massacre, which, for those involved, invokes the broader symbolism of youth heroism and sacrifice for the nation.[4]

The interweaving of the national and local, then, may privilege a particular kind of story, a triumphal story that resonates with popular national beliefs about the centrality of sacrifice for the national resistance struggle. This kind of narrative gives meaning to local struggles by inscribing them into the nation's story and suggesting that those who died did so for the good of the nation. What may be left out are experiences that do not fit with a glorified version of the past, including small, localised, stories of 'ordinary', everyday endurance, stories of death due to hunger, disease and malnourishment, stories of community-level violence and betrayal, and women's experiences of

3 Interview with member of the 12 November Committee, Dili, 9 July 2009.
4 Interview with NGO activist, Los Palos, 7 June 2008.

surviving the conflict. For example, it is instructive that, as of late 2011, there were few local-level memorials or commemorations to mark events relating to the internal civil conflict or East Timor political-party violence (Leach 2008). Accounts from Muapitine also suggest there was a heated debate within the *suco* about whether the monument should include the names of all those who died during the Indonesian occupation, including those who were killed by FALINTIL forces (and who might therefore have been 'traitors').[5] Local memory practices are rarely purely 'local' initiatives either: they are heavily supported by national NGOs and international organisations, which provide funding and logistical support for monuments and public commemorations. National NGOs helped to organise the Kraras commemorations, for example, and while the construction of the Muapitine monument was a local initiative, the idea emerged during the CAVR's truth-seeking activities in the village, and the monument was funded by the CAVR and an international NGO.

Although these practices have their own politics, power struggles and exclusions, and may also be constrained by national and international discourses, their locally embedded and collective nature does appear to enable remembering, mourning and making sense of the past in ways that differ markedly from the narratives of the national elite and the UN. That many local memory projects foreground the experiences of the *povu ki'ik* disrupts the leadership's emphasis on remembering and recognising 'veterans' and 'heroes' who fulfilled leadership roles during the resistance struggle. These practices, by suggesting that the suffering of ordinary people continues into the present, also unsettle the political leadership's entreaty to focus on the future rather than the past. Through the remembering – and in some cases 'forgetting' – of the past, local memory practices are also providing a basis for the mourning and honouring of loved ones, the resumption of everyday life, albeit fragile and tentative, and the fostering of links of solidarity amongst survivors of violence. These practices should be understood as a part of the pursuit of 'justice' by East Timorese survivors. In contrast to UN transitional justice advocates and their nation's leaders, who have attempted to draw a sharp line between the past and the future, local memory projects demonstrate that realising justice is an ongoing, localised and collective process that involves fidelity to the dead, keeping the stories of the past alive and reconstructing the world of the living.

Local memory practices: struggles for recognition

Although many local memory practices involve political struggles at some level, and bring to the fore competing viewpoints about which events should

5 Interviews in Muapitine, 6–8 August 2007.

be remembered and how they should be memorialised, some practices are political in a more overt sense, in that they seek to engage with and demand a response from the state. In this section, I argue that some local memory practices are part of a broader struggle for official recognition and reparation by certain individuals and groups who perceive themselves to be excluded from the nation-building process, and who derive their authority to speak from their collective experiences of suffering.

In their study of victims' groups in Argentina, Humphrey and Valverde (2007: 181) show how private grief can become a form of 'political mourning' by groups seeking to demand recognition from the state. Political mourning, they write, is directed toward the recovery of what is perceived to be absent – 'real rights and justice' for those at the margins of the state (Humphrey and Valverde 2007: 187). In the context of East Timor, where endemic poverty is experienced as a shattering of expectations and popular beliefs that good things would flow from independence, similar, if less organised, struggles are apparent. In this context, some local memory practices can be understood, in part, as expressions of the popular narrative of 'unpaid wages' – discussed in Chapter 5 – that evokes the idea that the *povu ki'ik*, who sacrificed their lives for the liberation struggle, have yet to be recompensed and have been abandoned by the nation's leaders.

These dynamics were evident in the public commemorations of the Kraras massacre in 2008. Community members invited the President to inaugurate the village monument in the presence of other national political leaders. Observers report that the first day of the two-day event was primarily a dialogue between political leaders and the community about the practical needs of the community.[6] While the commemoration involved a reflection on the past, it also served as a means for the community to draw the attention of political leaders to the ongoing effects of past suffering in the present, which led to the provision of funding to the community for a solar panel to generate electricity.

Similarly, the Liquica massacre commemorations of 2008 coincided with a community meeting organised by the International Centre for Transitional Justice (ICTJ), *Yayasan Hak, Fokupers*, and the Justice and Peace Commission of Baucau to provide information to victims on transitional justice mechanisms and to encourage them to begin networking with each other. Families of victims, community leaders, NGOs, the local Liquica administration, including education and health departments, and national member of Parliament Fernanda Borges[7] were invited to both the meeting and commemorations. A petition was then presented to the National Parliament on behalf of families of victims, entitled *Haluha Mak Labele, Justica Mak Dalan Los*

6 Interview with staff member international NGO, Dili, 9 July 2009.

7 Leader of the Kota political party.

('Forgetting is not Possible, Justice is the Right Path'). Framing their demands by reference to the lack of justice for victims of the Liquica church massacre, the petition called on the National Parliament to recognise 6 April as a *Loron Istorika* (Historical Day) for East Timor. It also called on the Parliament to debate the *Chega!* recommendations and to make a law regarding reparations for victims, including health assistance, scholarships for orphans, and financial assistance to assist victims and their families to develop their economic capacity, and demanded trials for human rights violations that occurred in 1999. Finally, the petition contained an expression of dissatisfaction about certain CAVR commissioners who had gone on to become commissioners in the bilateral East Timor–Indonesian CTF, suggesting that they had 'forgotten their principles'.[8] A similar petition was presented to the Parliament in 2009 to mark the tenth anniversary of the massacre, which reiterated these demands. It continued to express discontent about those who joined the CTF, noting:

> CVA [CTF] was created comprised of Timorese who never dreamed of independence but used the Timorese people's money to go back and forth Dili-Dempassar, with [no] great concern for the families of victims and other who were killed, who cry and pray for those killed because of independence, going and coming but never finding any work, and never receiving attention from most of the leaders who in the hard times lived in foreign countries or abroad.
>
> (In La'o Hamutuk 2010)

This petition suggests that the Liquica community's dissatisfaction with the CTF is about more than a failure of the Commission to deliver the 'truth' or contribute to criminal prosecutions. It also invokes a concern that those who joined the CTF accepted lucrative salary packages and travel perks. The comment that families of victims were killed because of their role in the independence struggle also gestures towards the national resistance narrative by contrasting the sacrifices of the *povu ki'ik* with the experiences of those who lived in foreign countries 'in the hard times' (including a number of members of the current political leadership). While strongly grounded in the local, then, the Liquica community petition is also indicative of the way in which local memory practices can retell the nationalist story of sacrifice and struggle for political purposes.

The increasing dialogue between local memory practices and political leaders cannot be understood without reference to the involvement and influence of victims' groups, which are themselves supported by international and national human rights organisations. Since 1999, a number of victims'

8 Copy on file with author.

organisations and groups representing families of victims have been established in Dili and the districts. Among the most active of these in the early years of the post-referendum period were widows' groups in the districts of Covalima, Maliana and Liquica. Formed in the aftermath of the 1999 violence and supported by the women's organisation *Fokupers*, the groups were initially established to provide mutual support to survivors, to address issues of economic survival, and to continue the demand for justice and disclosure regarding the whereabouts of those who were 'disappeared' (Wandita et al 2006). The names of the groups – *Mate Restu* (Remains of the Dead) in Covalima, *Rate Laek* (Without Graves) in Liquica, and *Novi Novi* (Ninety-Nine) in Maliana – evoke the women's shared experiences of suffering and loss.

Through their involvement in the widows' groups, these East Timorese women are seeking to make life liveable once more. As already observed, gender was an important factor in shaping both common and particular experiences of the Indonesian conflict. While it was largely men who were imprisoned, killed or 'disappeared', women were left to provide economically for themselves and their families. While women often did not hold formal positions within the resistance hierarchy, they fulfilled critical functions, for example acting as cooks, couriers and intelligence for the armed front. As widows, women were also vulnerable to violence and sexual exploitation from both the Indonesian military and members of their own communities. In a context in which discussion of women's experiences have largely been subsumed, or repressed, within the broader narrative of the resistance struggle, the widows' groups enable the recognition of shared experiences, as the women meet together to offer support and solidarity to one another. Importantly, members also assist one another in practical ways by engaging in collective economic activities, such as working in each other's fields and establishing co-operatives to sell products such as cassava and rice. For East Timorese widows, the resumption of these 'everyday' and practical economic activities is significant in itself. As one member of *Mate Restu*, in Covalima, explains:

> Working in our *to'os* [fields] together is good. It helps our livelihoods. It helps us to forget our *terus* [suffering]. We are together, we forget our thinking, [we are] *ramai* [happy/lively].[9]

The women's positive views about the importance of collective economic activities contrast with their expressions of disillusionment about the official transitional justice processes, and their weariness with telling their stories, noted at the very beginning of this book: 'What are we to talk

9 Interview in Suai, Covalima, 25 June 2007.

about? Whether we talk or not it is just the same.'[10] For these women, the decision *not* to continue recounting their stories of pain to 'official' people – including to Western researchers such as myself – has been an empowering act. The anthropologist Rosalind Shaw (2007), who has conducted research with survivors in Sierra Leone, describes such acts as 'directed forgetting'. Thus, while these women perceive that continually to tell their stories to a seemingly deaf listener may keep them trapped in the past, *not to speak* about past experiences can become a way of integrating experiences into everyday life by refocusing on the future and on livelihoods. This is not to suggest that the women literally expect to 'forget' or erase their memories, but that they seek, perhaps, to deploy them in ways that differ from the kinds of story-telling demanded by the transitional justice process and their political leaders, and to contain them in a way that will help them to live their lives (see Shaw 2007: 194).

The widows' groups have also enabled a small number of women to take on public roles that had previously been denied to them, through which they are involved in political activities and able to advocate for issues such as justice and reparations. Thus, while initially established to provide mutual support, over the years some members have developed a commitment to working on issues beyond their own immediate concerns and are now actively involved in development work within their broader communities, or in human rights advocacy on behalf of East Timorese 'victims' more generally.[11] Thus the three widows' groups met with then UN High Commissioner for Human Rights Mary Robinson during her 2002 visit to East Timor and presented their demands for the prosecution of serious crimes perpetrators. *Rate Laek* was also the initiator of the petition in 2008 to the National Parliament on behalf of Liquica victims, which demanded the implementation of the *Chega!* recommendations. In addition, the group has been active in lobbying the government for a national day of commemoration of the April 1999 Liquica church massacre and the need for victims' reparations. The women involved in these groups also specifically articulate the political intentions of their work. As Ana Maria, one of the founders of *Rate Laek*, describes:

> We formed *Rate Laek* in 2000. There were twelve of us at that time . . . Because we felt that one voice is not enough, we felt that people would listen to us if there were more.[12]

Similarly, Fernanda, another founder of *Rate Laek*, suggests that one of the main benefits of the widows' group is that it has enabled the women to be

10 Ibid.
11 Ibid.
12 Interview in Liquica, 4 July 2008.

'known to the world'.[13] As she describes: '*Rate Laek* has helped me – through *Rate Laek* people know us. The world knows if we mention this name; Kofi Annan, Mary Robinson, know us.'[14]

For widows who have occupied marginal positions in their communities, the re-establishment of 'ordinary' life and the claiming of public, political space is significant in itself. Yet navigating this space is also precarious. While, paradoxically, widowhood may offer a kind of freedom that married life, with its assigned domestic roles, may not allow, the widows' engagement in public activities must still be undertaken within certain prescribed codes of behaviour. Widows are expected to behave in certain 'deserving' ways if they are to receive the support of community leaders and their families; they should project an aura of sadness and suffering, they should not dress well and they should not be too prominent in public life. They must also take care to ensure that their moral and sexual reputations are not called into question, particularly given their vulnerability to sexual exploitation.[15] In addition, widows are often amongst the poorest members of a community, especially if they have no extended family to support them (UNDP 2006: 2; Martins and Kendall 2002). Many will continue living with the families of their late husbands, and are conscious of being an economic burden. In this context, any steps to assume prominent roles in public life may be viewed with suspicion.

The members of East Timorese widows groups have taken care to navigate this fragile space by framing their identities as 'victims' and 'mothers', and their activities as 'self-help' and 'mutual support', rather than as public and political in nature. As discussed in the previous chapter, they may also seek to legitimate their experiences by situating them within the broader context of their husband's roles in the resistance struggle. These observations resonate with the work of Fiona Ross and Mamphela Ramphele in the context of South Africa (see Ross 2003). Describing women whose deceased husbands were prominent members of the anti-apartheid resistance as 'political widows', Ramphele suggests that they occupy a precarious social position in which they derive their authority to speak from their relationships with their 'heroic' and fallen husbands:

> The political role of the political widow derives from her relationship with her husband: she is not seen as woman but someone standing in for a fallen man. She becomes the ultimate honorary man . . . her agency is not completely eliminated, but constrained. To the extent that she can renegotiate the terms of her engagement, she is able to enlarge her

13 Interviews in Muapitine 6–8 August 2007.

14 Ibid.

15 Interview with Nela, former director Fokupers, Dili, 2 July 2008.

> socio-political sphere as a public figure. It is a tough balancing act, fraught with danger.
>
> (Ramphele, in Ross 2003a: 34)

The limits placed on East Timorese widows' groups speak to the assumptions in transitional justice discourses around 'victimhood', which tend to portray victims as passive, voiceless and devoid of agency. They also illuminate the continuing power of national resistance narratives and the deeply patriarchal nature of East Timorese society, in which women's experiences of violence and their diverse contributions to the resistance struggle continue to be excluded from the triumphal, forward-looking, nation-building narratives of the political elite. The difficulties involved in negotiating these different stories are highlighted in the comments of the co-ordinator of the *Uma Feto* (Women's House) in Suai, which works with widows of the conflict, who explained: 'Widows want to take part in political activities, but people think badly of them. They think they are only looking for a man.'[16]

In recent years, other victims' organisations, including the Dili-based Association of Ex-Political Prisoners (ASSEPOL) and the 12 November Committee, have grown increasingly prominent. Their influence derives in part from the fact that their members are prominent male political figures, many of whom are also veterans of the armed or Clandestine resistance. ASSEPOL was formed soon after the referendum to advocate for the needs of those who had been imprisoned during the Indonesian occupation, many of whom were tortured, and the families of those who had died in prison or disappeared. The organisation is now working with a well-known Australian activist and journalist on the Living Memory Project, which aims to create a video archive based on interviews with these ex-prisoners.[17] The 12 November Committee, formed in 2008, continues to advocate for the creation of a national register to account for those who disappeared during the1991 Santa Cruz massacre, and the construction of a national monument, and hopes to build and archive to preserve documents and stories from the massacre.[18]

So, for some East Timorese survivors, remembering the past has become the starting point for a new, albeit fragile, politics. This politics draws its strength from experiences of collective suffering and a belief that the *povu ki'ik* must not be forgotten in the new independent nation. Some East Timorese survivors have been able to forge links of solidarity with each other in recognition of their common experiences. In some cases, they have begun to take on

16 Interview in Dili, 19 May 2007.

17 See http://sea.lib.niu.edu/inst/living.html for a description of the project.

18 Interview with member of the 12 November Committee, Dili, 9 July 2009.

public roles beyond their own local communities to demand justice. These demands encompass a diverse range of issues, from the need for the recovery of bodies of the dead and prosecutions, to the importance of economic assistance to address ongoing experiences of impoverishment and to recompense the *povu ki'ik* for their sacrifices. By highlighting that victims' suffering has not ended and that the struggle for justice remains unfinished, local acts of 'political mourning' further complicate official discourses of healing, forgiveness, transition and the remembrance of a triumphal past. Nonetheless, the agency, autonomy and 'home-grown' nature of victims' groups should not be overstated. As I now discuss in more detail, victims' groups have been intensively cultivated by national and international NGOs. Without this support, it is likely that many of their activities would not be sustainable.

The dialogue between victims' groups and NGOs

The growing prominence of local memory practices, and their increasing engagement with the formal political sphere, need to be understood within a broader political context of ongoing civil society advocacy campaigns for justice. Since 1999, prominent activists and national human rights NGOs,

Figure 6.3 Demonstration against the CTF, Dili, East Timor (text of banner reads 'Justice must come from the courts, not political compromises') (La'o Hamutuk)

including *Yayasan Hak* (Rights Foundation), *Fokupers* (East Timor Women's Communication Forum), the Justice and Peace Commission and *La'o Hamutuk* (Walking Together), have actively supported local victims' groups, and lobbied the East Timorese government and the international community for prosecutions of serious crimes. United by the phrase 'no reconciliation without justice', they have argued that prosecuting perpetrators of crimes against humanity and war crimes, and recognising the harms committed against victims, must be central to East Timor's nation-building process (Figure 6.3).

Importantly, East Timorese human rights activists are of a different generation from their political leaders. They came of age during the Indonesian occupation rather than during the period of Portuguese colonisation, were educated in the Indonesian language, and many attended Indonesian universities, where they formed strong links with Indonesian human rights activists and the international East Timor solidarity movement. The language of international human rights is thus more familiar to them than to their political leaders and they are, to some extent, less embroiled in the internal political divisions stemming from 1974–75.

Adding to the voices of young human rights activists, the East Timorese Catholic Church – in particular Bishop Belo, the former Bishop of Dili – has also firmly promoted the need for prosecutions for serious crimes. This stance was evident in a 'pastoral appeal', in June 2002, in which he was implicitly critical of parliamentary discussions of amnesty. Belo argued that:

> Insufficient human and financial resources in our institutions of justice cannot be used as an excuse to forgo litigation of perpetrators of high crimes against humanity in our country. On the contrary, it is precisely for these reasons that we should strengthen our institutions of justice so that the rule of law may prevail in our land, rather than the rule of power of occupation times.
>
> (Bishop Belo 2002)

Since Belo's replacement by Dom Ricardo da Silva in 2004, the East Timorese Catholic Church's public stance on questions of prosecutions has been muted and has shifted towards a more traditional, pastoral role. Nonetheless, the Church has not been wholly quiet and, in April 2005, the Bishops of Dili and Baucau wrote to the UN Secretary General outlining the Church's position on justice for crimes against humanity, stating:

> It is the right and duty of Catholics and all citizens to seek the truth and to promote and defend justice. On this basis, the Catholic community will continue to insist on the moral and legal accountability of all individuals that committed human rights violations and crimes against humanity in East Timor from 1975–1999.
>
> (Bishop Alberto Ricardo and Bishop Basilio do Nascimento 2005)

The letter was written in the context of the Commission of Experts' (COE) visit to East Timor, which, as discussed in Chapter 2, was established by the UN Secretary General to review the progress of prosecutions of serious violations of human rights and make recommendations. In light of the establishment of the bilateral CTF, in August 2005, NGOs and sections of the Church were concerned that the UN Security Council had not yet scheduled a discussion of the COE's report, which had recommended the reconsideration of an international criminal tribunal in the light of Indonesia's flawed attempts to prosecute serious crimes perpetrators through the Ad Hoc Human Rights Court. Bishop Dom Ricardo da Silva reiterated the Church's position on prosecutions at the recent National Consensus Dialogue for political leaders in Dili in June 2009.

During the UNTAET period, national human rights NGOs grew increasingly disillusioned with the UN's approach to justice. Relations between the SCIU and NGOs were initially strained by the unit's tendency to ignore their significant expertise and knowledge of human rights violations, and its general unwillingness to consult with the population. Over time, NGOs began increasingly to highlight the inadequate nature of the serious crimes model and the failure of the UN – contrary to its strong rhetoric – to implement effective mechanisms to prosecute Indonesian perpetrators. This disenchantment was firmly entrenched by the time of independence in 2002, when *Yayasan Hak* issued a statement lamenting that 'East Timor is gaining its independence without gaining justice, and without seeing any hope that there will ever be justice' (Yayasan Hak 2002).

In 2002, the East Timorese Alliance for an International Tribunal (*Alliansi*/the Alliance) was formed, comprising national NGOs, church representatives, victims' families and students, to more effectively co-ordinate advocacy work on justice. The basic position of the Alliance is that there must be accountability for the serious crimes committed in 1999 and during the Indonesian occupation, and that, because these involve crimes against humanity, genocide and war crimes, they are subject to universal jurisdiction and the international community has a responsibility for their prosecution. The Alliance has actively sought an international tribunal for East Timor similar to those established for the former Yugoslavia and Rwanda. Active at the international, regional and national levels, it lobbies the UN Human Rights Council (formerly the UN Commission on Human Rights), builds alliances with the international East Timor solidarity movement and key human rights organisations (among them Human Rights Watch, Amnesty International and the International Center for Transitional Justice), and networks with other victims' rights organisations across Asia.

While links to transnational advocacy networks have given the justice campaign additional lobbying power, they have not always been an advantage in the domestic political context. As in other post-conflict contexts, East Timor's political elite has too easily been able to dismiss the justice agenda as 'foreigner-driven' (see generally Brahm 2007: 62–72). The justice campaign has also been hamstrung by myriad other factors, such as national NGOs' lack of experience and declining levels of funding in the post-independence period, as donor priorities have shifted away from civil society to supporting the new state (see Hunt 2008: 297–313). NGO leaders have also struggled to define their relationship to an East Timorese government composed of former resistance leaders (Hunt 2009: 49), and their relatively young age has arguably limited their influence in a society that reveres the armed struggle. Nonetheless, since independence, the Alliance has become increasingly critical of the East Timorese leadership's 'forward-looking' reconciliation agenda. It has based its argument for prosecutions on Article 160 of the East Timorese Constitution on Serious Crimes, which states: 'Acts committed between 25th April 1974 and 31st December 1999 that can be considered crimes against humanity, genocide or war crimes shall be liable to criminal proceedings with the national or international courts.'

Since the 2006 crisis, the Alliance has also lobbied the national government on the need for a strong and impartial criminal justice system, and has drawn links between the failure to hold to account perpetrators of past serious crimes and the development of a culture of impunity in the present. It has suggested that the crisis was indicative of a widespread lack of confidence in the 'rule of law', and a climate in which perpetrators believe that they can act without fear of legal consequences. In an open letter to the UN Secretary General, the Alliance and international human rights activists suggested that the reactions of Dili residents to the 2006 events were those of a traumatised population, and that the severe shortcomings of the local and international justice processes have helped to create a 'culture of impunity' in which some actors believe it is literally possible to 'get away with murder and other crimes' (Alliance, ACTJET and IFET 2006). Similarly, the NGO *La'o Hamutuk* noted that the failure to hold the perpetrators of war crimes and crimes against humanity to account has created a culture conducive to human rights violations, in which 'new perpetrators expect to get away with their crimes, while victims see no option for justice other than taking it into their own hands' (La'o Hamutuk 2009a). While NGOs continue to lobby for an international criminal tribunal, the 2006 crisis has helped to foster a broadening of justice advocacy to include a focus on effective criminal justice not only for past crimes, but also for crimes in the present. The demands of NGOs, then, are both past- and future-oriented: criminal justice, they argue, is needed to satisfy individual victims of human rights violations, and to construct a new shared future based on the institutional protection of human rights and the 'rule of law.'

In addition, beyond their focus on the formal justice system, national human rights NGOs have also linked the violent events of 2006 to unresolved political divisions amongst the leadership. Like survivors, they are acutely aware that 'reconciliation' has been expected of local communities rather than the nation's elites, and have called on the East Timorese leaders to learn from their past mistakes. For example, the East Timor Crisis Reflection Network, formed in 2006, called upon the leaders of political parties to 'show political maturity and courage to carry out political reconciliation among each other'. In a press release, it suggested that:

> It is important that the leaders show to their people that they have reconciled themselves and can bring confidence to the communities and Timorese people in order to overcome the crisis of confidence and trust. All leaders should also recognise and have the courage to say that they made mistakes and should apologise to all Timorese that suffered from this crisis. This is important in order to contribute to communal reconciliation among Timorese people.
>
> (ETCRN 2006)

As in many other post-conflict contexts, relations between East Timorese NGOs and official truth-seeking mechanisms have not always been smooth (see generally Brahm 2007; Hayner 2011). NGOs were initially sceptical of the CAVR; while they were not in principle opposed to the Commission's aims, they were concerned that it might sap donor resources that would be better directed to building a more effective criminal justice system (see, for example, La'o Hamutuk 2001). They also worried about the balance of national and international staff within the CAVR, and the extent to which it would divert international attention from the issue of Indonesian military impunity (see La'o Hamutuk 2001). Thus, as *La'o Hamutuk* put it:

> there are questions about whether it is truly directed by East Timorese people, appropriate to the needs of this nation and serving the priorities of the East Timorese population. And how much has it cost this country in lost opportunities to hold major perpetrators accountable for their crimes?
>
> (La'o Hamutuk 2003)

The CTF aroused even deeper suspicions amongst the NGO community. Criticising the CTF as 'illegitimate', key NGOs maintained that it had been established to avoid calls for an international tribunal, and that it lacked transparency, clarity and popular support.[19] Indeed, during the period of its operation, the CTF was referred to disparagingly as 'Timor Fried Chicken' by the broader NGO community due to its unfortunate abbreviation.

19 See, for example, an open letter to the presidents of Indonesia and East Timor in May 2007 from national and international NGOs: http://www.uniya.org/news/news_23may07.html (accessed 15 July 2010).

Since the public release of the CAVR and CTF reports in 2006 and 2008, NGO criticism has softened, and activists have begun to see their potential as advocacy and educational tools. They actively lobbied the National Parliament to debate and implement the recommendations of *Chega!* and the CTF report. Alliances between East Timorese and Indonesian activists are also being strengthened on the basis of a mutual interest in lobbying their respective parliaments to implement the CTF recommendations, to prosecute senior members of the Indonesian military and to strengthen the democratic culture in both countries.

Recent years have also witnessed a discernable shift in the advocacy of East Timorese NGOs towards a greater emphasis on reparations. After many years of campaigning for an international tribunal, activists have become aware that the focus on prosecutions has not always addressed the practical material concerns of many victims. As Nela, former director of Fokupers, explains, NGOs began to recognise the difficulties of distinguishing between survivors' demands for effective criminal justice, the recovery of the remains of the dead and economic assistance, given the intertwined nature of these issues:

> When we speak to women survivors about justice they also say their daily lives are important. They want to send their children to school, they want to know where their husbands' bodies are . . . Some say that if we don't help their lives it is just the same.[20]

Chega! – in particular its substantial recommendations section, which was informed by views of victims – has perhaps contributed to this shift in the justice campaign.

The broadening and deepening of NGOs' justice agenda suggests that there is a dynamic relationship between their activities and local memory practices. Victims' demands for practical, material assistance can be seen reflected in the NGOs' growing focus on reparations. In turn, NGOs and the CAVR have had an effect on the development, and tenor, of local memory practices. The CAVR's truth-seeking activities encouraged some local communities to initiate the construction of monuments. In a very practical sense, NGOs have provided financial support for the establishment of victims' groups, funds for commemorations and monuments, and for transport to Dili for victims' events and demonstrations. Nonetheless, human rights advocates continue to express frustration about the extent to which issues such as poverty, illiteracy, difficulties with travel and lack of access to radio, television and print media in rural areas create obstacles to the development of a sustainable and broad-based victims' movement. These constraints have also led to the uneven development of local victims' groups. Groups that have survived tend

20 Interview with Nela, Dili, 2 July 2008.

to be located in more accessible areas, while those engaged in victims' rights advocacy at the national level represent an even more privileged group of articulate individuals who are well connected to NGOs. The central role that NGOs have played in cultivating victims' groups has also meant that, until recently, the membership of these groups has predominantly comprised victims of the 1999 violence – a reflection, perhaps, of the centrality of this period of history to young East Timorese activists.

The increasing engagement of local victims' groups with the formal political sphere is partly a reflection, then, of the influence and intensive support of national and international human rights advocates. While not seeking to overstate the organised nature of local victims' groups, or to underestimate their fragility, it is apparent that the discourse of victims' rights is enabling *some* individuals to identify themselves as 'victims' in order to articulate their personal grief and anger in the public sphere and to appeal to the state to listen to, and address, their concerns. The current campaign for reparations also suggests that victims' desires for material assistance have, to some extent, influenced NGOs' justice campaign. Given the current level of dependence on NGOs, however, it remains a question whether these groups will be sustainable in the long term, and whether they have the potential to shift the justice movement beyond the priorities of elite national NGOs and international organisations and to contribute to a broadening of the justice debate. In the next section, I reflect more deeply on the possibilities and limits of the emerging politics of victims' rights in East Timor, including who, and what, may be excluded from it.

The possibilities and limits of victims' rights politics

In recent years, a more expansive concept of victimhood has begun to emerge that pays greater attention to the diverse forms of harm experienced during the twenty-four-year Indonesian occupation. This may be a consequence in part, of the CAVR's attempts to shed light on these experiences, and to focus on sensitive issues such as East Timorese political-party violence and violence against women. It may also be a product of the growing political voice of victims themselves. Interestingly, there has also been some attention to the violence of the pre-Indonesian period. For example, in 2006, human rights NGO *Yayasan Hak* initiated a campaign focused on the experiences of East Timorese comfort women during the period of Japanese occupation, which requests an official apology and reparations from the Japanese government.[21]

21 Interview with Yayasan Hak staff member, Dili, 15 July 2009.

Reflecting on the experience of working with the widows' groups, Nela, the former director of *Fokupers*, explains that human rights NGOs have begun to recognise the problems that an exclusive focus on 1999 victims has created. She explains that *Fokupers* was initially preoccupied with how to assist widows from the 1999 violence due to the immediacy of these issues; for logistical reasons such as transport, it focused primarily on women living in rural capitals. Now, *Fokupers* recognises that this can be problematic if other women perceive that only certain '1999 widows' are getting assistance, and the organisation has begun to encourage these groups to expand their livelihood activities to include other impoverished women and, in some cases, men from these communities. At the same time, Nela is concerned that some of the widows' groups have developed a dependence on *Fokupers* assistance and an attachment to their identity as victims, to the extent that they do not want other women to join their group. As she describes:

> When we started working on these things we didn't have experience working with victims. We focused on 1999 and forgot about 1975 . . . Now the 1999 women feel they are the only ones who are important.[22]

Civil society leaders have also begun to acknowledge that NGOs have tended to 'speak on behalf of' victims rather than strengthening their own political voice, and in this sense, have replicated the mistakes of the government by purporting to understand victims' best interests. Maleve, for example, a prominent human rights activist and victim's representative from Lautem, explains his growing awareness that only 'some' victims were being represented:

> *Yayasan Hak* and the *Alliansi* always organise demos but it's always me, Edio, Sisto in the front. It's time to let others speak out . . . Sometimes I see the things that *Yayasan Hak* have produced using very technical language, and I ask whether any victims have been involved? They [NGOs] can't just bring victims into Dili. They should create mechanisms so that they can talk to the government themselves. Only victims can represent victims. I always speak at public gatherings but I also know that I can't represent all victims.[23]

Over time, then, NGOs have strengthened victims' own political voices to enable them to participate in public debates and have become more aware of victims' diverse experiences of harm. They have augmented their support for victims who live in remote areas and for victims from the pre-1999 period, to

22 Interview with Nela, Dili, 2 July 2008.
23 Interview with Maleve, Lautem, 7 June 2008.

enable them to participate in existing victims' groups. They have also encouraged the establishment of new victims' groups at the district, subdistrict and *suco* levels. The recognition that victims need their own national voice also led NGOs to organise a national 'Victims Congress' in September 2009, which brought together 150 victims and their families from around the country in Dili. This led to the formation of a national Victims' Network, with representatives in each district, to co-ordinate advocacy work in relation to justice, reconciliation and reparations. In the lead-up to the proposed parliamentary debate on the CAVR and CTF recommendations, NGOs assisted members of this network to gather monthly in front of the Parliament with a banner reading *'Bondia Deputadu, la bele haluha ita-nia promite'* ('Good morning, Parliamentarians, don't forget your promises').

Despite these developments, there may be limits to the extent to which it is possible to cultivate a shared national victims' voice in East Timor. Notwithstanding the constraints of inaccessible terrain, poverty and illiteracy, and the fragility of victims' groups, victims are not a unified group. Marked by diverse experiences of the conflict, their views are shaped by multiple factors, including gender, political background, socio-economic status, locality and age. Groups such as the 12 November Committee and ASSEPOL, composed of prominent male political leaders, have very different priorities from the widows' groups. Describing the aims of the organisation as 'moral' rather than 'political', the director of the 12 November Committee suggests that the organisation's key priority is to recover the bones of the 12 November victims, and to rebury them in order to give them value and honour. As self-described activists, those involved in the 12 November Committee also view themselves, and those who were killed in the massacre, as veterans rather than victims. The Committee places priority on socio-economic justice – by requesting government assistance for those who were deprived of schooling because of their role in youth resistance struggles – over criminal justice. As the director explains:

> Our objectives are the same as other victims' groups, but our methods are different. We are not so interested in an international tribunal because it is so difficult. We look at what we can do more easily.[24]

Similarly, Kristina, from Liquica, considers herself to be a victim, due to losing both of her parents and her brothers and sisters who were active in the Clandestine movement, and because she herself was imprisoned by FALINTIL for a year in a 'bush' prison in the early 1980s. Yet she distinguishes herself from 1999 victims, including the women involved in *Rate Laek*, whom she

24 Interview with director of the 12 November Committee, Dili, 9 July 2009.

believes have had very different experiences of violence and whose socio-economic situation is far removed from hers:

> 1975 is not the same as 1999 . . . Our experiences are very far apart. Their husbands have only just died in 1999 . . . The 1999 victims eat well, drink well. I am not the same as 1999 victims. I ate *ai farina* [cassava] in the jungle, I don't have a *cadeira* [chair, position]. The 1999 victims live well because their husbands worked for the government. They were not *ema biasa* [ordinary people] like me.[25]

Kristina suggests that undue attention has been paid to 1999 victims at the expense of those who suffered earlier in the Indonesian occupation, which, to her, was far worse. 'Comparing 1975 and 1999, 1999 was like a dream,' she explains. 'But in the *ai laran* [jungle] we didn't know the time, the date, our age – we ate *ai farina* [cassava].'[26]

Kristina's comments point to the limitations of a politics of victims' rights when it comes to recognising and encompassing a diversity of experiences. Kristina does not identify with all victims; she identifies with a small group of women from her village who were imprisoned together with her, at a particular point in time, in a FALINTIL bush prison, underscoring the strongly localised nature of victim identity (and identity in general) in East Timor. Kristina also wants to establish her own victims' group:

> I need to look for those who had the same experiences as me in the past . . . We need to organise separately. We need to have our own group [in Bazatete.] . . . I want to make a group so that the state can see that we are together.[27]

Although she distinguishes her experiences from those of the 1999 victims, Kristina's comments suggest that she has been influenced by the discourse of victims' rights, in that she believes that establishing her own group would help her to gain visibility and influence the government. Kristina's comments also allude to the extent to which while victimhood can form the basis for commonality and solidarity, it could also potentially become a basis for competing claims to recognition based upon a narrative of 'who suffered the most' or, perhaps more accurately, who suffered 'legitimately' (ie because of their support for the liberation struggle). Contestations over what constitutes legitimate victimhood have also arisen within the newly formed National Victims' Network, in which there has been some debate as to whether victims of FALINTIL and FRETILIN

25 Interview in Liquica, 28 July 2007.
26 Ibid.
27 Ibid.

violence, and women who had had sexual relations with the Indonesian military, should be entitled to participate in the network's activities.[28]

In the East Timor context, where many of the rural population feel excluded from rights and resources in the new nation state, the potential for competing claims to recognition is particularly acute. As discussed in previous chapters, structural violence – manifested through the widespread and chronic experiences of malnutrition, maternal mortality, illiteracy and fear that were part of the fabric of everyday life under the Indonesian occupation and Portuguese colonial rule – continues to have ongoing ramifications in the form of economic hardship, particularly for rural subsistence farmers. This has not been helped by the widening wealth inequalities between Dili and the rural areas and the disruptions of the 2006 crisis.

Further exacerbating the potential for competition is the fact that, as discussed in Chapter 4, the government has its own priorities for conferring recognition and distributing scarce state resources. It has favoured veterans, who conform to a particular heroic national identity, and other interest groups who are perceived as a political threat to national security or are viewed as a means of shoring up the political support of constituencies.[29] This approach, which is reflected in the provision of cash payments to 'petitioners', families of police officers killed by the military and those who were internally displaced due to the conflict (IDPs), is cultivating resentment amongst those who feel they have missed out. This includes the rural poor and those who describe themselves as victims, groups which, needless to say, are not considered to be threats by the current government and who do not fit within the national resistance narrative. Thus some victims express anger that the 'petitioners' have received assistance to 'reintegrate' into the community. Comments such as 'Why are all the petitioners who created problems for the state, and broke the law, receiving assistance, while we who sit quietly are receiving nothing?' were made by a number of interviewees. In addition, some 1999 victims have expressed frustration that those who were internally displaced in 2006 due to the 'crisis' have received economic assistance to rebuild their homes, while the earlier victims have yet to receive any assistance for their losses. As a prominent victims' advocate and member of *Rate Laek* stated on national radio: 'It's better if we 1999 victims just organise ourselves and go and live in a refugee camp.'[30] These developments suggest that identity politics has become one of the few avenues available to disenfranchised and marginalised East Timorese for asserting their claims for recognition and assistance.

28 Interview with staff member international NGO, Dili, 16 April 2011.

29 Lipscomb suggests that the creation of state programmes that offer direct benefits to constituents has become increasingly prevalent due to the fact that no one political party has a majority in the legislature at present (Lipscomb 2010: 4).

30 Comments heard on 20 July 2008.

As the most prominent feature of the emerging politics of victims' rights, the current campaign for reparations can be seen to contain both possibilities and limitations, in terms of its capacity to encourage solidarity, rather than competition, amongst a diverse group of victims and between victims and other marginalised groups. One positive feature of the draft law on reparations that NGOs and victims' groups are currently lobbying the Parliament to adopt is that it does not distinguish between victims on the basis of their support for the independence struggle; it is also inclusive of victims from the entire period of the Indonesian occupation (and the internal political conflict between FRETILIN and UDT). In addition, the main criteria for receiving individual reparations in the form of health and rehabilitation services, educational subsidies for children, vocational training, mental health services and assistance with the reburying of the remains of missing persons is 'vulnerability'.[31] The law's emphasis on need, as opposed to legitimacy of suffering and the breadth of its temporal time frame, might enable it to help to foster a more inclusive definition of victimhood. The fact that the law includes a range of collective measures, such as a national commemorations programme and a programme to assist communities seriously affected by the conflict through the provision of infrastructure and livelihoods projects within the scope of the law, might also help to encourage the building of social solidarity within local communities.

Nonetheless, even if it is adopted in its current form, the implementation of the reparations law, and the verification of victims' claims, are likely to occur in a highly charged context in which narratives of victimhood are shaped by contested ideas about what constitutes 'legitimate' suffering and participation in the resistance struggle. This threatens give rise to disputes at the local and national levels about who is deserving of victim status. Indeed, these kinds of issues have emerged in the veterans' process, in which community tensions have arisen regarding the legitimacy or otherwise of individuals' claims to veteran status.[32] Another potentially problematic aspect of the law is that only those who experienced a range of identifiable 'human rights violations' will be entitled to individual reparations.[33] This will potentially exclude

31 A 'vulnerable victim' is defined as a victim who continues to suffer from difficulties in the form of physical or mental damages, or from financial difficulties, as a result of one or more of the following human rights violations: torture; permanent physical or mental disability; the disappearance or summary execution of a spouse or their descendants; the forcible removal of parents; sexual violations or sexual slavery (Framework of the National Reparations Programme, Draft Law No II, Art 4).

32 Field observations 2007 and 2008.

33 These violations are defined as torture, a violation that resulted in permanent physical or mental disability, close relatives of victims of disappearances or summary execution, forced removal of parents, sexual violations or sexual slavery of those who were born as a result of an act of rape or sexual slavery (Framework of the National Reparations Programme, Draft Law No II, Art 4).

the many East Timorese people who experienced the less visible and more 'everyday' forms of harm, such as poverty, malnutrition and the death of family members due to illness, during the occupation. In other words, as Gledhill (2003: 211) observes, a problem with claims for redress made on the basis of historical injustice is that they often rest on an identity claim in the present, in which those who cannot successfully appropriate that identity, but might be considered equally disadvantaged, are unable to make the same kind of claim. Finally, by encouraging the channelling of local demands in the language of individual rights, rather than collective needs, the reparations law may also work to 'fix' identities in a particular way, 'imposing narrower limits on an understanding of agency than might be possible necessary or desirable' (Ross 2005: 233), and restricting the possibilities for building solidarity amongst those who have experienced diverse forms of harm (Ross 2003b: 179).

The emerging politics of victims' rights in East Timor, then, and in particular the current campaign for reparations, has mixed consequences. Given the current context of identity politics, there is a potential for the individualist language of rights to foster competition between different kinds of victims, and between victims and other marginalised groups, all struggling for scarce resources and recognition, contributing to an emerging 'hierarchy of the deserving'. By the same token, and not wanting to overstate the influence of a victims' rights politics on national political developments, the growing political voice of some victims also indicates that 'official' narratives of justice and nation-building are being actively renegotiated and reconstructed from below, and that the language of rights may hold the potential to open up possibilities of political expression for some of those who have been marginalised in 'official' transitional justice discussions. By shedding light on diverse – and previously undisclosed – experiences of harm, this politics may help to shift the focus away from heroic triumphal nation-building narratives towards the diverse experiences of the *povu ki'ik* and to broaden and deepen the justice debate.

Conclusion

While it is tempting to celebrate the growing visibility of local memory practices and the emergence of a victims' rights politics as representing an active and engaged local sphere, I do not want to overplay the extent to which 'the margins' in East Timor have become sites of creativity and agency. Fiona Ross's observations about the kind of life being led by dwellers within an urban slum community in South Africa seems apposite when describing the agency embodied in the acts of East Timorese survivors. Ross writes:

> People struggle against forms of vulnerability and social invisibility and they sometimes succeed in making gains. Thus margins are sites of both

> subjugation and creativity, zones in which possibility and constraint play off one another, often in unpredictable ways.
>
> (Ross 2010: 208)

Like the South African township dwellers of whom Ross writes, East Timorese survivors are doing their best to reconstruct their everyday lives, remember and mourn the past, and fulfil customary responsibilities to the dead in the wake of the Indonesian occupation. Yet, they are also grappling with experiences of profound loss, and the constrictions imposed by ongoing poverty, food insecurity, illiteracy, geography and poor health. The long conversations I had with East Timorese members of widows' groups also revealed the extent to which the renegotiation of everyday life in the aftermath of the conflict is deeply *gendered*, constrained by masculinist nation-building narratives and the social mores imposed by a conservative and Catholic society. The practices East Timorese survivors are engaged in, then, are not 'choices, in the sense implied by liberal notions of the sovereign subject' (Ross 2010: 211). Rather than being oriented along 'definite paths, pursuing definite claims and establishing particular identifiable rights' (Fitzpatrick and Tuit 2004: xix), their actions have more of an 'improvisational quality' (Ross 2010: 211).

In this context, attempts at remaking the world take on a range of different forms. At some levels, the official transitional justice process and national nation-building process remain marginal to the reconstruction of everyday life and the imagining of a collective future that is taking place in local communities. Exhibiting its own politics and power struggles, the local level is where the re-establishment of relationships and social bonds that were fractured during the Indonesian occupation is taking place, through activities such as rebuilding *uma luliks* (sacred houses), reburying the dead, and conducting ceremonies to put to rest the spirits of loved ones. These practices point to the personalised, localised and ongoing demands of justice. Invoking responsibilities to the spirit world and to the living, local memory practices illuminate the centrality of customary responsibilities to care for the dead. They underscore the ongoing need to remember and mourn the past, transmit memories to the younger generation as part of a struggle against forgetting, to rebuild fractured relationships and to improve the lives of victims and their children in the present. Embedded in the realm of ordinary everyday life, these practices complicate national and international narratives of justice by resisting final 'closure' and at times contesting the appropriation of personal experiences for broader nation-building purposes.

That some survivors of violence are beginning to see themselves as political agents, making public demands for recognition and reparations from the state, suggests that some local memory practices also have a relationship with international and national conceptions of justice and nation-building. Although the contours of this victims' rights politics remain far from fixed, it delineates how local victims' groups have been influenced by the discourse of human rights promoted by the CAVR and NGOs. Local actors imbue this discourse with new meanings, including by introducing a socio-economic dimension into 'justice' advocacy. I have raised some concerns about the fact that this politics – and in particular the current campaign for reparations – is taking shape within a broader context of scarce state resources and widespread poverty in which a variety of groups compete for access to resources and official recognition. In this context, there is potential for the campaign for reparations to bring to the fore new tensions amongst different *kinds* of victims, and between victims and other interest groups. At the same time, the emergence of a politics of victims' rights can be seen as a positive development. By calling attention to 'unfinished business' and victims' continuing experiences of *injustice*, this politics is a sign that official discourses of justice and nation-building are being actively remade from below and, in this sense, are being 'vernacularised'. New discussions about the past are taking place, and they have the capacity to lead to the emergence of new, locally grounded conceptions of 'justice' at the national level that are based on the experiences of the *povu ki'ik*.

The dynamic nature of local memory practices, and the ongoing struggle for recognition and resources, also highlights some of the unexpected and paradoxical consequences of the transitional justice process. It is a sign that 'official' narratives emanating from the international sphere are being assigned new meanings within a highly charged national sphere in which the government has its own priorities for distributing scarce state resources, based on its own preferred narratives of national identity. National and international narratives are also interacting with a dynamic and fluid local sphere where they are being imbued with new meanings. These developments indicate that the official transitional justice process has become embedded within a broader social and political process, where it is being shaped, contested and transformed by a myriad of different actors – among them international and national NGOs, the East Timorese leadership, local victims' groups and other marginalised groups – and is gaining its meaning as part of a broader dialogue about the past. In the drive towards 'closure', a new form of politics is emerging in which victims have the potential to be key actors.

Chapter 7

Rethinking transitional justice

More than a decade on from the referendum, East Timor continues to grapple with the aftermath of its violent past. Questions about how to deal with issues of impunity and accountability, whether and how to provide reparations to victims or grant amnesties to militia members, how to maintain ongoing relations with its large neighbour and former occupier, and how to forge a new future through the shaping of collective memory remain pressing preoccupations for the political leadership. For ordinary East Timorese, a gradual reconstruction of everyday life is under way in local attempts to locate and bury the remains of the dead, to rebuild fractured relationships with neighbours and family, and to transmit memories to, and create a better life for, the next generation. These highly charged and complex issues, which are at once intensely personal and openly political, go to the heart of the ongoing process of seeking 'justice' in the post-referendum period.

By way of conclusion, this chapter reflects on the main findings of this book, which demonstrate the *dynamic* nature of transitional justice. I then offer some reflections on what 'rethinking' transitional justice entails for practitioners, justice activists and scholars, both in East Timor and beyond. Given the important influence of these actors in defining what constitutes 'official' transitional justice discourse and practice, there is an onus on them to be reflexive. Reimagining transitional justice, I suggest, is more than a 'technical' task. While there is, of course, a place for improving techniques and practices, I argue that transitional justice scholars, practitioners and justice activists need to reflect more deeply on the intricate, dynamic and long-term nature of seeking justice in the wake of conflict. These reflections would inform a reconceptualisation of transitional justice as an ongoing, locally grounded, social and political conversation.

Transitional justice in East Timor: an ongoing conversation

This book has unsettled the narratives of transition, retribution, or 'settling accounts', and restoration that underpinned the UN-sponsored transitional justice process in East Timor. I have done this by exploring the interplay between narratives of justice promoted by actors within the international, national and local spheres. I have shown that developing a 'thicker' understanding (as per McEvoy 2008) of the nature of these interactions is critical for appreciating the rich, multilayered and dynamic nature of transitional justice, including how 'official' narratives are reconfigured within specific national and local contexts, in often unexpected ways.

We have seen that, for a plethora of reasons, neither the transitional justice process nor the East Timorese leadership have been able to provide a definitive 'justice' response that could provide an authoritative basis for building shared values and a shared political community. Rather, in the gaps between local expectations and the form of justice that has been officially delivered, a conversation is continuing about how best to 'deal with the past'. What can be observed is that official transitional justice discourse and practice has contributed to the emergence of new narratives (based around concepts of victims' rights), encouraged emerging forms of identification (based around victimhood) and contributed to a new form of victim politics. Emphasising unreconciled experiences and unfinished business, this politics is unfolding at a time when the constituents and tensions of nation formation are laid bare. The boundaries of this politics are being shaped and contested by a range of different actors with varying degrees of political power: the national government and opposition parties; national and international human rights organisations; the UN; victims' groups; widows' groups; and other interest groups.

The unsettled and fluid nature of these developments highlights that dealing with the past is a continuing process, rather than confined to a specific 'transitional' period. This process is being moulded by East Timor's specific historical and geopolitical circumstances, and is unfolding within a context in which there are pre-existing power relations and pre-existing debates about the meanings of the past and the nature of 'justice'. It is also being shaped and constrained by East Timor's colonial legacies, the imperative of building workable relations with Indonesia, and the new nation's fragile and unequal position within the 'international community'. These dynamics suggest that the transitional justice process in East Timor is perhaps best described as an ongoing social and political conversation between international, national and local actors.

Rethinking transitional justice: implications for practitioners and scholars

What insights might East Timor's experiences offer to transitional justice practitioners? One key implication that flows from acknowledging the dynamic nature of 'dealing with the past' is that it is necessary for those involved in the establishment of trials and truth commissions to correct the 'celebratory impulse' (Scheper-Hughes and Bourgois 2004: 27) that leads to a tendency to portray these mechanisms as short-term, legal or therapeutic 'solutions' to violence, and to reflect more deeply on their possibilities and limitations, power relations, paradoxes and exclusions. This process of reflexivity could help to open the way for the emergence of a more grounded, locally embedded, approach to transitional justice.

A starting point for this rethinking involves questioning the assumptions about the link between transitional justice mechanisms and the goals of rule of law, reconciliation, deterrence and transition; space needs to be made for contradiction and tension. One key contradiction is the fact that even well-intentioned transitional justice initiatives are constrained by broader political forces (including the practical and normative demands of state-building projects), which reflect the power inequities between the 'developed' and the 'developing' world. These relations of power, often reconstituted by externally devised transitional justice processes, are at odds with the tendency of international actors to see their interventions as neutral or technical. Better awareness of the limits of transitional justice also requires accepting that trials and truth commissions, while having a role to play, are unlikely to fully address local demands for justice, which encompass a range of intertwined issues and needs. It is certainly the case that transitional justice practitioners could think more creatively about how to address more of these needs. For example, in the East Timor context, community dissatisfaction with the transitional justice process may well have been assuaged to some extent by initiatives that gave greater attention to the urgent material, health and cultural/spiritual reburial needs of survivors, putting more resources into exhuming and identifying the dead and listing the missing, and improving community outreach (including honest communication about the limits of the Serious Crimes Process and CAVR). Even with these reforms, it is unlikely that an official transitional justice process, due to its inherently limited interpretation of justice, finite resources, short time frame and the broader political constraints upon its work, would have completely responded to local expectations. Further complicating this is the fact that only a relatively small number of survivors ever have the opportunity to participate in truth commissions, with even fewer seeing their claims become the subject of trial proceedings. Finally, the way in which transitional justice mechanisms intersect with pre-existing national and local beliefs, value systems and disputes also produces new forms of political engagement and new justice conversations, which in turn need to be acknowledged as part of the process of transitional justice.

The point I seek to make here is not that all of these contradictions, limitations and local power dynamics can necessarily be 'overcome'; rather, it is that a greater awareness of their existence would help practitioners to resist the seductive promises of transitional justice discourse and instead acknowledge the contingent, partial and political (rather than technical, neutral and therapeutic) nature of these processes. Such reflection is necessary to build different kinds of relationships between international transitional justice practitioners and national and local actors. These relationships would situate international practitioners as one set of actors among many in a shared, open-ended conversation that is responsive to the demands of specific local contexts.

Andrew Schaap's (2005; 2006) work on political reconciliation offers a good starting point for thinking about what this transitional justice conversation might look like. Rather than assuming that social conflict has a clear end point, Schaap conceptualises reconciliation as a process of ongoing political interaction through which individuals can develop relationships with others. Drawing on the insights of Hannah Arendt, he sees the process of reconciliation as providing 'space for politics in which individuals can appear before each other, and people can engage in a collective effort to transform the world or enter a discourse about how the world appears to each of them' (Schaap 2005: 60). The open-ended discussions and negotiations that he imagines do not depend on individuals holding similar viewpoints. That is, the fact that the world appears differently to those who are involved with each other in the public realm should not be seen as 'an impediment to public life, a source of conflict that should be overcome' (Schaap 2005: 61); rather, this 'difficult, restless and unceasing negotiation' (Norval 1999: 510) should be acknowledged as a sign of openness and ongoing responsiveness to others, and as intrinsic to the process of reconciliation itself. This process, of course, is not without risk. Such discussions may well lead to further conflict rather than consensus or resolution. However, Schaap (2006: 255) maintains that this risk is a necessary one, in that creating community is contingent upon the political action of citizens and cannot be instituted from 'above'. Moreover, the attempts by national elites and international transitional justice practitioners to present reconciliation as a restorative and healing process will merely act to paper over, rather than resolve, those conflicts (Schaap 2005: 21).

Approaching transitional justice as an open-ended, political conversation pushes practitioners to move beyond a preoccupation with short-term 'outcomes' in the form of prosecutions or truth commission reports, and toward considering what role these mechanisms could play in fostering inclusive national and local discussion on justice and the significance of the past. Giving greater priority to issues of national and local participation in the design of official transitional justice mechanisms would encourage these kinds of discussions, as would seeking to understand and address the structural barriers that prevent certain kinds of individuals – including women and others with less power in local communities – from taking part in formal transitional justice processes. More than this, however, a crucial shift must be to move the conceptual framework beyond the standardised toolkit approach, which envisages both trials and truth commissions as short-term, technical and neutral mechanisms that can be introduced over and above the political sphere. Meaningful national conversations about official transitional justice mechanisms (and other justice priorities) are required prior to their establishment, to reduce the extent to which these mechanisms are 'internationalised but isolated from their societies' (Chandler 2006: 166). Diverse discussions about the past need also to be fostered long after the substantive work of a truth commission or trial is completed. The flexible mandates of truth commissions, and their capacity to involve the participation of a diverse range of community members, suggests that they are better placed to make this kind of contribution than criminal trials; indeed, in the East Timor context, *Chega!* has shown itself to have the potential to open up new discussions on a range of previously 'taboo' topics (particularly if it can be translated into a meaningful form for a non-literate audience). Nonetheless, there is also a need for practitioners to give more attention to conducting less formal, locally embedded, conversations, which could enable a broad range of community members to discuss, debate and negotiate the past, and through this process to 'remake the world'. Ultimately, however, a commitment to an open-ended, political approach to transitional justice entails letting go of the belief that these discussions will lead to final 'restoration', the 'settling of accounts' or 'transition' in the short term, and acknowledging that they are more likely than not to give rise to a new set of debates and conversations.

Recognising the dynamic, social and political dimensions of transitional justice also poses challenges for scholarship. One key implication is that more attention should be devoted to studying the ongoing effects of official transitional justice processes, including how they intersect with national and local narratives, and the consequences of this interaction, rather than focusing solely on the delivery of verdicts and the production of truth commission reports. A related implication is the need to conceptualise transitional justice as a multifaceted process that is given meaning and shape by a myriad of 'official' and 'unofficial' actors. By widening the parameters of transitional justice beyond 'official' legal and quasi-legal mechanisms, to consider the intricate and ongoing interactions between international, national and local actors, scholars could help to develop a more dynamic conception of transitional justice that is grounded in, and responsive to, local realities.

Rethinking transitional justice: implications for East Timorese justice activists and NGOs

Acknowledging that transitional justice is an ongoing social and political process also has implications for East Timorese justice activists and NGOs, and their international supporters, amongst whom I count myself. One of the roles that these actors can play is to help to ensure that official justice mechanisms and processes are responsive to the needs and priorities of a diverse group of survivors. In addition, perhaps more so than practitioners, activists have the capacity to attend to the 'small stories' that do not easily fit the grand linear narratives of retribution and restoration, and to support the pursuit of justice both within and beyond the parameters of the law.

As I have elucidated, East Timorese activists have played an important role in exposing the failures of international and national justice initiatives. Their advocacy continues to highlight that the prosecution of senior members of the Indonesian military is a critical component of 'justice' in the East Timor context. While not suggesting that this campaign should be abandoned, it is important to also recognise – as activists themselves are beginning to do – that the single-minded pursuit of an international criminal tribunal does not grasp the multifaceted and varied justice demands of East Timorese survivors. At times, this campaign has inadvertently reproduced the 'seductive' assumptions of transitional justice discourse by assuming that justice will be realised through a short-term, internationally driven legal process that is introduced over and above the national and local political spheres. The organisation of a national victims' congress in late 2009 and NGOs' support for a national victims' association suggests that activists have become aware of the need to strengthen victims' own political voices to enable them to represent their own interests. The emergence of a reparations campaign indicates that there is also an increasing acknowledgement that justice advocacy must include a socio-economic dimension. The recent campaign by *Yayasan Hak*, seeking redress for 'comfort women' in East Timor during the Japanese occupation, also indicates that activists are widening their lens to consider the experiences of violence during the pre-Indonesian period. As victims' groups themselves become increasingly engaged in national justice debates, they are likely to further reshape justice advocacy.

Despite these promising shifts, there remains further scope for justice activists and NGOs to develop a more expansive and transformative justice vision that encompasses the experiences of a broader group of survivors. One challenge might involve ensuring that existing advocacy pays more attention to the 'everyday' experiences of violence, including poverty, malnutrition and poor health that affected the large numbers of East Timorese people during the Indonesian occupation. This requires going beyond the boundaries of the current reparations campaign, which, while representing an increasing responsiveness to victims' material circumstances, also has the potential to exclude those who cannot be categorised as a 'victim' within the limited parameters of the law. For example, this campaign does not sufficiently take account of the experiences of widows whose husbands or children died during the Indonesian occupation due to a lack of food or medicines, nor does it acknowledge the frustrations of many East Timorese who perceive that the conflict denied them an education and opportunities, and hence kept them mired in poverty. Attending to these diverse and everyday experiences might lead activists to consider how justice advocacy could become part of a political call for the collective transformation of the poor economic conditions, health and education of the disadvantaged and marginalised in East Timor. It would also entail reminding the Indonesian state, and the Western governments that supported the occupation, of their responsibilities to address the ongoing effects of past violence by providing collective reparations in the form of development assistance.

In developing a more inclusive, collective vision of justice within the East Timorese community, activists might find it valuable to adopt Mahmood Mamdani's concept of 'survivors justice', which seeks to transcend the bipolar notions of victim and perpetrator in order to imagine a new community of 'all those who continue to be blessed with life' in the aftermath of conflict (Mamdani 2001a: 272–3). Envisaged as a means to help to build an inclusive community in Rwanda, where many ordinary people were implicated in the genocide, Mamdani's concept of survivors' justice may well have resonance in East Timor, where there is an acute awareness in local communities of the many ways in which ordinary people were affected by, and implicated in, the violence of the Indonesian occupation. Activists could also seek to engage more deeply with the political leadership's discourse of social justice, which focuses on the collective needs of the East Timorese people and their shared experiences of struggle, martyrdom and heroism, and endeavour to make this vision one that is truly inclusive of diverse experiences of the conflict.

Like transitional justice practitioners, activists and NGOs need also to consider increasing support for local, collective, efforts to commemorate the past and honour the dead. East Timorese activists are already engaged in some important initiatives in this regard. Funds for community memorialisation, reburials and commemoration ceremonies are also some of the elements of the proposed reparations programme currently being discussed by the East Timorese Parliament. Support for these kinds of initiatives is critical in that the local level is where the rebuilding of relationships, the reconstruction of everyday life and the negotiation of the future is taking place. While not without their own politics, local memory practices enable people to remember and mourn the past in personal, as well as collective, ways, and to tell stories that may challenge the boundaries erected by of transitional justice practitioners, the national leadership *and* justice advocates. Given the extent to which the Indonesian occupation sowed deep fear and mistrust within local communities, these practices are particularly important for building a community of survivors. By assisting communities to build on these activities and enter into a dialogue with the political leadership, justice activists could also help to bring about a more inclusive *national* conversation about the past that is grounded in the experiences of the *povu ki'ik*, including women, survivors of East Timorese political-party violence and others who remain marginalised within official nation-building discourses. This conversation could help to guard against premature 'closure' by serving as a reminder to political elites of the need for *ongoing* remembrance and memorialisation.

It is important to reiterate that, in offering these suggestions, I do not wish to imply that the continuing struggle for prosecutions of members of the

Indonesian military should be jettisoned. Indeed, the campaign for an international tribunal for this purpose continues to resonate amongst the East Timorese population, in part because it symbolises the broader struggle for recognition of the long-term structural oppression that they experienced at the hands of the Indonesian military, and the complicity of Western states. By contesting the official Indonesian narrative about what 'really happened' in 1999 and during the earlier years of the occupation, prosecutions would also help to reconstitute a basis for ongoing discussions between the two nations about these issues. Through the accountability campaign, East Timorese and Indonesian activists are also forging links of solidarity based on their common interest in challenging the prominence, power and impunity of the Indonesian military, including the ongoing violence being perpetrated in provinces such as Aceh and West Papua. Instead, my argument is simply that it is reasonable to conclude that an international tribunal will not fully respond to the justice demands of East Timorese survivors. As has become clear in this book, these demands encompass multiple, intertwined issues, including desires for the recovery and burial of the bodies of missing family members, the public shaming of wrongdoers and the restoration of survivors' status in their communities, official recognition of past and ongoing experiences of violence, economic assistance, and respect and care for the dead. Responding to these diverse and highly personalised demands requires thinking both within, and beyond, the prescriptive parameters of the criminal law. It entails acknowledging that the pursuit of justice is an ongoing process that needs to involve the active participation of survivors themselves.

Rethinking transitional justice

This book does not suggest that trials and truth commissions have no role to play in the pursuit of justice in post-conflict societies. What it does argue, however, is the need to correct the 'celebratory impulse' that fuels the tendency of transitional justice practitioners to portray these mechanisms as having the capacity to 'resolve' complex legacies of conflict. East Timor's experiences show that transitional justice is a far more dynamic, ongoing process than the narratives of retribution, restoration and transition imply. It is necessary to widen the parameters of what is taken to constitute transitional justice beyond official legal and quasi-legal mechanisms to consider the ways in which international, national and local narratives intersect in specific contexts. Transitional justice is an open-ended, locally grounded conversation; it is not a short-term, technical project. By acknowledging this, scholars, practitioners and justice activists may ultimately be in a better position to engage with, and respond to, the complexity of justice demands in post-conflict societies.

Bibliography

Aarons, M. (2006) 'Beloved Companheiros: What Happened in East Timor', *The Monthly*, August.

—— (2008) 'Justice Betrayed: Post-1945 Responses to Genocide', in D. A. Blumenthal and T. L. H. McCormack (eds) *The Legacy of Nuremberg: Civilising Influence or Institutionalised Vengeance?* (pp. 69–97), Leiden: Martinus Nijhoff.

Agliomby, J. (2000) 'Timorese Pay Price for Stability', *The Guardian*, 15 November. Online. Available http://www.theguardian.co.uk (accessed 17 December 2009).

Allen, J. (1999) 'Balancing Justice and Social Unity: Political Theory and the Idea of a Truth and Reconciliation Commission', *The University of Toronto Law Journal*, 49(3): 315–53.

Alliance/ACTJET/IFET (Timor-Leste Alliance for an International Tribunal, Australian Coalition for Transitional Justice in East Timor and International Federation for East Timor) (2006) 'Letter to the UN Secretary-General on Justice', 21 July. Online. Available http://www.etan.org/ifet/ (accessed 10 February 2010).

Amnesty International (2005) 'Timor-Leste: Denial of Justice?' (Public Statement, 29 November). Online. Available http://www.etan.org/et2005/november/default.htm (accessed 10 January 2009).

Anderson, B. (1983) *Imagined Communities*, London: Verso.

—— (1993) 'Imagining East Timor', *Arena Magazine*, 4(Apr–May).

Anghie, A. (2005) *Imperialism, Sovereignty and the Making of International Law*, Cambridge: Cambridge University Press.

ANTARA News (2006) 'President Called on to Ask Clarification from Xanana', 27 January. Online. Available http://www.etan.org/et2006/january/21/27pres.htm (accessed 5 June 2009).

Ashplant, T. G., Dawson, G. and Roper, M. (eds) (2000) *The Politics of War Memory and Commemoration: Contexts, Structures and Dynamics*, Oxford: Routledge.

Asia Society (2006) 'Asia Source Interview with Jose Ramos Horta', 20 March. Online. Available http://www.asiasource.org/news/special_reports/horta2.cfm (accessed 14 May 2010).

Babo-Soares, D. (2003) 'Branching from the Trunk: East Timorese Perceptions of Nationalism in Transition', unpublished PhD thesis, Australian National University.

—— (2005) '*Nahe Biti*: Grassroots Reconciliation in East Timor', in E. Skaar, S. Gloppen and A. Suhrke (eds) *Roads to Reconciliation* (pp. 225–46), Lanham, MD: Lexington Books.

BBC News (2006) 'Army Chief Denies Timor Killings', 22 January. Online. Available http://news.bbc.co.uk/2/hi/asia-pacific/4637190.stm (accessed 10 February 2010).

Beauvais, J. (2001) 'Benevolent Despotism: A Critique of UN State-Building in East Timor', *Journal of International Law and Politics*, 33: 1101–78.

Bhuta, N. (2001) 'Great Expectations: East Timor and the Vicissitudes of Externalised Justice', *Finnish Yearbook of International Law*, 12: 165–89.

—— (2005) 'Between Liberal Legal Didactics and Political Manichaeism: The Politics and Law of the Iraqi Special Tribunal', *Melbourne Journal of International Law*, 10: 245–71.

—— (2009) 'Democratisation, State-Building and Politics as Technology', in B. Bowden, H. Charlesworth and J. Farrall (eds) *The Role of International Law in Rebuilding Societies after Conflict* (pp. 38–63), Cambridge: Cambridge University Press.

Bishop Alberto Ricardo and Bishop Basilio Nascimento (2005) 'The Catholic Church of East Timor Position on Justice for Crimes against Humanity' (Presented to the Commission of Experts appointed by the Secretary General, 9 April). Online. Available http://www.etan.org/et2005/july/01/01cathlc.htm (accessed 15 January 2010).

Bishop Belo (2002) 'A Pastoral Appeal: On Amnesty and the Settlement of Crimes against Humanity', 29 June. Online. Available http://www.etan.org/et2002c/july/01–06/01apastr.htm (accessed 15 January 2010).

Blau, S. (2007) 'Should the Past Remain Buried? Examining the Contributions Forensic Archaeology and Anthropology Can Make to Post-Conflict Justice', in D. Kingsbury and M. Leach (eds) *East Timor: Beyond Independence* (pp. 141–8), Melbourne: Monash University Press.

Booth, J. W. (2001) 'The Unforgotten: Memories of Justice', *American Political Science Review*, 95(4): 777–90.

Border, T. A. (2003) 'A Taxonomy of Victims and Perpetrators: Human Rights and Reconciliation in South Africa', *Human Rights Quarterly*, 25: 1088–116.

Brahm, E. (2007) 'Transitional Justice, Civil Society and the Development of the Rule of Law in Post-Conflict Societies', *International Journal of Not-for-Profit-Law*, 9(4): 62–72.

Brown, A. (2009) 'Security, Development and the Nation-Building Agenda: East Timor', *Conflict, Security and Development*, 9(2): 141–64.

Burchill, R. (2009) 'From East Timor to Timor-Leste: A Demonstration of the Limits of International Law in the Pursuit of Justice', in J. Doria, H.-P. Gasser and M. C. Bassiouni (eds) *The Legal Regime of the ICC: Essays in Honour of Prof. Igor Blishchenko* (pp. 255–96), Leiden and Boston, MA: Martinus Nijhoff.

Callinicos, A. (2008) 'Jacques Derrida and the New International', in S. Glendinning and R. Eaglestone (eds) *Derrida's Legacies* (pp. 80–9), New York: Routledge.

Campbell-Nelson, K. (2003) 'East Timor Women Must Tell of Atrocities by Indonesians', *The Jakarta Post*, 9 and 10 June.

Carothers, T. (2002) 'The End of the Transition Paradigm', *Journal of Democracy*, 13(1): 5–21.

—— (2003) *Promoting the Rule of Law Abroad: The Problem of Knowledge* (Rule of Law Series, Democracy and Rule of Law Project), Washington DC: Carnegie Endowment for International Peace.

CAVR (Commission for Reception Truth and Reconciliation) (2001) *Progress Report on Selection Panel Consultations*, 14 November (Copy on file with author).

—— (2004a) 'CAVR Update Dec 03–Jan 04'. Online. Available http://www.cavr-timorleste.org/en/CAVRupdate.htm (accessed 10 July 2010).

—— (2004b) *Women and the Conflict April 1974–Oct 1999: Report of the CAVR Research Team on Women and the Conflict* (Copy on file with author), Dili: CAVR.

—— (2005a) *Chega!*, Dili: CAVR.

—— (2005b) *Women and the Conflict* (CAVR Public Hearing Book), Dili: CAVR.

—— (2005c) *Timor-Leste: Massacres* (CAVR Public Hearing Book), Dili: CAVR.

—— (2005d) *Timor-Leste: Political Imprisonment* (CAVR Public Hearing Book), Dili: CAVR.

—— (2007) *The Internal Political Conflict* (CAVR Public Hearing Book, pre-publication copy), Dili: CAVR.

Chandler, D. (2004) 'The Problems of "Nation-Building": Imposing Bureaucratic "Rule from Above"', *Cambridge Review of International Affairs*, 17(3): 577–91.

—— (2006) *Empire in Denial: The Politics of State-Building*, London: Pluto Press.

Charlesworth, H. and Chinkin, C. (2000) *The Boundaries of International Law: A Feminist Analysis*, Manchester: Manchester University Press.

Chesterman, S. (2002) 'East Timor in Transition: Self-Determination, State-Building and the United Nations', *International Peacekeeping*, 9(1): 45–76.

—— (2004) *You, the People: The United Nations, Transitional Administration and State-Building*, Oxford: Oxford University Press.

Chiam, M. (2008) 'Different Models of Tribunals', in D. A. Blumenthal and T. L. H. McCormack (eds) *The Legacy of Nuremberg: Civilising Influence of Institutionalised Vengeance?* (pp. 205–28), Leiden and Boston, MA: Martinus Nijhoff.

Chopra, J. (2000) 'The UN's Kingdom of East Timor', *Survival*, 42(3): 27–39.

—— (2002) 'Building State Failure in East Timor', *Development and Change*, 33(5): 979–1000.

CIGI (The Centre for International Governance Innovation) (2011) *Security Sector Reform Monitor: Timor-Leste* (SSRM, January, No. 4) Waterloo, ON: CIGI.

Cleary, P. (2007) *Shakedown: Australia's Grab for Oil*, Crow's Nest, NSW: Allen & Unwin.

Cleveland, T. (2005) '"We Still Want the Truth": The ANC's Angolan Detention Camps and Postapartheid Memory', *Comparative Studies of South Asia, Africa and the Middle East*, 25(1): 63–77.

CNRT (National Council for Timorese Resistance) (2000a) *Resolution Commission 3: Outcomes of the CNRT National Congress, 21–30 August 2000* (Copy on file with author), Dili: CNRT.

—— (2000b) 'CNRT on Recent Events in West Timor: Calls for an International Tribunal; Postponement of CGI Meeting', 13 September. Online. Available http://etan.org/news/2000b/CNRT2.htm (accessed 30 November 2009).

Cohen, D. (2002) *Seeking Justice on the Cheap: Is the East Timor Tribunal Really a Model for the Future?* (East–West Center Analysis No. 61), Honolulu, HI: East–West Center.

—— (2003) *Intended to Fail: The Trials before the Ad Hoc Human Rights Court in Jakarta* (Occasional Paper Series, August), New York: International Center for Transitional Justice.

—— (2006) *Justice on the Cheap Revisited: The Failure of the Serious Crimes Trials in East Timor* (East–West Center Analysis No. 80), Honolulu, HI: East–West Center.

Cohen, S. (1995) 'State Crimes of Previous Regimes: Knowledge, Accountability and the Policing of the Past', *Law and Social Inquiry*, 20(1): 7–50.

—— (2001) *States of Denial: Knowing about Atrocities and Suffering*, Cambridge: Polity Press.

COI (Commission of Inquiry) (2006) *Report of the United Nations Independent Special Commission of Inquiry for Timor Leste*, 2 October, Geneva: United Nations High Commission for Human Rights.

Colvin, C. J. (2003) 'Brothers and Sisters, Do Not Be Afraid of Me: Trauma, History and the Therapeutic Imagination in the New South Africa', in K. Hodgkin and S. Radstone (eds) *Contested Pasts: The Politics of Memory* (pp. 153–68), Oxford and New York: Routledge.

—— (2008) 'Purity and Planning: Shared Logics of Transitional Justice and Development', *International Journal of Transitional Justice*, 2(3): 412–25.

Constituent Assembly of East Timor (2002) *Constitution of the Democratic Republic of Timor-Leste*, East Timor: Constituent Assembly of East Timor.

Crockford, F. (2007) 'Contested Belonging: East Timorese Youth in the Diaspora', unpublished PhD thesis, Australian National University.

CTF (Commission of Truth and Friendship) (2008) *Per Memoriam Ad Spem* ['From Memory to Hope']: *Final Report of the Commission for Truth and Friendship*, March, Indonesia/East Timor: Commission of Truth and Friendship.

Curtain, R. (2006) 'Crisis in East Timor: Looking for the Causes to Find Solutions', *Australian Policy Forum*, 06(25A).

Czarnota, A. (2001) 'Law as Mnemosyne and as Lethe: Quasi-Judicial Institutions and Collective Memories', in E. Christodoulidis and S. Veitch (eds) *Lethe's Law: Justice, Law and Ethics in Reconciliation* (pp. 115–28), Oxford and Portland, OR: Hart Publishing.

Darian-Smith, E. (2000) 'Structural Inequalities in the Global Legal System', *Law and Society Review*, 34(3): 809–28.

—— (2004) 'Ethnographies of Law', in A. Sarat (ed.) *The Blackwell Companion to Law and Society* (pp. 545–68), Oxford: Blackwell Publishing.

Das, V. (2003) 'Trauma and Testimony: Implications for Political Community', *Anthropological Theory*, 3(3): 293–307.

—— (2007) *Life and Words: Violence and the Descent into the Ordinary*, Berkeley, CA, and London: University of California Press.

—— and Kleinman, A. (2001) 'Introduction', in V. Das, A. Kleinman, M. Lock, M. Ramphele and P. Reynolds (eds) *Remaking a World: Testimony, Trauma and Social Suffering* (pp. ix–xxvii), Berkeley, CA, and London: University of California Press.

de Araujo, M. (2005) 'Oxfam and Partners in East Timor: Creating a Voice for Women and Carving a Space for that Voice', in D. Grenfell and A. Trembath (eds) *Challenges and Opportunities: International Organisations and Women in Timor-Leste* (pp. 13–16), Melbourne: Globalism Institute, RMIT.

De Greiff, P. (2006) 'Justice and Reparations', in P. De Greiff (ed.) *The Handbook of Reparations* (pp. 451–77), Oxford: Oxford University Press.

Dembour, M.-B. and Kelly, T. (eds) (2007a) *Paths to International Justice: Social and Legal Perspectives* (Cambridge Studies in Law and Society), Cambridge: Cambridge University Press.

—— (2007b) 'Introduction: The Social Lives of International Justice', in T. Kelly and M.-B. Dembour (eds) *Paths to International Justice: Social and Legal Perspectives*

(Cambridge Studies in Law and Society) (pp. 1–25), Cambridge: Cambridge University Press.

Derrida, J. (1999) 'Hospitality, Justice, and Responsibility: A Dialogue with Jacques Derrida', in M. Dooley and R. Kearney (eds) *Questioning Ethics: Contemporary Debate in Philosophy* (pp 65–83), New York and Oxford: Routledge.

—— (2002) 'Force of Law: The Mystical Foundation of Authority', M. Quaintance (trans.), in G. Anidjar (ed.) *Acts of Religion* (pp. 228–98), New York and Oxford: Routledge.

Dodd, M. (2000) 'Calls for East Timor Reconciliation', *The Age*, 18 December. Online. Available http://members.pcug.org.au/ wildwood/Truth.htm (accessed 20 December 2009).

Dolan, C. and Large, J. (2004) *Evaluation of UNHCR's Repatriation and Reintegration Programme in East Timor 1999–2003*, Geneva: United Nations High Commission for Refugees Evaluation and Policy Analysis Unit.

Douzinas, C. (2000) *The End of Human Rights*, Portland, OR: Hart Publishing.

—— (2002) 'Identity, Recognition, Rights or What Can Hegel Teach Us about Human Rights?', *Journal of Law and Society*, 29(3): 379–405.

—— (2005) 'Violence, Justice, Deconstruction', *German Law Journal*, 6(1): 171–8.

—— (2007) *Human Rights and Empire: The Political Philosophy of Cosmopolitanism*, Oxford: Routledge-Cavendish.

Dwyer, L. and Santikarma, D. (2006) 'Speaking from the Shadows: Memory and Mass Violence in Bali', in B. Pouligny, S. Chesterman and A. Schnabel (eds) *After Mass Crime: Rebuilding States and Communities* (pp. 190–214),Tokyo: United Nations University Press.

Elliot, J. (2005) *Using Narrative in Social Research: Qualitative and Quantitative Approaches*, Thousand Oaks, CA: Sage Publications.

ETAN (East Timor Action Network) (2008) 'Sexual Violence against East Timorese Women During the Japanese Occupation', October. Online. Available http://www.etan.org/issues/ww2.hth (accessed 10 February 2010).

ETCRN (East Timor Crisis Reflection Network) (2006) 'How to Achieve Justice and Reconciliation in Timor Leste' (Press release, 17 November). Online. Available http://www.etan.org/et2006/november/25/18how.htm (accessed 10 June 2010).

Evans, J. (2005) 'Colonialism and the Rule of Law: The Case of South Australia', in G. Godfrey and G. Dunstall (eds) *Crime and Empire 1840–1940: Criminal Justice in Local and Global Context* (pp. 57–75), Oxford: Willan Publishing.

Fairclough, N. (1995) *Critical Discourse Analysis*, London and New York: Longman.

Farmer, P. (2003) *Pathologies of Power: Health, Human Rights and the New War on the Poor*, Berkeley, CA: University of California Press.

Federer, J. (2005) *The UN in East Timor: Building Timor-Leste, a Fragile State*, Darwin: Charles Darwin University Press.

Field, A. (2004) 'Places of Suffering and Pathways to Healing: Post-Conflict Life in Bidau, East Timor', unpublished PhD thesis, James Cook University.

Fitzpatrick, P. (1992) *Modernism and the Grounds of Law*, Oxford: Routledge.

—— and Tuitt, P. (2004) 'Introduction', in P. Fitzpatrick and P. Tuitt (eds) *Critical Beings: Law, Nation and the Global Subject* (pp. xi–xx), Aldershot: Ashgate.

Franke, K. M. (2006) 'Gendered Subjects of Transitional Justice', *Columbia Journal of Gender and Law*, 15(3): 813–28.

Fraser, N. (2000) 'Rethinking Recognition', *New Left Review*, 3(May–June): 107–20.

—— (2003) 'Social Justice in the Age of Identity Politics', in N. Fraser and A. Honneth (eds) *Redistribution or Recognition: A Political Philosophical Exchange* (pp. 7–109), London and New York: Verso.

Freire, P. (1970) *Pedagogy of the Oppressed*, Myra Mergman Ramos (trans.), New York: Herder and Herder.

FRETILIN (2000) *Resolution No. 5: Regarding Unity and Tolerance* (Resolution from the National FRETILIN Congress, May), Susana Barnes (trans.) (Copy on file with author), Dili: FRETILIN.

—— (2007) 'From the People, with the People, and for the People: We Want Justice for Crimes' (Press release, 1 June) (Copy on file with author), Dili: FRETILIN.

Fritz, N. (2005) 'Made to Order? Transitional Justice Initiatives in the Developing World, or the Truths We Should Be Telling', in C. L. Eisgruber and A. Sajo (eds) *Global Justice and the Bulwarks of Localism* (pp. 317–31), Leiden and Boston, MA: Martinus Nijhoff.

Galtung, J. (1994) *Human Rights in Another Key*, Cambridge: Polity.

Gear, S. (2002) *Wishing Us Away: Challenges Facing Ex-Combatants in the 'New' South Africa* (Centre for the Study of Violence and Reconciliation, Violence and Transition Series, Vol. 8). Online. Available http://www.sasoldier.com/data/06_sadflinks/UsedPDFs/Wishing_Us_Away_%20Challenges_facing_ex-combatants_in_the_New_South_Africa.pdf (accessed 10 December 2011).

Gledhill, J. (2003) 'Rights and the Poor', in R. A. Wilson and J. P. Mitchell (eds) *Human Rights in Global Perspective* (pp. 209–29), New York: Routledge.

Goldstone, A. (2004) 'UNTAET with Hindsight: The Peculiarities of Politics in an Incomplete State', *Global Governance*, 10: 83–98.

—— (2012 forthcoming) 'Building a State and "State-Building": East Timor and the UN, 1999–2012', in M. Berdal and D. Zaum (eds) *Political Economy of State-Building: Power after Peace*, Oxford: Routledge.

Graydon, C. (2005) 'Local Justice Systems in Timor-Leste: Washed up, or Watch this Space?', *Development Bulletin*, 68(Oct): 66–70.

Gready, P. (2011) *The Era of Transitional Justice: The Truth and Reconciliation Commission in South Africa and Beyond*, Oxford and New York: Routledge.

Grenfell, D. (2004) 'East Timor: Colonialism, Nation-Building and the Politics of Oil', *Arena*, 22: 45–52.

—— (2008) 'Reconciliation: Violence and Nation-Formation in Timor-Leste', in D. Grenfell and P. James (eds) *Rethinking Insecurity, War and Violence: Beyond Savage Globalization?* (pp. 181–93), Oxford: Routledge.

——, Walsh, M., Trembath, A., Noronha, C. M. and Holthouse, K. (2009) *Understanding Community: Security and Sustainability in Four Aldeia in Timor-Leste* (Research Report Produced for the Globalism Research Centre), Melbourne: RMIT University.

Grenfell, L. (2006) 'Legal Pluralism and the Rule of Law in Timor Leste', *Leiden Journal of International Law*, 19: 305–37.

Gunn, G. (1999) *Timor Lorosae: 500 Years*, Macau: Livros do Oriente.

—— and Vltchek, A. (2007) 'Timor Leste and Indonesia: Between a Rock and a Hard Place', *The Asia Pacific Journal*, 18 October.

Gunter, J. (2007) 'Communal Conflict in Viqueque and the "Charged" History of '59', *Asia Pacific Journal of Anthropology*, 8(1): 27–41.

Gusmao, K. R. X. (2005a) Address by H. E. The President of the Republic Kay Rala Xanana Gusmao on the Occasion of the Presentation of the Final Report of the

Commission for Reception, Truth and Reconciliation (CAVR) (Dili, Salão Nobre, Lahane Palace, 31 October).

—— (2005b) Speech on the Occasion of the Handing over of the Final Report of the CAVR (National Parliament, East Timor, 28 November).

—— (2006) Address by H. E. The President of the Republic Kay Rala Xanana Gusmao on the Occasion of the UN Security Council 5351st Meeting on the Situation in East Timor (UN Doc S/Pv.5351, 23 January).

—— (2007) Speech of H. E. The Prime Minister of Timor Leste, Kay Rala Xanana Gusmao, at the Swearing-in Ceremony of the Members of the Government (Dili, 8 August).

Halbwachs, M. (1980) *Collective Memories*, New York: Harper & Row.

Halderman, F. (2007) *Another Kind of Justice: Transitional Justice as Recognition* (Center for Human Rights and Global Justice Working Paper No. 14), New York: NYU School of Law.

Harper, E. (2005) 'Delivering Justice in the Wake of Mass Violence: New Approaches to Transitional Justice', *Journal of Conflict and Security Law*, 10(2): 149–85.

—— (2007) 'Constructing a Legal System in East Timor: Challenges to Introducing International Legal Norms and Principles into Post-Conflict States under UN Administration', unpublished PhD thesis, University of Melbourne.

Harris-Rimmer, S. G. (2007) 'Orphans or Veterans?', *Texas International Law Journal*, 42(3): 323–44.

—— (2008) 'Transitional Justice and the Women of East Timor', unpublished PhD thesis, Australian National University.

—— (2010) *Gender and Transitional Justice: The Women of East Timor*, Oxford and New York: Routledge.

Haslam, E. (2007) 'Law, Civil Society and Contested Justice at the International Criminal Tribunal for Rwanda', in M.-B. Dembour and T. Kelly (eds) *Paths to International Justice: Social and Legal Perspectives* (Cambridge Studies in Law and Society) (pp. 57–82), Cambridge: Cambridge University Press.

Hayner, P. (2011) *Unspeakable Truths: Transitional Justice and the Challenge of Truth Commissions*, New York: Routledge.

Henry, N. (2005) 'Disclosure, Sexual Violence and International Jurisprudence: A Therapeutic Approach', unpublished PhD thesis, University of Melbourne.

—— (2009) 'Witness to Rape: The Limits and Potential of International War Crimes Trials for Victims of Wartime Sexual Violence', *International Journal of Transitional Justice*, 3(1): 114–34.

Hill, H. (2002) *Stirrings of Nationalism in East Timor: FRETILIN 1974–1978*, Otford, NSW: Otford Press.

Hinton, A. L. (2010) 'Introduction: Toward an Anthropology of Transitional Justice', in A. L. Hinton (ed.) *Transitional Justice: Global Mechanisms and Local Realities after Genocide and Mass Violence* (pp. 1–24), Piscataway, NJ: Rutgers University Press.

Hirst, M. (2008) *Too Much Friendship, Too Little Truth: Monitoring Report on the Commission of Truth and Friendship in Indonesia and Timor-Leste* (ICTJ Occasional Paper Series, January), New York: International Center for Transitional Justice.

—— (2009) *An Unfinished Truth: An Analysis of the Commission of Truth and Friendship's Final Report on the 1999 Atrocities in East Timor* (ICTJ Occasional Paper Series, March), New York: International Center for Transitional Justice.

—— and Varney, H. (2005) *Justice Abandoned? An Assessment of the Serious Crimes Process in East Timor* (ICTJ Occasional Paper Series, March), New York: International Center for Transitional Justice.

Hohe, T. (2002) 'Totem Poles: Indigenous Concepts and "Free and Fair" Elections in East Timor', *International Peacekeeping*, 9(4): 69–88.

—— and Nixon, R. (2003) *Reconciling Justice: 'Traditional' Law and State Judiciary in East Timor* (Report for the United States Institute for Peace, January), Washington DC: United States Institute for Peace.

Honneth, A. (1995) *The Struggle for Recognition: The Moral Grammar of Social Conflicts*, Cambridge: Polity.

—— (2001) 'Recognition or Redistribution: Changing Perspectives on the Moral Order of Society', *Theory, Culture and Society*, 18(2): 43–55.

Huang, R. and Gunn, G. (2004) 'Reconciliation as State-Building in East Timor', *Lusotopie*, 19–38.

Hughes, C. (2009) *Dependent Communities: Aid and Politics in Cambodia and East Timor*, Ithaca, NY: Cornell Southeast Asia Program.

—— and Pupavac, V. (2005) 'Framing Post-Conflict Societies: International Pathologisation of Cambodia and the Post-Yugoslav States', *Third World Quarterly*, 26(6): 873–89.

Humphrey, M. (2003) 'From Victim to Victimhood: Truth Commissions and Trials as Rituals of Political Transition and Individual Healing', *The Australian Journal of Anthropology*, 14(2): 171–87.

—— (2005) 'Reconciliation and the Therapeutic State', *Journal of Intercultural Studies*, 26(3): 203–20.

—— and Valverde, E. (2007) 'Human Rights, Victimhood, and Impunity: An Anthropology of Democracy in Argentina', *Social Analysis*, 51(1): 179–97.

Hunt, J. (2008) 'Local NGOs in National Development: The Case of East Timor', unpublished PhD thesis, RMIT University.

Huyse, L. (2003) *Reconciliation after Violent Conflict: Introduction and Overview of the IDEA Reconciliation Handbook* (Paper Presented at the IDEA–OHCHR Seminar, 'From Divided Past to Shared Future: Reconciliation in Post-Conflict Societies', Palais Wilson, Geneva, 26 September).

Hyland, T. and Murdoch, L. (2006) 'We Were Put in Crates', 12 February. Online. Available http://www.theage.com.au/news/world/we-were-put-incrates/2006/02/11/1139542445484. html (accessed 15 February 2010).

ICG (International Crisis Group) (2006) *Resolving East Timor's Crisis* (Asia Report No. 120, 10 October), Jakarta/Brussels: ICG.

—— (2011a) *Timor-Leste: Reconciliation and Return from Indonesia* (Asia Briefing No. 122, 18 April), Dili/Brussels: ICG.

—— (2011b) *Timor-Leste's Veterans: An Unfinished Struggle?* (Asia Briefing No. 129, 18 November), Dili/Brussels: ICG.

ICTJ (International Center for Transitional Justice) (2005) 'Timorese Parliament Should Release Truth Commission Report Immediately' (Press release, 28 November). Online. Available http://www.etan.org/et2005/november/default.htm (accessed 10 January 2009).

—— (2010) *Impunity in Timor-Leste: Can the Serious Crimes Investigation Team Make a Difference?* (ICTJ Report, June), Brussels: ICTJ.

—— and Kontras (Commission for the Disappeared and Victims of Violence) (2011) 'Derailed: Transitional Justice in Indonesia Since the Fall of Soeharto', 7 April.

Online. Available http://ictj.org/sites/default/files/ICTJ-Kontras-Indonesia-Derailed-Report-2011-English_0.pdf (accessed 10 December 2011).

Jacobsen, C. G., Brand-Jacobsen, K.-F. and Galtung, J. (2002) *Searching for Peace*, London: Pluto Press.

Jolliffe, J. (ed.) (1976) *Revolutionary Poems in the Struggle against Colonialism: Timorese Nationalist Verse {by} Fransisco Borjada Costa*, Sydney: Wild and Woolley.

—— (1978) *East Timor: Nationalism and Colonialism*, St Lucia: University of Queensland Press.

—— (2003) 'Timor PM Slams UN on War Criminals', *Asia Times*, 15 May. Online. Available http://www.atimes.com/atimes/Southeast_Asia/EE15Ae03.html (accessed 10 January 2010).

Joyo Indonesian News (2003) 'Jakarta "Perplexed" by E Timor PM's Call for Intl Tribunal', 10 June.

JSMP (Judicial Systems Monitoring Programme) (2002) *The General Prosecutor* v *Joni Marques and nine others* (the *Los Palos case*) (JSMP Trial Report), Dili: JSMP.

—— (2004a) *The Lolotoe Case: A Small Step Forward* (JSMP Trial Observation Report), Dili: JSMP.

—— (2004b) *The Future of the Serious Crimes Unit* (JSMP Issue Report, January), Dili: JSMP.

—— (2005) *Overview of the Justice Sector* (March), Dili: JSMP.

—— (2007) *Justice Update* (June), Dili: JSMP.

Kammen, D. (2003) 'Master–Slave, Traitor–Nationalist, Opportunist–Oppressed: Political Metaphors in East Timor', *Indonesia*, 76(Oct).

Katzenstein, S. (2003) 'Hybrid Tribunals: Searching for Justice in East Timor', *Harvard Human Rights Journal*, 16: 245–78.

Kelsall, T. (2009) *Culture under Cross-Examination: International Justice and the Special Court for Sierra Leone*, Cambridge: Cambridge University Press.

Kent, L. (2004) *Unfulfilled Expectations: Community Views of the Reconciliation Process* (Report for the Judicial Systems Monitoring Programme). Online. Available http://www.jsmp.minihub.org/Reports/otherresources (accessed 25 October 2010).

—— (2006) *Independent Evaluation of the Commission on Cadres of the Resistance (CAQR)* (Report for the World Bank, April), Dili: World Bank.

Kiernan, B. (2003) 'The Demography of Genocide in South-East Asia: The Death Tolls in Cambodia, 1975–79, and East Timor, 1975–80', *Critical Asian Studies*, 35(4): 585–97.

King's College (2003) *A Review of Peace Operations: A Case for Change, East Timor* (10 March, pre-publication copy), London: Conflict, Security and Development Group, King's College.

Kingsbury, D. and Leach, M. (2007) 'Introduction', in D. Kingsbury and M. Leach (eds) *East Timor: Beyond Independence* (pp. 1–16), Melbourne: Monash University Press.

Kingston, J. (2006) 'Balancing Justice and Reconciliation in East Timor', *Critical Asian Studies*, 38(3): 271–302.

Kiss, E. (2000) 'Moral Ambition within and beyond Political Constraints: Reflections on Restorative Justice', in R. I. Rotberg and D. Thompson (eds) *Truth v. Justice* (pp. 68–98), Princeton, NJ, and Oxford: Princeton University Press.

Kitley, P. (2000) *Television, Nation and Culture in Indonesia*, Athens, OH: Ohio University Press.

Lam, S. (2005) 'Timor: No Compensation Wanted for Occupation', *Radio Australia*, 1 December. Online. Transcript available at http://www.asia-pacific-solidarity.net/southeastasia/easttimor/netnews/2005/end_12v4.htm#Justice%20lost%20in%20East%20Timor%20friendship (accessed 12 June 2010).

Lambourne, W. (2009) 'Transitional Justice and Peacebuilding after Mass Violence', *International Journal of Transitional Justice*, 3(1): 28–48.

La'o Hamutuk (2001) 'Sites of Justice-Related Efforts', *La'o Hamutuk Bulletin*, 2(6/7).

—— (2003) 'Reviewing the East Timor Commission for Reception, Truth and Reconciliation', *La'o Hamutuk Bulletin*, 4(5).

—— (2007) 'Timor-Leste's 50 Year Loss of Sovereignty', *La'o Hamutuk Bulletin*, 8(2): 10–12.

—— (2009a) 'Justice for Timor-Leste Remains an Unfulfilled International Obligation' (La'o Hamutuk Briefing Paper, August). Online. Available http://www.laohamutuk.org/reports/09bgnd/JusticeEn.pdf (accessed 10 February 2010).

—— (2009b) 'Maternus Bere Indicted for Crimes Against Humanity in Suai Church Massacre and other Laksaur Militia Activities', 13 November. Online. Available http://www.laohamutuk.org/Justice/99/bere/09MaternusBere.htm (accessed 15 June 2010).

—— (2010) 'Land Rights and Justice', *La'o Hamutuk Bulletin*, 11(1–2).

—— (2011) 'RDTL General State Budget for 2012', 3 October, updated 2 December. Online. Available http://www.laohamutuk.org/econ/OGE12/10OJE2012En.htm (accessed 10 December 2011).

Larke, B. (2009) 'And the Truth Shall Set You Free: Confessional Trade-offs and Community Reconciliation in East Timor', *Asian Journal of Social Science*, 37(4): 646–76.

Leach, M. (2002) 'Valorising the Resistance: National Identity and Collective Memory in East Timor's Constitution', *Social Alternatives*, 21(3): 43–7.

—— (2007) 'History Teaching: Challenges and Alternatives', in D. Kingsbury and M. Leach (eds) *East Timor: Beyond Independence* (pp. 193–207), Melbourne: Monash University Press.

—— (2008) 'Difficult Memories: The Independence Struggle as Cultural Heritage in East Timor', in W. Logan and K. Reeves (eds) *Places of Pain and Shame: Dealing with Difficult Memories* (pp. 144–61), Oxford: Routledge.

Leebaw, B. (2004). *New Approaches to Transitional Justice: Combining Restorative Justice and Prosecution* (Paper Presented at the Annual Meeting of the International Studies Association, Montreal, Canada, 17–20 March).

—— (2008) 'The Irreconcilable Goals of Transitional Justice', *Human Rights Quarterly*, 30(1): 95–118.

Libscomb, L.-A. (2010) *Beyond the Truth: Can Reparations Move Peace and Justice Forward in Timor-Leste?* (East–West Center Analysis No. 93, March), Honolulu, HI: East–West Center.

Linton, S. (2001) 'Cambodia, East Timor and Sierra Leone: Experiments in International Justice', *Criminal Law Forum*, 12: 185–286.

Lusa (2005) 'Admitting War Excesses: Alkatiri Rebuts 3,000 Death Toll', 21 December. Online. Available http://www.asia-pacific-solidarity.net/southeastasia/easttimor/netnews/2005/end_12v4.htm#Admitting%20war%20'excesses',%20Alkatiri%20rebuts%203,000%20death%20toll (accessed 10 February 2010).

Lynch, C. and Nakashima, E. (2006) 'East Timor Atrocities Denied', *Washington Post*, 21 January.

MacGinty, R. (2008) 'Indigenous Peace-Making versus the Liberal Peace', *Cooperation and Conflict*, 43(2): 139–63.

McEvoy, K. (2008) 'Letting Go of Legalism: Developing a "Thicker" Version of Transitional Justice', in K. McEvoy and L. McGregor (eds) *Transitional Justice from Below: Grassroots Activism and the Struggle for Change* (pp. 15–46), Portland, OR: Hart Publishing.

—— and McGregor, L. (2008a) *Transitional Justice from Below: Grassroots Activism and the Struggle for Change*, Portland, OR: Hart Publishing.

—— and —— (2008b) 'Transitional Justice from Below: An Agenda for Research, Policy and Praxis', in K. McEvoy and L. McGregor (eds) *Transitional Justice from Below: Grassroots Activism and the Struggle for Change* (pp. 1–13), Portland, OR: Hart Publishing.

McWilliam, A. (2005) 'Houses of Resistance in East Timor: Structuring Sociality in the New Nation', *Anthropoligical Forum*, 15(1): 27–44.

—— (2007a) 'Introduction: Restorative Custom – Ethnographic Perspectives on Conflict and Local Justice in Timor', *Asia Pacific Journal of Anthropology*, 8(1): 1–8.

—— (2007b) 'Meto Disputes and Peacemaking: Cultural Notes on Conflict and its Resolution in West Timor', *Asia Pacific Journal of Anthropology*, 8(1): 75–91.

Mallinder, L. (2008) *Amnesty, Human Rights and Political Transitions: Bridging the Peace and Justice Divide*, Oxford and Portland, OR: Hart Publishing.

Mamdani, M. (2001a) *When Victims Become Killers: Colonialism, Nativism, and the Genocide in Rwanda*, Princeton, NJ: Princeton University Press.

—— (2001b) 'A Diminished Truth', in W. James and L. Van der Vijver (eds) *After the TRC: Reflections on Truth and Reconciliation* (pp. 58–61), Athens, OH: Ohio University Press/Swallow Press.

Mani, R. (2002) *Beyond Retribution: Seeking Justice in the Shadows of War*, Cambridge: Polity Press.

March, S. (2008) 'Horta Pushes Amnesty Laws' (Dili, 13 July, AAP). Online. Available at http://www.etan.org/et2008/7july/19/13horta.htm (accessed 27 July 2010).

Markell, P. (2007) 'Recognition and Redistribution', in J. Dryzek, B. Honig and A. Phillips (eds) *Oxford Handbook of Political Theory* (pp. 450–69), Oxford: Oxford University Press.

Martinkus, J. (2002) 'Beyond Justice', *The Bulletin*, 11 June: 34.

Martins da Silva, M. and Kendall, S. (2002) *Issues for Women in East Timor: The Aftermath of the Indonesian Occupation* (Conference Paper for 'Expanding our Horizons: Understanding the Complexities of Violence against Women', University of Sydney, 18–22 February).

Mearns, D. (2002) *Looking Both Ways: Models for Justice in East Timor*, Sydney: Australian Legal Resources International.

Mehta, U. S. (1990) 'Liberal Strategies of Exclusion', *Politics and Society*, 18(4): 427–54.

Meister, R. (2002) 'Human Rights and the Politics of Victimhood', *Ethics and International Affairs*, 16(2): 91–119.

Merry, S. E. (2006a) *Human Rights and Gender Violence: Translating International Law into Local Justice*, Chicago, IL: University of Chicago Press.

—— (2006b) 'Transnational Human Rights and Local Activism: Mapping the Middle', *American Anthropologist*, 108(1): 38–51.

—— (2009) *Human Rights as Global Law and as Transnational Political Resource: Unpacking the Vernacularization Process* (Paper Presented at the Annual Meeting of the ISA's 50th Annual Convention, 'Exploring the Past, Anticipating the Future', New York Marriott Marquis, 15–18 February). Online. Available http://www.allacademic.com/meta/p310922_index.html (accessed 12 December 2010).

Mertus, J. (2000) 'Truth in a Box: The Limits of Justice through Judicial Mechanisms', in I. Amadiume and A. An-Na'im (eds) *The Politics of Memory: Truth, Healing and Social Justice* (pp. 142–61), New York: Zed Books.

Miller, Z. (2008) 'Effects of Invisibility: In Search of the "Economic" in Transitional Justice', *International Journal of Transitional Justice*, 2(3): 266–91.

Minow, M. (1998) *Between Vengeance and Forgiveness: Facing History after Genocide and Mass Violence*, Boston, MA: Beacon Press.

Molnar, A. K. (2010) *Timor Leste: Politics, History and Culture*, Oxford: Routledge.

Moon, C. (2008) *Narrating Political Reconciliation*, London: Lexington Books.

Moreton-Robinson, A. (2000) *Talkin' up to the White Woman: Aboriginal Women and Feminism*, St Lucia: University of Queensland Press.

Nagy, R. (2008) 'Transitional Justice as Global Project: Critical Reflections', *Third World Quarterly*, 29(2): 275–89.

National Planning Commission (2002) *East Timor: National Development Plan* (May), Dili: National Planning Commission.

National Statistics Directorate (2010) *Timor-Leste Demographic and Health Survey 2009–10* (Preliminary Report, March), Dili: National Statistics Directorate.

Nevins, J. (2002a) 'The Making of "Ground Zero" in East Timor in 1999: An Analysis of International Complicity in Indonesia's Crimes', *Asian Survey*, 42(4): 623–41.

—— (2002b) '(Mis)Representing East Timor's Past: Structural-Symbolic Violence, International Law, and the Institutionalization of Injustice', *Journal of Human Rights*, 1(4): 523–40.

—— (2005) *A Not So Distant Horror: Mass Violence in East Timor*, Ithaca, NY: Cornell University Press.

—— (2007) 'Truth, Lies and Accountability: In Search of Justice for East Timor', *Boston Review*, Jan/Feb.

Niner, S. (ed.) (2000) *To Resist is to Win! The Autobiography of Xanana Gusmao with Selected Letters and Speeches*, Richmond, Vic: Aurora Books/David Lovell Publishing.

—— (2001) 'A Long Journey of Resistance: The Origins and Struggle of CNRT', in R. Tanter, M. Selden and S. R. Shalom (eds) *Bitter Flowers, Sweet Flowers: East Timor, Indonesia and the World Community* (pp. 15–29), Lanham, MD: Rowman and Littlefield Publishers.

—— (2009) *Xanana: Leader of the Struggle for Independent Timor-Leste*, Melbourne: Australian Scholarly Publishing Pty Ltd.

—— (2011) '*Hakat Klot*, Narrow Steps', *International Feminist Journal of Politics*, 13(3): 413–35.

Norval, A. J. (1998) 'Memory, Identity and the (Im)Possibility of Reconciliation: The Work of the Truth and Reconciliation Commission in South Africa', *Constellations*, 5(2): 250–65.

—— (1999) 'Truth and Reconciliation: The Birth of the Present and the Reworking of History', *Journal of Southern African Studies*, 25(3): 499–519.

OHCHR (Office of the High Commissioner for Human Rights) (2000) *Report of the International Commission of Inquiry on East Timor to the Secretary General* (UN Doc S/2000/59, January), Geneva: OHCHR.

—— (2006) *Rule of Law Tools for Post-Conflict States*, New York and Geneva: OHCHR.

Orford, A. (1997) 'Locating the International: Military and Monetary Interventions after the Cold War', *Harvard International Law Journal*, 38: 443–85.

—— (1999) 'Muscular Humanitarianism: Reading the Narratives of the New Interventionism', *European Journal of International Law*, 10(4): 679–711.

—— (2003) *Reading Humanitarian Intervention*, Cambridge: Cambridge University Press.

—— (2006) 'Commissioning the Truth', *Columbia Journal of Gender and Law*, 15(3): 851–83.

Otto, D. (1999) 'Everything is Dangerous: Some Poststructural Tools for Rethinking the Universal Knowledge Claims of Human Rights Law', *Australian Journal of Human Rights*, 5(1): 17–47.

Paris, R. (2004) *At War's End: Building Peace after Civil Conflict*, Cambridge: Cambridge University Press.

Phan, G. (dir.) (2006) *A Hero's Journey* (Documentary Film, also known as *Where the Sun Rises*), East Timor: Luxlucis.

Pigou, P. (2004) *The Community Reconciliation Process of the Commission for Reception, Truth and Reconciliation* (Evaluation Report for the UNDP), Dili: UNDP Timor-Leste.

Post-CAVR (Commission for Reception Truth and Reconciliation) Secretariat (2006) *Post-CAVR Update* (September–October), Dili: Post-CAVR Secretariat.

Powell, A. (2007) 'Generation Y: Re-Writing the Rules on Sex, Love and Consent', unpublished PhD thesis, University of Melbourne.

Pupavac, V. (2004) 'International Therapeutic Peace and Justice in Bosnia', *Social and Legal Studies*, 13(3): 377–401.

Radstone, S. (2007) 'Trauma Theory: Contexts, Politics, Ethics', *Paragraph*, 30(1): 9–29.

Rajagopal, B. (2008) 'Invoking the Rule of Law in Post-Conflict Rebuilding: A Critical Examination', *William and Mary Law Review*, 49: 1347–76.

Ramos-Horta, J. (1987) *Funu: The Unfinished Saga of East Timor*, Lawrenceville, NJ: The Red Sea Press.

—— (2006) Address by Dr José Ramos-Horta at his Swearing-in Ceremony as Prime Minister of the Democratic Republic of Timor-Leste (Dili, 10 July). Online. Available http://www.etan.org/et2006/july/15/10address.htm (accessed 8 July 2009).

—— (2011) President's Speech on the Anniversary of Independence (Dili, 28 November). Online. Available http://presidenttimorleste.tl/2011/12/presidents-speech-on-28th-november-the-anniversary-of-independence/ (accessed 10 December 2011).

Rapoza, P. (2006). 'Hybrid Criminal Tribunals and the Concept of Ownership: Who Owns the Process?', *American University International Law Review*, 21: 525–40.

Rawnsley, C. (2004) *East Timor: A Theology of Death – Massacres, Memorials, Rites and Reconciliation* (Proceedings of 'Peace Works', Third Triennial Conference of Women Scholars of Religion and Theology, Melbourne, 23–26 January). Online. Available http://www.wsrt.com.au (accessed 10 February 2010).

Rawski, F. (2002) 'Truth-Seeking and Local Histories in East Timor', *Asia-Pacific Journal on Human Rights and the Law*, 3(1): 77–96.
Reiger, C. and Wierda, M. (2006) *The Serious Crimes Process in Timor-Leste: In Retrospect* (ICTJ Prosecutions Case Studies Series, March), New York: International Center for Transitional Justice.
Rigney, L.-I. (2001) 'A First Perspective of Indigenous Australian Participation in Science: Framing Indigenous Research towards Indigenous Australian Intellectual Sovereignty', *Kaurna Higher Education Journal*, 7(Aug).
RI and GOTL (Republic of Indonesia and Government of Timor Leste) (2004) 'Joint Press Release of Foreign Minister of the Republic of Indonesia and the Democratic Republic of Timor-Leste' (Press release, 22 December). Online. Available http://www.kbri-tokyo.go.id/menue/information/press/joint-press-release-ri-timorleste.htm (accessed 6 February 2009).
RI and UNTAET (Republic of Indonesia and the United Nations Transitional Administration in East Timor) (2000) 'Memorandum of Understanding between the Republic of Indonesia and the United Nations Transitional Administration in East Timor Regarding Cooperation in Legal, Judicial and Human Rights Related Matters', 5–6 April. Online. Available http://www.unmit.org/legal/Other-Docs/mou-id-untaet.htm (accessed 3 January 2010).
Robins, S. (2009) 'Whose Voices? Understanding Victims' Needs in Transition (Review Essay)', *Journal of Human Rights Practice*, 1(2): 320–31.
—— (2010) *An Assessment of the Needs of Families of the Missing in Timor-Leste* (Report for the Post War Reconstruction and Development Unit, February), York: University of York.
Robinson, G. (2003) *East Timor: Crimes against Humanity* (Report Commissioned by the OHCHR, July), Geneva: OHCHR.
—— (2010) *If You Leave us Here, We Will Die: How Genocide was Stopped in East Timor*, Princeton, NJ: Princeton University Press.
Rohland, K. and Cliffe, S. (2002) *The East Timor Reconstruction Program: Successes, Problems and Trade-offs* (World Bank Conflict Prevention and Reconstruction Unit Working Paper No. 2, November), Washington DC: World Bank.
Rombouts, H. (2002) 'Importance and Difficulties of Victim-Based Research in Post-Conflict Societies', *European Journal of Crime, Criminal Law and Criminal Justice*, 10(2/3): 216–32.
Roosa, J. (2007a) 'East Timor's Truth Commission', *Pacific Affairs*, 80(4): 563–7.
—— (2007b) 'How Does a Truth Commission Find out What the Truth is? The Case of East Timor's CAVR', *Pacific Affairs*, 80(4): 569–80.
Ross, F. C. (2003a) *Bearing Witness: Women and the Truth and Reconciliation Commission in South Africa*, London: Pluto Press.
—— (2003b) 'Using Rights to Measure Wrongs: A Case Study of Method and Moral in the Work of the South African Truth and Reconciliation Commission', in J. P. Mitchell and R. A. Wilson (eds) *Human Rights in Global Perspective: Anthropological Studies of Rights, Claims and Entitlements* (pp. 163–82), New York: Routledge.
—— (2005) 'Women and the Politics of Identity: Voices in the South African Truth and Reconciliation Commission', in V. Broch-Due (ed.) *Violence and Belonging* (pp. 214–35), Oxford: Routledge.
—— (2010) *Raw Life, New Hope: Decency, Housing and Everyday Life in a Post-Apartheid Community*, Cape Town: University of Cape Town Press.

Roughneen, S. (2009) 'East Timor: Justice in the Dock', *ISN Security Watch*, 16 July. Online. Available http://www.isn.ethz.ch/isn/Current-Affairs/Security-Watch/Detail/?lng=enandid=103345 (accessed 10 July 2010).
Sarat, A. and Kearns, T. R. (1996) 'Legal Justice and Injustice: Towards a Situated Perspective', in A. Sarat and T. R. Kearns (eds) *Justice and Injustice in Law and Legal Theory* (pp. 1–18), Ann Arbor, MI: University of Michigan Press.
Schaap, A. (2005) *Political Reconciliation*, New York: Routledge.
—— (2006) 'Agonism in Divided Societies', *Philosophy and Social Criticism*, 32(2): 255–77.
Scheper-Hughes, N. (1995) 'The Primacy of the Ethical: Propositions for a Militant Anthropology', *Current Anthropology*, 36(3): 409–40.
—— (2006) 'Dangerous and Endangered Youth: Social Structures and Determinants of Violence', in M. H. Hirsch (ed.) *Inclusion and Exclusion in the Global Arena* (pp. 287–318), New York: Routledge.
—— and Bourgois, P. (2004) 'Introduction: Making Sense of Violence', in N. Scheper-Hughes and P. Bourgois (eds) *Violence in War and Peace: An Anthology* (pp. 1–31), Oxford: Blackwell Publishing.
Shaw, R. (2005) *Rethinking Truth and Reconciliation Commissions: Lessons from Sierra Leone* (USIP Special Report, February), Washington DC: United States Institute for Peace.
—— (2007) 'Memory Frictions: Localizing the Truth and Reconciliation Commission in Sierra Leone', *International Journal of Transitional Justice*, 1(2): 183–207.
—— and Waldorf, L. (2010) 'Introduction: Localizing Transitional Justice', in R. Shaw, L. Waldorf and P. Hazan (eds) *Localizing Transitional Justice: Interventions and Priorities after Mass Violence* (pp. 3–26), Stanford, CA: Stanford University Press.
Shklar, J. (1964) *Legalism*, Boston, MA: Harvard University Press.
Silva, K. (2008) 'Reciprocity, Recognition and Suffering: Political Mobilizers in Independent East Timor', *Vibrant*, 2: 156–78.
Simpson, G. (2007) *Law, War and Crime: War Crimes Trials and the Reinvention of International Law*, Cambridge: Polity Press.
Smith, L. T. (2003) *Decolonizing Methodologies*, London and New York: Zed Books.
SPSC (Special Panels for Serious Crimes) (2001) *The Prosecutor* v *Joseph Leki* (Case No 5: 2000, Judgment 11 June 2001, Dili: Special Panels for Serious Crimes).
—— (2002) *The Prosecutor* v *Joao Franca da Silva (alias Jhoni Franca)* (Case No 4a: 2001, Judgment 5 December 2002, Dili: Special Panel for Serious Crimes).
Sriram, C. L. (2007) 'Justice as Peace? Liberal Peacebuilding and Strategies of Transitional Justice', *Global Society: Journal of Interdisciplinary International Relations*, 21(4): 579–91.
—— and Ross, A. (2007) 'Geographies of Crime and Justice: Contemporary Transitional Justice and the Creation of "Zones of Impunity"', *International Journal of Transitional Justice*, 1: 45–65.
Stahn, C. (2001) 'Accommodating Individual Criminal Responsibility and National Reconciliation: The UN Truth Commission for East Timor', *American Journal of International Law*, 95: 952–66.
Stanley, E. (2008) 'The Political Economy of Transitional Justice in Timor-Leste', in K. McEvoy and L. McGregor (eds) *Transitional Justice from Below: Grassroots Activism and the Struggle for Change* (pp. 167–188), Oxford: Hart Publishing.
—— (2009) *Torture, Truth and Justice: The Case of Timor-Leste*, Oxford: Routledge.

Stover, E. (2005) *The Witnesses: War Crimes and the Promise of Justice in The Hague*, Philadelphia, PA: University of Pennsylvania Press.

Subotic, J. (2009) *Hijacked Justice: Dealing with the Past in the Balkans*, Ithaca, NY: Cornell University Press.

Suhrke, A. (2001) 'Peacekeepers as Nation-Builders: Dilemmas of the UN in East Timor', *International Peacekeeping*, 8(4): 1–20.

Taylor, C. (1994) 'The Politics of Recognition', in A. Gutmann (ed.) *Multiculturalism: Examining the Politics of Recognition*, Princeton, NJ: Princeton University Press.

Taylor, J. G. (1999) *East Timor: The Price of Freedom*, London and New York: Zed Books.

Tempo Seminal (2008) '*Eis Prizoneirus Politik Lamenta Hahalok PNTL-UNPOL*' [Ex Political Prisoners Lament the Behaviour of PNTL-UNPOL]', 14 July.

Tierney, W. G. (2003) 'Undaunted Courage: Life History and the Postmodern Challenge', in N. K. Denzin and Y. S. Lincoln (eds) *Strategies of Qualitative Inquiry* (pp. 291–318), Thousand Oaks, CA: Sage Publications.

TIME Asia (2001) 'Interview: What Happens Next? Independence Leader and Presidential Hopeful Xanana Gusmao Talks with TIME about East Timor's Challenges', 3 September. Online. Available http://members.pcug.org.au/~wildwood/01augnext.htm (accessed 10 February 2010).

Traube, E. (2007) 'Unpaid Wages: Local Narratives and the Imagination of the Nation', *The Asia Pacific Journal of Anthropology*, 8(1): 9–25.

Trinidade, J. (2011) *Lulik: The Core of Timorese Values* (Paper Presented at 'Communicating New Research on Timor-Leste', Timor-Leste Studies Association Conference, Dili, 30 June).

Tsing, A. (2005) *Friction: An Ethnography of Global Connection*, Princeton, NJ: Princeton University Press.

Turner, C. (2008) 'Delivering Lasting Peace, Democracy and Human Rights in Times of Transition: The Role of International Law', *International Journal of Transitional Justice*, 2: 126–51.

UNCHR (United Nations Commission on Human Rights) (1999) *Report of the High Commissioner for Human Rights on the Human Rights Situation in East Timor* (UN Doc E/CN.4/ S-4/CRP.1, 17 September), Geneva: UNCHR.

UNDP (United Nations Development Programme) (2006) *Timor Leste: The Path out of Poverty, Integrated Rural Development* (Timor Leste Human Development Report 2006), Dili: UNDP.

—— (2010) *Human Development Report 2010*, New York: Oxford University Press.

—— (2011) *Human Development Report Timor-Leste 2011: Managing Natural Resources for Human Development*, Dili: UNDP.

UNGA (United Nations General Assembly) (1999) *Report of the Expert Group to Conduct a Review of the Effective Operation and Functioning of the International Criminal Tribunal for the Former Yugoslavia and the International Criminal Tribunal for Rwanda* (UN Doc A/54/634). Online. Available http://daccess-dds-ny.un.org/doc/UNDOC/GEN/N00/230/32/IMG/N0023032.pdf?OpenElement (accessed 10 November 2010).

UNHCR (United Nations High Commission for Refugees) (2001) 'Outraged at Light Sentence', *UN Wire*, 4 May. Online. Available http://www.unwire.org/unwire/20010504/14604_story.asp (accessed 20 December 2009).

Unidjaja, F. D. (2003) 'RI, East Timor to Discuss Residual Issues', *The Jakarta Post*, 20 June.

Uniya (2006) *Justice and Reconciliation in East Timor: Australia and the CAVR* (Report by the Uniya Social Justice Centre, November), Sydney: Uniya.

UNMIT (United Nations Integrated Mission in Timor-Leste) (2007) *Human Rights Developments in Timor-Leste August 2006-August 2007* (Report by Human Rights and Transitional Justice Section), Dili: United Nations.

UN News Centre (2003) 'Timor-Leste not UN Indicts Indonesian General for War Crimes' (UNMISET Statement, 26 February). Online. Available http://www.un.org/apps/news/story.asp?NewsID=6273andCr=timorandCr1= (accessed 1 August 2010).

UNSC (United Nations Security Council) (1999a) *UNTAET Mandate, Security Council Resolution 1272* (S/RES/1272, 25 October). Online. Available http://www.un.int/usa/sres1272.htm (accessed 19 May 2010).

—— (1999b) *Security Council Resolution 1264* (S/RES/1264, 15 September). Online. Available http://daccess-dds-ny.un.org/doc/UNDOC/GEN/N99/264/81/PDF/N9926481.pdf?OpenElement (accessed 23 October 2010).

—— (2000) *Report of the United Nations Security Council Mission to East Timor and Indonesia, 9–17 November 2000* (UN Doc S/2000/1105). Online. Available http://daccess-dds-ny.un.org/doc/UNDOC/GEN/N00/754/03/PDF/N0075403.pdf?OpenElement (accessed 30 November 2010).

—— (2001) *Security Council Resolution 1338* (S/RES/1338, 31 January). Online. Available http://daccess-dds-ny.un.org/doc/UNDOC/GEN/N01/234/39/PDF/N0123439.pdf?OpenElement (accessed 27 November 2011).

—— (2004a) *Special Report of the Secretary General on the United Nations Mission of Support in East Timor* (UN Doc S/2004/117, 13 February). Online. Available http://daccess-dds-ny.un.org/doc/UNDOC/GEN/N04/233/19/IMG/N0423319.pdf?OpenElement (accessed 25 September 2011).

—— (2004b) *Security Council Resolution 1543* (S/RES/1543, 14 May). Online. Available http://www.unhcr.org/refworld/docid/411361714.html (accessed 30 November 2010).

—— (2006a) *UN Security Council 5351st Meeting: The Situation in East Timor* (UN Doc S/Pv.5351, 23 January).

—— (2006b) *UNMIT Mandate, UN Security Council Resolution 1704* (SC/RES/1704, 25 August). Online. Available http://www.un.org/Depts/dpko/missions/unmit/mandate/htm (accessed 17 December 2009).

—— (2006c) *Statement of Secretary General to 5457th Meeting of the Security Council* (13 June), New York: UN Department of Public Information.

UNSG (United Nations Secretary General) (2000a) *Report of the Secretary General on the UN Transitional Administration in East Timor* (UN Doc S/2000/738, 26 July), New York: United Nations.

—— (2000b) *Identical Letters Dated January 2000 from the Secretary General to the President of the General Assembly, the President of the Security Council and the Chairperson on Human Rights* (UN General Assembly Doc A/54/726, S/2000/59, 31 January), New York: United Nations.

—— (2002) *Report of the Secretary General on the United Nations Transitional Administration in East Timor* (UN Doc S/2002/432, 14 April), New York: United Nations.

—— (2004) *The Rule of Law and Transitional Justice in Conflict and Post-Conflict Societies* (UN Doc S/2004/616, 23 August), New York: United Nations.

—— (2006) *Report of the Secretary General on Justice and Reconciliation for Timor-Leste* (UN Doc S/2006/580, 26 July), New York: United Nations.

—— (2010) *Report of the Secretary-General on the United Nations Integrated Mission in Timor-Leste for the Period from 24 September 2009 to 20 January 2010* (UN Doc S/2010/85, 12 February), New York: United Nations.

UNTAET (United Nations Transitional Administration in East Timor) (2000a) *Regulation 2000/11 on the Organization of Courts in Timor-Leste* (6 March). Online. Available http://www.un.org/en/peacekeeping/missions/past/etimor/untaetR/Reg11.pdf (accessed 10 May 2010).

—— (2000b) *On the Establishment of Panels with Exclusive Jurisdiction over Serious Criminal Offences* (UNTAET Regulation 2000/15, 6 June), Dili: UNTAET.

—— (2001) *On the Establishment of a Commission for Reception, Truth and Reconciliation in East Timor* (UNTAET Regulation 2001/10, 13 July). Online. Available http://www.un.org/peace/etimor/untaetR/Reg10e.pdf (accessed 5 June 2010).

Verdeja, E. (2006) 'Reparations in Democratic Transitions', *Res Publica*, 12: 115–36.

Verdery, K. (1999) *The Political Lives of Dead Bodies: Reburial and Post-Socialist Change*, New York: Columbia University Press.

Waldorf, L. (2006) 'Mass Justice for Mass Atrocity: Rethinking Local Justice as Transitional Justice', *Temple Law Review*, 79(1): 1–87.

Walsh, P. (2000) *East Timor's Political Parties and Groupings* (ACFOA Development Issues Paper, March), Dili: Australia Council for Overseas Aid.

—— (2011) *At the Scene of the Crime: Essays, Reflections and Poetry on East Timor, 1999–2010*, Preston, Vic: Mosaic Press.

Wandita, G., Campbell-Nelson, K. and Long-Pereira, M. (2006) 'Learning to Engender Reparations in Timor-Leste: Reaching Out to Female Victims', in R. Rubio-Marin (ed.) *What Happened to the Women? Gender and Reparations for Human Rights Violations* (pp. 284–335), New York: Social Science Research Council.

Webster, D. (2007) 'History, Nation and Narrative in East Timor's Truth Commission Report', *Pacific Affairs*, 80(4): 581–91.

Weedon, C. (1987) *Feminist Practice and Poststructuralist Theory*, Oxford: Blackwell.

Wilke, C. (2007) 'Recognizing Victimhood: Politics and Narratives of Rehabilitation in Germany', *Journal of Human Rights*, 6(4): 479–96.

Wilson, B. (2010) 'Smoke and Mirrors: The Development of the East Timorese Police 1999–2009', unpublished PhD thesis, Australian National University.

Wilson, R. A. (2001) *The Politics of Truth and Reconciliation in South Africa*, Cambridge: Cambridge University Press.

Wise, A. (2004a) 'Nation, Transnation, Diaspora: Locating East Timorese Long-Distance Nationalism', *SOURJOURN*, 19(2): 151–80.

—— (2004b) 'Embodying Exile: Trauma and Collective Identities among East Timorese Refugees in Australia', *Social Analysis*, 48(3): 24–39.

World Bank (2003) *Timor-Leste: Poverty in a New Nation – Analysis for Action*, Washington DC: World Bank.

—— (2006) 'Closing Press Conference in Timor-Leste with Paul Wolfowitz', 10 April. Online. Available http://web.worldbank.org/WBSITE/EXTERNAL/NEWS/0,contentMDK:20882055~pagePK:64257043~piPK:437376~theSitePK:4607,00.html (accessed 10 February 2010).

—— (2008) *Defining Heroes: Key Lessons from the Creation of Veterans Policy in Timor-Leste* (Report of the Timor-Leste, Papua New Guinea and Pacific Islands Country Management Unit No. 45458-TP, 30 September), Washington DC: World Bank.

World Bank and Directorate of National Statistics (2008) *Timor Leste Poverty in a Young Nation* (November), Dili: World Bank/Directorate of National Statistics.

Yayasan Hak (2002) 'Independence Day: Cause for Celebration or Damnation of International Complicity in the Illegal Occupation of East Timor?' (Statement, 20 May). Online. Available http://www.etan.org/et2002b/may/12–18/18hak.htm (accessed 10 January 2010).

Zamora, L. P. (1998) *The Useable Past: The Imagination of History in Recent Fiction of the Americas*, Cambridge: Cambridge University Press.

Index

Page numbers in **bold** indicate figures

For Product Safety Concerns and Information please contact our EU representative GPSR@taylorandfrancis.com
Taylor & Francis Verlag GmbH, Kaufingerstraße 24, 80331 München, Germany

www.ingramcontent.com/pod-product-compliance
Lightning Source LLC
Chambersburg PA
CBHW060745150926
51501CB00003B/101
9780415504362